AF822475

DIVINE BODIES

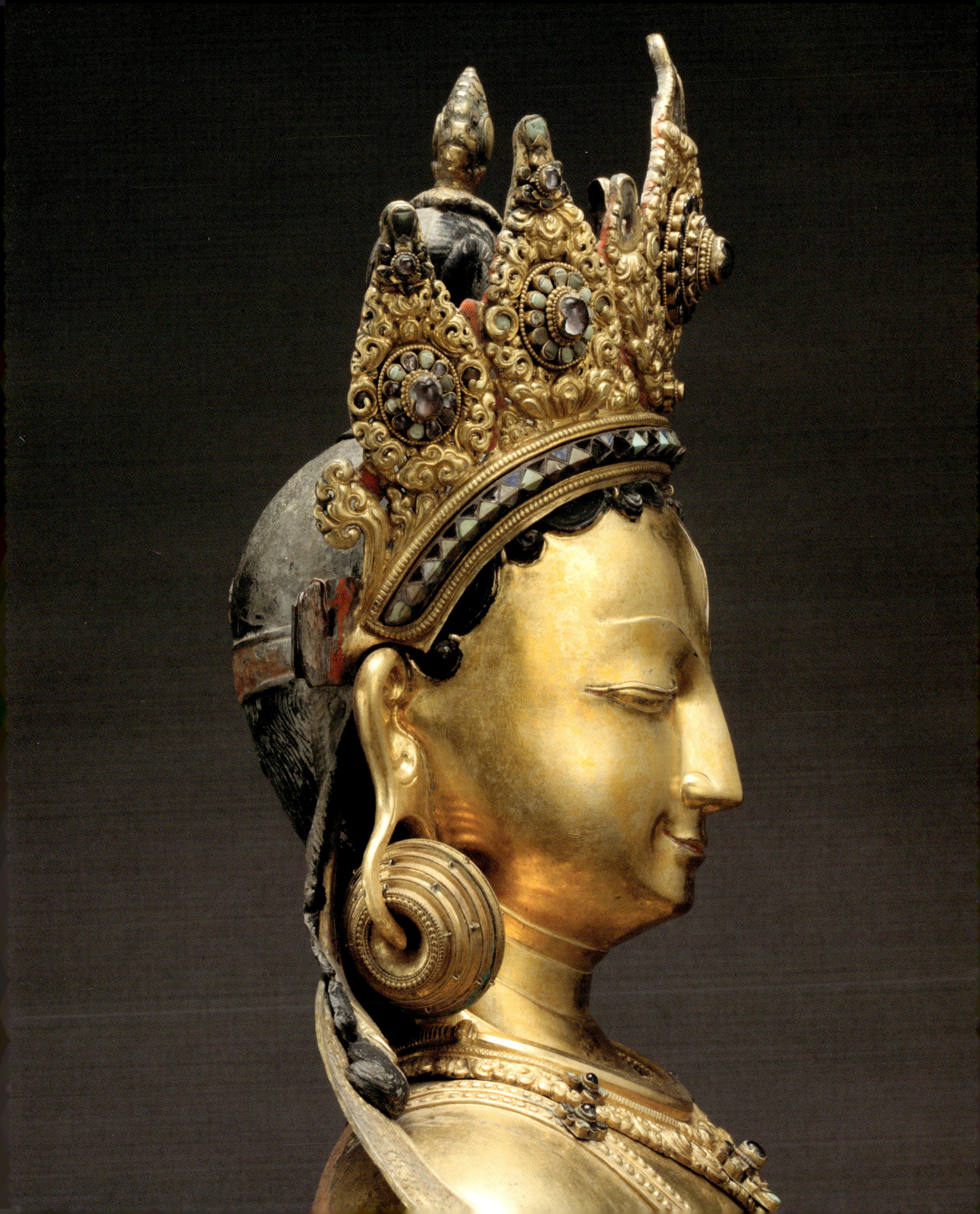

QAMAR ADAMJEE
JEFFREY DURHAM
KARIN G. OEN

Asian Art Museum
San Francisco

DIVINE BODIES

Sacred Imagery in Asian Art

Published by Asian Art Museum
Chong-Moon Lee Center for
Asian Art and Culture
200 Larkin Street
San Francisco, CA 94102
www.asianart.org

Printed and bound in the
United States

21 20 19 18 4 3 2 1 First edition

Produced by the Publications Department, Asian Art Museum of San Francisco
Clare Jacobson, Head of Publications

Designed by Connie Hwang Design
Edited by Tom Fredrickson
Proofread by David Sweet

Library of Congress Cataloging-in-Publication Data
Names: Adamjee, Qamar. Seeing in a sacred manner the shapes of things in the spirit. | Durham, Jeffrey, 1966-Body and cosmos. | Oen, Karin G., 1978-Bodies of work. | Asian Art Museum of San Francisco, organizer, host institution.
Title: Divine bodies : sacred imagery in Asian art / Qamar Adamjee, Jeffrey Durham, and Karin G. Oen.
Description: First edition. | San Francisco, CA: Asian Art Museum, 2018. | Includes bibliographical references.
Identifiers: LCCN 2017042706 | ISBN 9780939117833 (pbk. : alk. paper)
Subjects: LCSH: Human beings in art—Exhibitions. | Art, Asian—21st century—Themes, motives—Exhibitions. | Hindu art—Themes, motives—Exhibitions. | Buddhist art—Themes, motives—Exhibitions.
Classification: LCC N7625.5 .D58 2018 | DDC 700.95/0905—dc23
LC record available at https://lccn.loc.gov/2017042706

Published on the occasion of the exhibition *Divine Bodies* presented at the Asian Art Museum—Chong-Moon Lee Center for Asian Art and Culture, March 9–July 29, 2018.

Divine Bodies is organized by the Asian Art Museum. Presentation is made possible with the generous support of The Akiko Yamazaki and Jerry Yang Fund for Excellence in Exhibitions and Presentations, The Bernard Osher Foundation, Dixon and Carol Doll Family Foundation, Warren Felson and Lucy Sun, Blakemore Foundation, Rajnikant T. and Helen Crane Desai, John Maa, M.D., and Society for Art & Cultural Heritage of India.

The Asian Art Museum–Chong-Moon Lee Center for Asian Art and Culture is a public institution whose mission is to lead a diverse global audience in discovering the unique material, aesthetic, and intellectual achievements of Asian art and culture.

Distributed by:
North America, Latin America, and Europe
Tuttle Publishing
364 Innovation Drive
North Clarendon, VT 05759-9436
U.S.A.
Tel: 1 (802) 773-8930
Fax: 1 (802) 773-6993
info@tuttlepublishing.com
www.tuttlepublishing.com

Asia Pacific
Berkeley Books Pte. Ltd.
61 Tai Seng Avenue #02-12
Singapore 534167
Tel: (65) 6280-1330
Fax: (65) 6280-6290
inquiries@periplus.com.sg
www.periplus.com

Cover, ii, vii: The Buddhist deity White Tara, cat. no. 15 (details)
viii: The bodhisattva Avalokiteshvara, cat. no. 35 (detail)
x: The Hindu deity Parvati, cat. no. 19 (detail)
10: The Buddhist deity Guhyasamaja, cat. no. 22 (detail)
19, 28: Death of the Buddha Shakyamuni, cat. no. 3 (details)
20: *Myself Mona Ahmed*, cat. no. 45 (detail)
27: *Khajuraho_08*, cat. no. 33 (detail)
46: Head of a Buddha image, cat. no. 9 (detail)
54: The Buddhist deity Vajrabhairava, cat. no. 27 (detail)
88: The Hindu deity Shiva revealed in the linga, cat. no. 44 (detail)
110: Nature divinity, cat. 20 (detail)

All photographs are by the Asian Art Museum of San Francisco except for the following:
27, 84–87: © Vivan Sundaram courtesy sepiaEYE
38–43: © Gauri Gill; images courtesy the artist
44–45: David Hodge and Hi-Jin Kang Hodge
80–83: © Pamela Singh courtesy sepiaEYE. Photographs © Chika Kobari.
107T: Courtesy the artist
107B: Courtesy the artist and Frith Street Gallery, London

In the stillness of your presence, you can feel your own formless and timeless reality as the unmanifested life that animates your physical form. You can then feel the same life deep within every other human and every other creature. You look beyond the veil of form and separation. This is the realization of oneness.

—Eckhart Tolle

ix
Foreword
Jay Xu

1
Seeing in a Sacred Manner the Shapes of Things in the Spirit: Power and Wonder in Devotional Art
Qamar Adamjee

11
Body and Cosmos: From the Ancient to the Adamantine
Jeffrey Durham

21
Bodies of Work: Exploring the Human and the Divine in Series
Karin G. Oen

29
Transience and Transcendence

47
Embodying the Sacred

55
The Many Aspects of Divinity

89
Divine Metamorphosis

113
Notes

115
Bibliography

118
Contributors

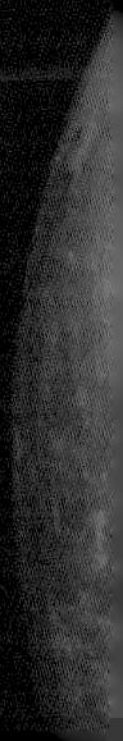

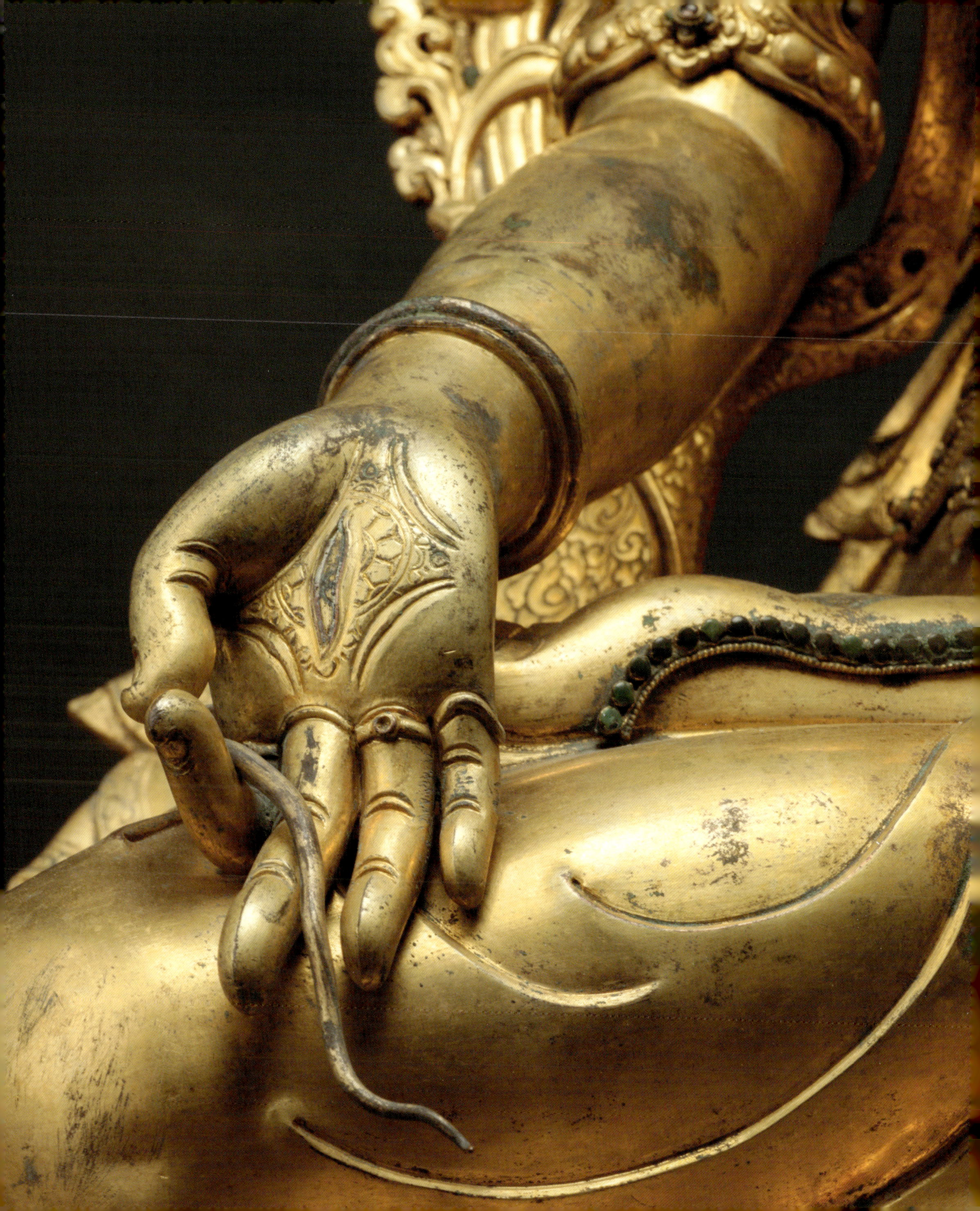

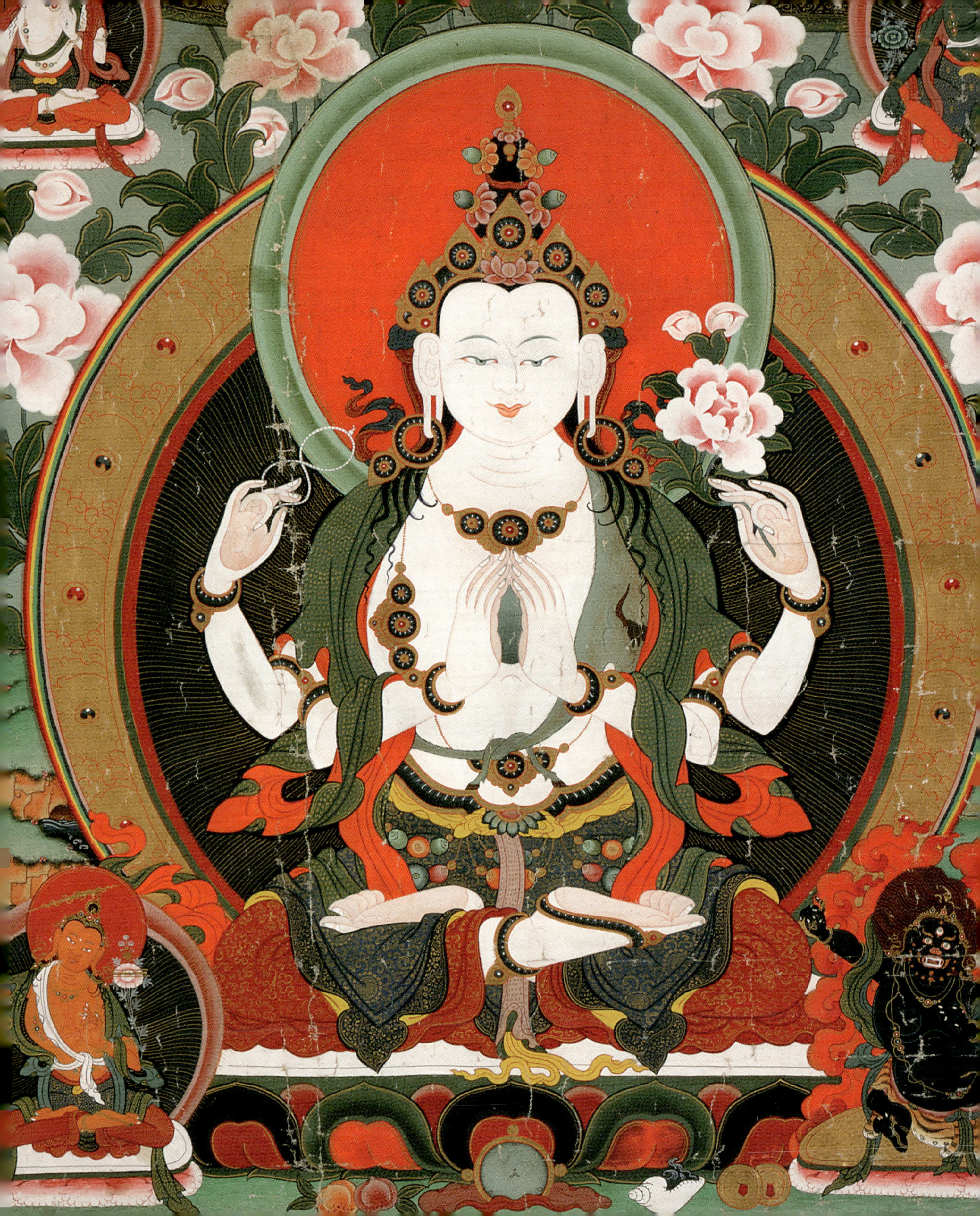

FOREWORD

JAY XU

Director, Asian Art Museum of San Francisco

What do you see when you look at a sacred image? Are you looking at the divine itself, or a representation of an otherwise invisible deity? Or perhaps you encounter some reflection of fundamental human concerns, focusing on the problems of life or of death?

Divine Bodies uses innovative methods of displaying and interpreting sacred art to explore these questions. For example, one aspect of the exhibition involves the extent to which sacred artworks reflect cultural norms about the body and its ideal configuration. Does the image of the Buddha change when the tradition he founded crosses cultural boundaries? If so, what is the reason for this? Is it because divine bodies provide a visual mirror to the perfection of divinities—but only if viewers can relate to their outward appearances? Or are there more profound forces at work here? If so, we hope our rather unorthodox approach will give you ample scope to explore and discover them.

This exhibition and accompanying catalogue celebrate the visual and intellectual ingenuity of the artists who translated the abstract, invisible divine into concrete, material form. From India and Tibet to China and Japan, painters and sculptors have striven to clothe the infinite divine in the perceptible vesture of concrete forms, kaleidoscopic colors, incessant dynamism, and profound symbolism. In so doing, they sought to bring ideas of divine presence and activity into the ordinary world bounded by our senses.

Thanks to everyone who helped to make this project a success. To curators and authors Qamar Adamjee, Jeffrey Durham, and Karin G. Oen for joining their diverse talents and expertises into creating a comprehensive work. Their thoughtful considerations of artworks from the collection of the Asian Art Museum of San Francisco and from contemporary artists allow us to look at sacred arts in new ways. I am grateful to the sponsors whose contributions made this exhibition and publication possible. Finally, thanks to those who arrive at this show and/or to this book with an open mind and an eagerness to understand the wealth of ways in which we humans seek to embody the divine—whether through artistic creativity or personal transformation. Through *Divine Bodies* the museum hopes to inspire new ways of thinking by connecting art to life and, in so doing, connecting us to each other.

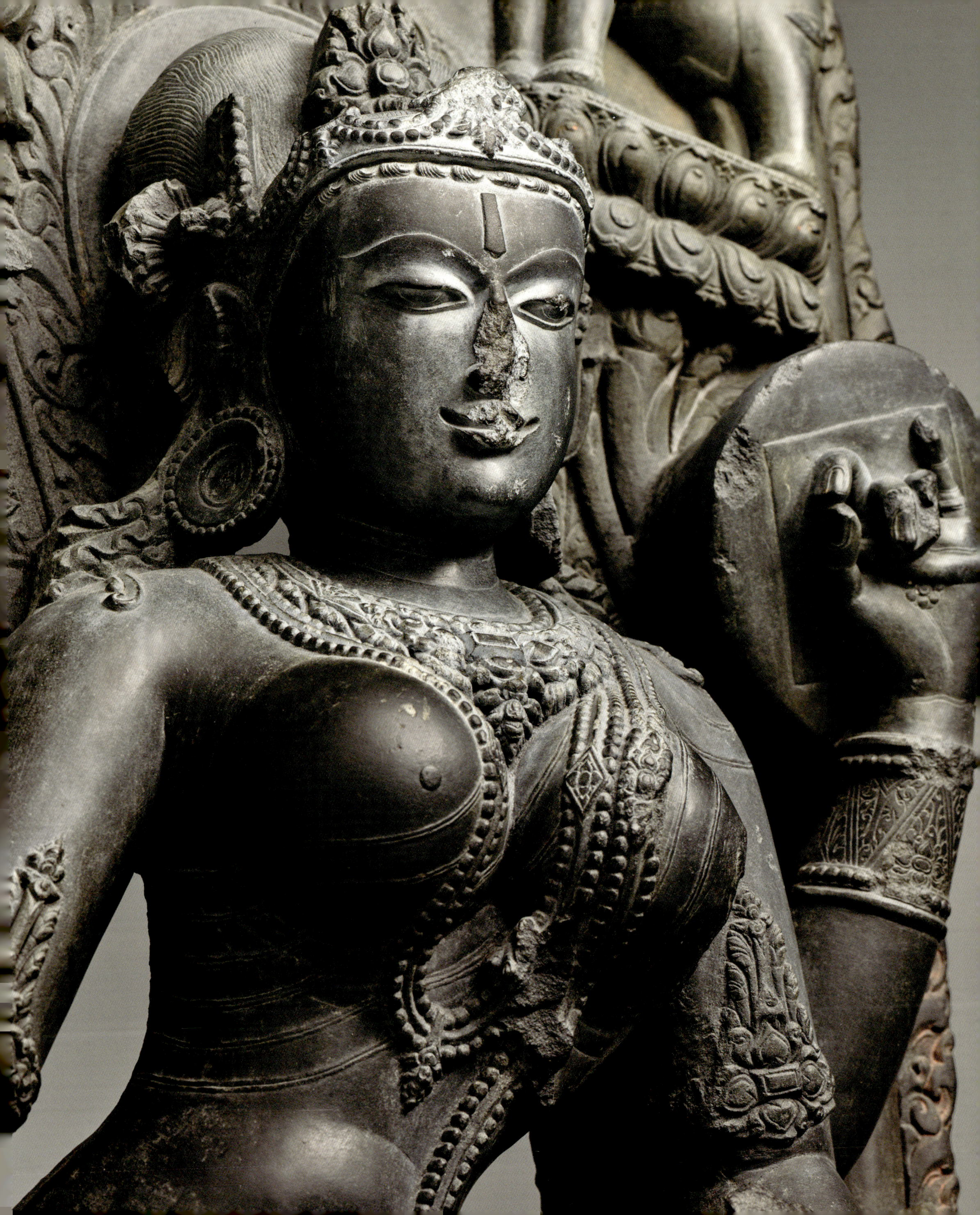

SEEING IN A SACRED MANNER THE SHAPES OF THINGS IN THE SPIRIT
POWER AND WONDER IN DEVOTIONAL ART

QAMAR ADAMJEE

How can one look at religious art with fresh eyes and see the humanness within? In what ways can we recognize in it a personal, spiritual resonance apart from theology? How can we also remain responsible to faith traditions and the markedly varied interpretations of texts and rituals that such images represent?

Divine Bodies explores these and other questions by initiating a dialogue between the sacred and the secular, past and present through historical artworks in the Asian Art Museum's collection and select works by contemporary artists.[1] Our interests here are the ways in which the human body is represented in (mainly) Hindu and Buddhist religious traditions. We see in figural devotional imagery a dialectical relationship between conceptualizations of divinity and the human form, manifestations of which are explored in the exhibition's four sections. It is impossible to generalize about religious concepts or the role of images in worship, especially considering the wide range of doctrinal specificities, regional diversity, and historical circumstances that have shaped them. At the same time, in surveying imagery portraying divinity in human form clear patterns emerge—patterns that remind us, as Jeffrey Durham discusses in his essay (pp. 11–18), that the sacred and human realms are closely intertwined. Thus, the artworks and ideas presented here are intended as provocations and an invitation to develop your own meanings by transcending conventional categories.

And while I stood there I saw more than I can tell, and I understood more than I saw; for I was seeing in a sacred manner the shapes of things in the spirit, and the shape of all shapes as they must live together like one being.

—Black Elk, Oglala Lakota (Sioux) spiritual leader (1863–1950)

Shift Perspectives, Shift Perceptions

Many people see the world today as having been marred by atrocities committed in the name of religion, and as a result they find little room for faith in their lives, being skeptical of, if not averse to, the practices and institutions of organized religion. At the same time, the global North has in recent decades witnessed a rising interest in nondenominational spirituality that perhaps fills some of the space once occupied by "religion." Contemporary (largely Western) understanding typically separates art and religion into distinct cultural spheres, and post-Enlightenment thought similarly pits reason and science against faith and belief. Yet in the early modern period, intersections among these categories were numerous and fluid, and some societies never understood them in such rigid terms. Art was often the membrane through which these categories were connected. Religious subjects (images of gods and holy figures, stories about their lives and teachings), objects, and places of worship have inspired artists across cultures and over time. Valuable material and creative resources have been invested into these projects, several of which are now considered among the world's greatest artworks. Many objects originally made for service to faith have endured the ravages of time to be preserved as cultural legacies: think, for example, of ancient Egyptian, Mesopotamian, Greek, or Roman sculpture; of paintings by Renaissance masters; of beautifully copied scriptures; of magnificent temples, churches, and mosques.

Art historian Robert DeCaroli, discussing Buddhist religious imagery, makes a useful distinction between *devotional images* and *art* that illustrates a central point in *Divine Bodies*. For most people today, art is associated with images one views as an act of leisure and contemplation and that contain meanings expressing their creator's ideas or values. Religious imagery is rarely understood in this way. Although they are works of human creation and may reflect the values of their time and makers, devotional images are invested with an extraordinary degree of power, agency, and authority. They are believed to possess the potential to affect the world around them.[2] For Hindus and Buddhists, the image *is* god and not simply a representation of the divine.[3]

The meaning of a sacred object is shaped by the context within which it is viewed and the personal attitudes that a viewer brings to it. A change of context shifts the nature of the power we allow an object to have over us. Where a religious devotee in a temple may experience a connection with the divine through a sculpture, a visitor to a museum may see in that object (now relocated to a gallery) an inspiring example of art. Thus, the implicitly transcendental nature of devotional objects resolves into a more earthbound status when they are presented in a museum and seen as artworks. In *Divine Bodies*, we aim to reduce this gap by considering the relationships between the physical (human) body and metaphysical (divine) concepts as they are made manifest in powerful artworks.

Bodies—Human and Divine

In many religious philosophies, the divine is understood as a force that creates, maintains, and/or controls order in the universe. It is often described as formless, infinite, beyond time; without beginning or end; present everywhere; seeing and knowing everything. With such an immense scope, a single "complete" representation of the divine is impossible. Even a casual glance at religious objects from different cultures and times shows that creative responses to the divine are as manifold (and sometimes as concrete) as the concept is vast and abstract.

In many traditions, conceptualizing gods in humanlike form presents the "unvisible as visible,"[4] resulting in images that offer devotees relatable paths of action, hope, and inspiration that give purpose and order to their lives. One may ask here, though, that if a god is indeed as mighty and vast as religions tell us, then would not the human form be an inadequate and limiting vessel with which to express divinity? To which we may respond: if the divine *is* all-encompassing and all-powerful, it is conceivable that it can assume *any* form, with the human body being one among a limitless set of possibilities—and perhaps the most accessible.

As individuals, we negotiate between our internal selves and the outside world through and with our bodies. Participation in this world is predicated on our bodily existence, and the external world becomes "real" only through the information gathered by our senses and given meaning to by perceptual processes. But the human body is much more than a biological substance. It is a culturally constructed system of meanings and a vehicle for communication.[5] We use body language, dress, and other markers to navigate between the internal and the external. In a way, then, the bodies or forms of gods can also be thought of as modes of communication expressing culturally bound essences of the divine, guiding the lives of devotees, shaping—and reflecting—their worldviews. A devotional image can thus make divine presence felt with immediacy and a personal connection.

Take the Buddha, for example. Though we have no contemporaneous "portrait" of him,[6] textual sources give detailed accounts of the Buddha's appearance, enumerating thirty-two characteristics that identify him as a "great man" (*mahapurusha* in Sanskrit). He is described as having long fingers, a golden complexion, white and even teeth, a perfectly proportioned body, limbs like a fig tree, etc.[7] These identifying marks (*lakshana*) are variously generic, highly specific, and often metaphorical, and they are important for symbolizing the Buddha's exemplary character, his past and future actions. While such descriptions do not facilitate a picture of what the historical Buddha actually looked like, artists have inscribed these key features on their images. Representations of the Buddha from the third century CE onward in India, China, Tibet, and beyond share such identifiable characteristics: eyes downcast in meditation, a gentle smile of compassion, a tuft of hair between his eyebrows (*urna*) sometimes thought to denote the ability to see beyond material appearances, and a protrusion on the crown of his head (*ushnisha*; artistically depicted as a topknot of hair) signaling his enhanced wisdom and enlightenment. Such images accrued their iconic status through constant replication in the chains of copies, appropriations, and adaptations that connected artistic and faith traditions across regions and cultures.[8] As an array of buddha heads from several Asian traditions shows (cats. 8–14), shared textual and oral descriptions have been variously interpreted and imagined by their makers. More interestingly, they demonstrate how the "ideal" of Buddhahood was identified in the faces of local peoples. While such representations draw upon the observed world, they are not strictly ethnographic, and artists—as well as theologians and priests—have relied on devotees' ability to read the overall meaning embedded in devotional images.

An individual is perhaps more easily able to identify with sacred imagery when the divine's infinite powers are expressed in human terms and mainly through body language. For instance, the benevolence of the Buddhist goddess of compassion, White Tara, is visible in her calm posture, gentle facial expression, and hand gestures (mudras) denoting wish fulfillment and the allaying of fear, while her perfectly proportioned and richly adorned body conveys her elevated status (cat. 15). In other instances, the divinity's suprahuman abilities are indicated by a modification of familiar physical features, typically with additional heads, arms, and eyes in what scholar Doris Srinivasan has called "the multiplicity convention."[9] Tara's powers thus manifest differently in her form as the fierce Vajra Tara (Thunderbolt Tara), in which she assumes three heads, fearsome expressions, and multiple arms, each bearing a weapon or attribute symbolizing a spiritual obstacle (ego, ignorance, anger, etc.) that she—and, with her help, the devotee—overcomes (cat. 16). The glory and majesty of the goddess remain unmistakable in both images, but the changing visible signs convey her different aspects.

Transience and Transcendence

Our bodies are never static: our emotional and mental states are continuously shifting, and our bodies physically change throughout our lives. Transience is a constant. The 122 interviewees, including philosophers and gardeners, economists and spiritual leaders, doctors and patients, in David Hodge and Hi-Jin Kang Hodge's video installation *Impermanence: The Time of Man* (cat. 7) eloquently reflect on topics such as death and change and their impact on everyday lives. Their moving responses emphasize that just as impermanence (*anitya*) is a central concept in Buddhism, so it is also a universal concern.

Death is perhaps the most striking manifestation of human transience, and the concept of "life" cannot be determined without its counterpoint and only certitude: death. Death is a fearful prospect, perhaps because we know nothing with certainty about what happens to us after our body stops functioning biologically. Religious traditions have offered answers in such concepts as a final judgment, heaven and hell, and multiple rebirths, among other alternatives. By openly considering the eventuality of death, devotional systems advocate ways of living a fulfilling and ethically guided life in the here and now, providing purpose and structure to an individual's life and enabling a functioning society.

But how is an individual to reconcile life with death? In Buddhism and Hinduism death is not thought of as an ending but rather as a stage in the journey of the self.[10] Great religious teachers, such as the Buddha and Jesus, for example, were human. Their historical deaths marked the genesis of their faiths, over the course of which their divinity became major subjects of (often contentious) theological debate. Many adherents consider both the Buddha and Jesus wholly divine beings, yet images of their physical demise—the dying Buddha and the crucified Christ (cats. 2 and 1)—appear as central features in devotional contexts. Their suffering or peaceful bodies serve as visual embodiments of their teachings and become guiding examples of ideal conduct for their followers. Some believe the very essence of the Buddha's body was eternally dispersed into the air upon his death, and this blessed presence is sometimes visualized in paintings as rainbow-colored radiance emitting from crematoria (cat. 3). The Buddha's ashes, which were divided at his death into ten parts and distributed among local communities, were enshrined as relics in funeral mounds called stupas. These became pilgrimage sites, facilitating the spread of his teachings across vast geographical distances. Small votive stupas (cats. 4 and 5), which once held the ashes or relics of devotees and were placed near the monumental stupas containing the Buddha's ashes, allowed the deceased to eternally remain in the Buddha's presence. The body, even in its physical absence, thus continued to symbolically endure and stay present.

In her series *Traces* and *Birth* (cat. 6), photographer Gauri Gill reflects on life, death, and all—or rather, the nothing—that we bring with us and leave behind in this world. Gill's quietly poignant photos capture the process of birth as a midwife delivers her granddaughter and document the anonymous graves of nomadic peoples in the remote and shifting deserts of Rajasthan. In these images, life and death become part of a continuous cycle. As Karin G. Oen notes in her essay in this volume (pp. 21–26), these photographs not only remind us of the impermanence of human life but also nourish the impulse to respect life.

The Many Aspects of Divinity

Sacred exemplars and teachings deal with life in all its totality, acknowledging the strengths, frailties, and contradictions inherent in human nature. States of being—whether positive or negative—such as compassion, a sense of justice, anger, jealousy, a lack of focus or discipline, and so on, can be seen as holding the potential to inspire—or inhibit—positive action. The qualities we recognize in ourselves are made visible in images of gods, which render internal psychological dispositions in physical form. In Hindu and Buddhist systems, individual manifestations of a given deity may take different forms, each with a distinctive appearance, specific name, and related mythic context and each expressing a particular quality. The Hindu god Shiva, for example, can appear as a sensual god whose inner perfection is reflected in a bodily beauty that holds the power of inspiring selfless devotion and a deeply intense personal connection for his adherents (cat. 21). The same deity's transgressive act of patricide is made visible in his naked, skull-garlanded, and ferocious form as Bhairava (cat. 24). Here, Shiva/Bhairava instills awe and fear, but as a penitential sinner, he also possesses the power to lead devotees to redemption.

A direct correlation between inner perfection of character and external beauty is articulated in Indic devotional systems. These ideas are shared across religious boundaries, though variously imagined as the unadorned Jain spiritual teacher Parshvanatha (cat. 18) and the sensuous and bejeweled Hindu goddess Parvati (cat. 19). As a simple, elegant sculpture of the bodhisattva of compassion, Avalokiteshvara, from Japan shows (cat. 17), concepts of what constitutes beauty are specific to culture, time, and place.[11]

Changing Roles, Changing Meanings

A divinity's discernable form can shift according to the context and the problem he or she sets out to address. The Hindu god Vishnu, for example, is understood by his devotees as the cosmic creator of the universe and the one who maintains order in it. His role as preserver of the universe is conveyed in his iconic devotional form as a four-armed standing figure (cat. 38). Here, the god's firmly controlled and balanced pose refers to textual descriptions of Vishnu as the "cosmic pillar" that supports and connects the heavens with the earth. He holds his distinct attributes (discus, conch shell, mace, and lotus flower) and stands dressed in kingly garments, jewelry, and a crown. In this manifestation, familiar symbols of worldly power combine with mythic attributes to form an image of transcendence.

According to Hindu traditions, Vishnu descends to earth on ten different occasions in ten different guises (avatars)—human, animal, or part animal—to protect and guide his followers when the forces of chaos reign supreme (cats. 39 and 40).[12] In each instance, Vishnu's avatars assume the form best suited to solve the particular mythic problem confronting them. Devotees recognize the narrative from their knowledge of textual and oral traditions and, facilitated by the artist's work, find personal meaning in the devotional image. It is not essential to know the backstory of Vishnu/Varaha's rescue of the earth goddess Bhu Devi to be awed by the sheer power and dynamism of the god as seen in a stone sculpture (cat. 40). Even in his part-boar, part-human aspect, Vishnu is identifiable by his four arms holding his four key attributes. And in his upward-thrusting, diagonally aligned form, the deity appears majestically—and cosmically—triumphant.

In his aspect of Avalokiteshvara, the Buddha also assumes some measure of shape-shifting. He can, for example, appear in simple humanlike form to offer a model of empathy to devotees (cat. 34) yet texts describe the metaphorically infinite extent of Avalokiteshvara's compassion. One tells of the occasion when his head split into ten parts when he despaired over the extent of suffering in this world. His spiritual father, the buddha Amitabha, came to his rescue and gave Avalokiteshvara courage by shaping the broken pieces into ten individual heads. Amitabha put his own head on top so that his spiritual son would have eleven heads to contemplate all the ways of helping others. Avalokiteshvara's multiheaded form (cat. 37) can thus be seen as a symbol of hope, forbearance, and compassion, as well as an acknowledgment of human suffering. In some other contexts, Avalokiteshvara also shifts gender—from male (cats. 36 and 37) to androgynous (cats. 34 and 35) to female. While an explanation commonly offered for this gender change is that the quality of compassion is a feminine attribute in East Asia, there are underlying philosophical reasons for it as well: gender is considered a conventional construct in some Buddhist texts, empty of self-existence. Given the proper perspective, it can accordingly be changed at will.

Divine transformation can, through this example, be seen as leveling and incorporating human and social conceptions of dualities.

In Hinduism, gender and its attendant roles are clearly articulated. Both the male and female principles (*purusha* and *prakriti*, respectively) are independently seen as forces of creation and agents of change, and together they constitute reality. In his abstract and nonrepresentational form as a phallic shape, the linga, Shiva is the embodiment of the creative force of the cosmos. He represents the hidden unity between apparent opposites, the energy supporting all existence, the beginning and the end (cat. 41). In other representations, he has a fully articulated human form, and, when accompanied by the goddess Parvati (who represents female divine energy), he is sometimes seen with a prominently erect phallus that recalls the linga (cat. 42). Together, Parvati and Shiva represent the creative powers of the universe, "the womb and the seed," as the text of the *Bhagavata Purana* states. This idea is made explicit in their conjoined form as Ardhanarishvara, "the Lord who is half female" (cat. 43). As with Avalokiteshvara, one is reminded that the transcendental, pure essence of the great god of the universe is beyond male/female gender differences or any other simplified binaries.

Photographer Dayanita Singh explores relationships involving gender, identity, and society in the series *Mona Ahmed*, a long-term project documenting the life of a eunuch and member of Delhi's hijra community (cat. 45). Born male and self-identified as female, hijras are considered a third sex in India. Paradoxically, they are seen as being closer to the divine than ordinary people but are socially marginalized, forced to live on the fringes of society. Singh's sympathetic portrayals of Mona Ahmed prompt us not only to consider the transformations of an erstwhile famed beauty through aging, but also to empathize with her personal emotional journey. Together, the images of the gods and Mona Ahmed question the validity of social and perceptual categorizations; when one shifts perspective, binaries can melt into a continuum.

Connectedness

The thread running through the artworks in the exhibition is the link between the physical world and the divine. Many people today feel that their lives are connected to something bigger than themselves, however they may define it. Research in fields such as quantum physics, neuroscience, and ecology has investigated questions related to the nature of creation, which philosophers and spiritual teachers across cultures have contemplated and devotional systems have presaged. Take, for example, the powerful image of a cosmic Buddha (cat. 46). Worlds within worlds are depicted here. The Buddha, seated on a throne, has the celestial Mount Meru mapped on his body; his own dying form appears on his torso, and the realms of this world, the underworld, and the heavens are included in the sculpture. The image raises an essential question: Is the Supreme Buddha infused in every part of the cosmos or do all parts of the cosmos together constitute the supreme Buddha? The answer is: both. Images such as this encourage us to rethink our relationship as individuals to the world in which we live and, beyond that, to consider anew our place in the universal and cosmic order.

In *Divine Bodies* we invite viewers to do more than just read the symbols inscribed in sacred Hindu and Buddhist images. We hope you will draw upon your experiences of the world and the awareness of your own internal and external selves to find personal inspiration in religious objects, regardless of your familiarity with or level of adherence to the traditions represented. We also want to evoke the power and authority embodied in this imagery and to prompt an appreciation for the potential it holds to shape—and reflect—humanity. And in the end, we'd like to remind you that viewing an artwork, like a spiritual experience, is one that, as scholar Robert Zwinjenberg notes, can never be translated entirely into words: "There is always a remainder, something in the picture that escapes translation...something that, strictly speaking, cannot be—and is in essence not meant to be—described."[13]

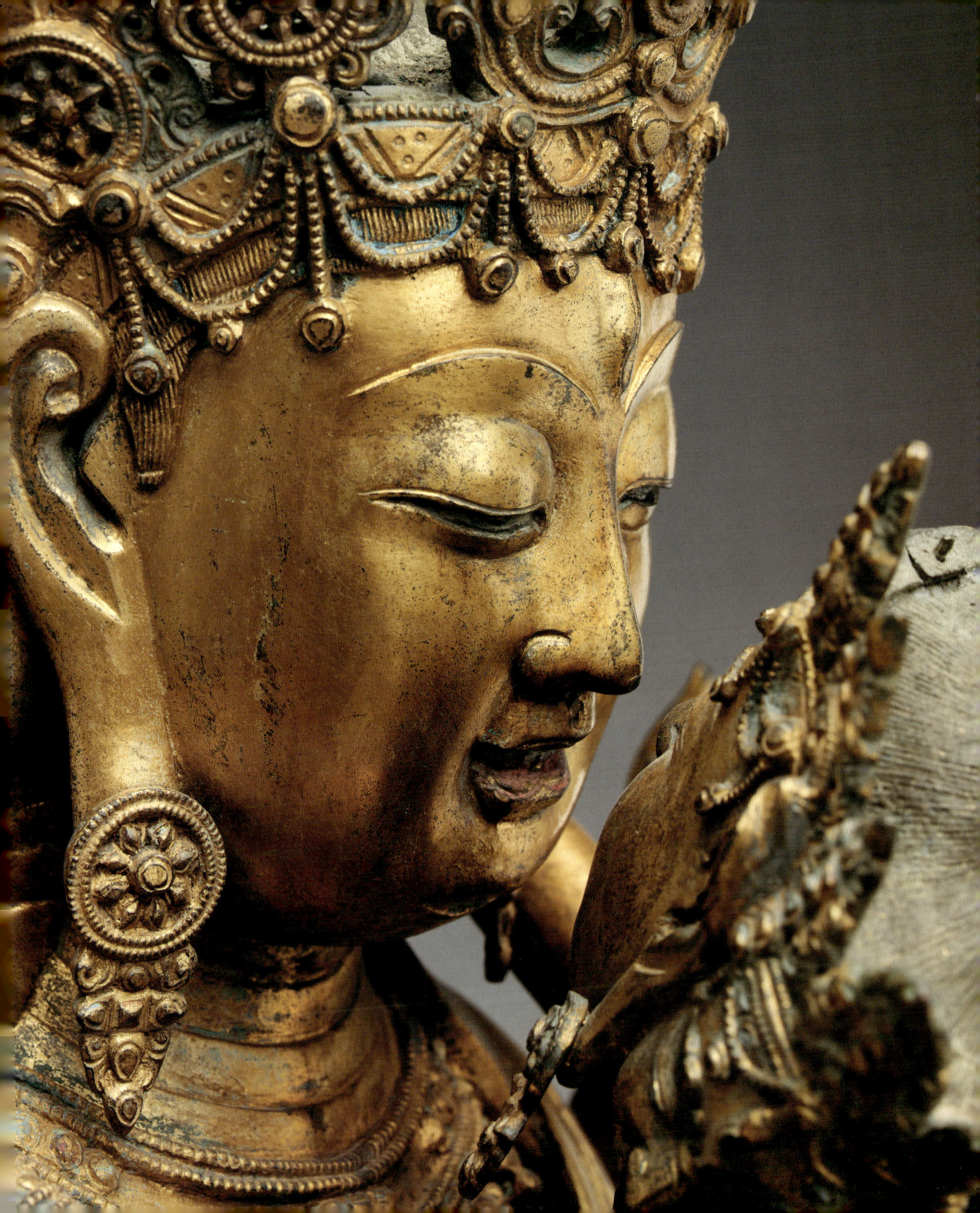

BODY AND COSMOS

FROM THE ANCIENT TO THE ADAMANTINE

JEFFREY DURHAM

The Human Body Organizes Physical Experience

The body is the fundamental apparatus through which human awareness organizes experience. This remains true whether the body is conceived literally, as the physical substratum of an organic being, or metaphorically, as a coordinated unity of otherwise disparate parts: a body of related texts (corpus), a body of fellow soldiers (corps), or a body of commercial colleagues (corporation). When the relations between the members of such bodies become disordered, coordinated continuity dissolves, and the result is again a body (corpse).

Our early ancestors were very much concerned with this last aspect of bodily existence. Indeed, some of the most ancient human interments reveal a clear intent to facilitate the continuity of consciousness beyond the limits of the physical body and the world it ordinarily inhabits. The means, used across an immense span of space and time, was through interment with red ochre—a symbolic analog of blood, the substance of life.[14] This practice suggests that many ancient humans experienced a cosmos in which it was thought possible to symbolically give life to that which was apparently not living, and thus for a being to be "alive" without a functioning physical substratum. For some scholars of religion, such noncorporeal persons may well have been the source for many mythic figures we today recognize as divinities.[15]

Ancient Artistic Bodies Appear in the "Divine" World

Along with burial and the apparent revivification of the body, the genesis of human symbolic activity coincided with a complementary artistic enterprise: an effort to articulate the structure, dynamics, and even residents of the world that the deceased might be deemed to inhabit. This effort appears in the abundant "parietal" artworks painted in caves primarily in France and Spain during the Paleolithic era. Here, human and theriomorphic figures intermingle on the walls of what would quite literally be an "underworld." In these caves, such famous images as the Shaman of Lascaux or the Sorcerer of Les Trois Frères become visitors to—and perhaps eventually denizens of—the land into which beings dissolve upon their decease.[16] Indeed, one prevailing interpretation of the cave environment maintains that it was created by and for shamans so that they might travel into the "land of the dead," that place inhabited preeminently by beings not possessed of ordinary physical bodies. Only when a person was taught, or initiated into, the procedure for visiting the world beyond the world would he or she then qualify as a "shaman."[17]

The genesis of the European cave paintings may lie in that peculiar faculty we call the human imagination, the portal between the visible and the invisible. In their making these paintings have become actual physical presences; they exist as artistic productions, right here in the world of ordinary experience. And this would have been the same situation faced by every potential shaman entering the cave environment, its mystery rendered all the more sacred by the divine presences represented therein, their "numinous"[18] power experienced with ever-new awe for each initiate.

The Divine and the Pragmatic Realms Are Connected

The underworld realms of dream and vision are not the only places where artists have identified and projected imagery revealing the divine. For just as darkened caves, flickering in torchlight and imbued with numinous presences, must have evoked from our ancestors an undeniable sense of awe, so must the vast reaches of the sky have aroused wonder and dread in equal measure.[19] Indeed, the vault of the sky is the first place where we can discern a precise parallel between the name and the nature of the place understood as divine.

What, then, is this principle of organization, the "divine"? Linguistically, the term derives from an old Latin root (*div-*) designating the sky, the place that "shines," as it is the abode of all the celestial luminaries—sun, moon, planets, and stars.[20] These visible phenomena have several key qualities that make them "divine": they are luminous, they do not pass away, and, what is most important for the human world of space and time, their appearance recurs in a more or less regular pattern.

Tracking such patterns in the celestial vault of the sky had many pragmatic applications. For example, human societies could correlate divine phenomena with naturally recurrent earthly events, such as the flooding of a river or the beginning of the vernal equinox. In so doing, they could optimize planting, harvesting, and storage of food supplies. Scholars have traced such activities to the very genesis of civilization.[21]

Many ancient societies therefore understood these recurrent apparitions, from planets to constellations, to comprise the perceptible forms of otherwise divine and transcendent beings—capable, if properly attended to, of providing for human needs. Such conclusions might indeed seem logical from at least one point of view, for these patterns do indeed seem eternally recurrent, undying, radiant, and thus, ipso facto, divine.

Divinity, then, exists at but one remove from the quintessentially pragmatic activity of producing, storing, and consuming food—obviously essential for the maintenance of the body. Thus is it clear that the divine and the human realms do not merely depend on one another for their very existence as such but are actually structured along similar, and in some cases strictly isomorphic, lines—just, as we shall see, like divine bodies.

The Divine Body and the Human Body Are Related

In classical Greece, the divine bodies of the Olympian gods were anthropomorphic: they looked human but possessed a perfection of form and luminosity beyond the ordinary.[22] Here, then, is a clear connection between the divine body and the human body—one that makes each relatable to the other. In fact, the favorite pastime of many male deities was making themselves "relatable" to the human females they fancied, in the process engendering any number of hybrid human-divine heroes.

Divine bodies in Asian art, on the other hand, are seldom representational in the Greek sense. That is, Asian artists seldom attempt to directly transcribe the visuality of some objectively existent divine entity. To be sure, they do find and depict clear similarities between the structure of the human and divine body. Such correlations as they occur in Asia, however, typically do not depend on any literal resemblance between the bodies of humans and divinities. Instead, divinity projects itself into form symbolically, and often geometrically. At the individual level, the symbolism linking divine and human involves a series of nested circles and squares linked by passageways; this is the system of chakras, or nerve plexuses, distributed along the spine that will be familiar to anyone who has visited a yoga studio.

At the level of the cosmos, symbolic bodies appear as systems of nested geometric forms known as mandalas. And just as the geometric chakra in the individual provides the subtle structure for a human body, so does the mandala provide the subtle structure for visualizing an entire cosmos—one in which it becomes possible to attain a divine body not subject to physical decay. Both the chakra system and the mandala system articulate and render accessible a shared insight: the geographies that structure the internal and the external worlds of experience mirror one another. For just as we visualize the orbit of stars around a sun as isomorphic to that of electrons around an atomic nucleus, phenomena that operate in a given way on one scale will tend to operate similarly on others.

It is perhaps these geometrically conceived "fractal" links between cosmic and individual bodies that provide a kind of structure that facilitates the participation of the devotee in the life of the deity. Indeed, the process appears in similar forms across the globe and in widely different cultural contexts. From the ancient Egyptian Osiris to the Greek Orpheus, from the Chinese P'an Ku to the Norse Ymir, the motif of a dying-and-rising god with whom humans may identify is one of the most important in archaic human religion. For when the human body, subject as it is to physical decay, can be assimilated to that which does not so decay, death is defeated.

The same is true of any number of living traditions as well. Thus in Buddhism as in Christianity, the death of the mythic savior is the sine qua non for the dissemination of each one's message. The Asian Art Museum's painting Death of the Buddha Shakyamuni (cat. 3) visually manifests this paradox, revealing simultaneously the death of the founder and the continuance of his spiritual presence in the rainbow light emanating from what, absent the power of his goodness (*punya* in Sanskrit), might be but whited sepulchers rather than eternal repositories of spiritual wisdom (*jnana*). Similarly, the Filipino Crucified Christ (cat. 1) emphasizes how the death of Jesus of Nazareth—and not necessarily either his existence or his teachings—is the essence of the tradition, without which its multifarious manifestations could never emanate. Paradoxically, the genesis of the tradition lies in the decease of its founder; the life of the divine spirit is incumbent upon the death of the human body.

The Distributed Presence of the Divine Body: Relics Catalyze Pilgrimage

In ancient India as in early Christianity, one means employed by religious traditions to disseminate their messages was through the transport and enshrinement of relics. If a given holy site possessed relics, it might become a center of pilgrimage, which would then stimulate trade and generate wealth.[23] Also: in both Indian and European contexts, the ability of holy relics to stimulate trade made them valuable—and hence frequently forged—commodities.

The Buddhist tradition in India presents a uniquely instructive case. For here, we know from textual and archaeological sources exactly how the process of gaining benefits from visiting the remains of a divine body worked: to see or make a donation to a relic generated positive karma, the force of good (*punya*). Since the term *panya* means wealth, the formula runs thus: making a donation of wealth (*panya*) to the relics of the Buddha generates goodness (*punya*).[24] The acquisition of goodness (*punya*) in turn leads to positive rebirth for the donor and wealth (*panya*) for the recipient of the donation, usually a group of monks in residence at a monastery. It is thus not difficult to see how, following the Buddha's suggestion, the community of monks (*samgha*) was able to take the teachings (*dharma*) to the four corners of the world through the agency of the dead body of the divine Buddha, in the process establishing the institution of Buddhism across Asia and indeed the world. How might such a lofty destiny be realized? In a word: symbolism.

Shakyamuni's Signs and Divine Destiny

The symbolic vocabulary whereby one might identify a buddha has its source in the earliest strata of Buddhist literature. Known literally as the thirty-two signs (*lakshana*) of a great man, the relevant indicators include everything from wheels on the palms of the hands and feet to a very large tongue and blue eyes.[25] These signs were apparently present at the birth of the Indian prince Shakyamuni, for when the seer Asita beheld "his foot marked with a wheel, his fingers and toes webbed, with a circle of hair between his eyebrows," he was awestruck, for the Buddha-to-be "shone as if he had come down from heaven... he shone like the young sun... with the radiant splendor of his limbs, he extinguished like the sun the splendor of the lamps."[26] Indeed, texts like this allow us to see precisely where the luminosity of the divine and the formal specificity of the body converge.

Beyond such specific signs of divine destiny, the Pali Canon contains an account whereby Shakyamuni enumerates the multifarious miracles that accompany the birth of a buddha. Prominent among these miracles is the fact that he emerges from the womb undefiled and instead exhibits a "splendor limitless and eminent," so luminous it outshines even the effulgence of the gods.[27] Indeed, from Dionysus Zagreus to Jesus of Nazareth and Padmasambhava of Tibet, miraculous births of some type are the rule among the mythic saviors with whom human communities have identified in their efforts to see and survive beyond the horizon of death.

The Absence of the Divine Body: Mauryan Symbolism

Despite the importance of the Buddha's body and its recognition as such in the dissemination and institutionalization of Buddhism, there is, when we examine the art historical corpus, something very strange about the body of the Buddha: for at least 250 years after Shakyamuni's death, he is never represented physically. What instead appears is a studied absence of the Buddha's body.

The Mauryan school of art, the earliest in India (fourth to second century BCE), depicts abundant legends from the Buddha's life in efflorescent detail. But where we might most want or expect to see the Buddha Shakyamuni himself, we instead see a symbolic substitute. In one place, sculptors may have carved a parasol to represent the Buddha's Great Departure from household life. In another, there appears a turban to represent Shakyamuni's ascent to the great heaven called Thirty-Three—but again no Shakyamuni.

The ideological reasons behind such eschewal of representation remain debatable from the textual or art historical perspective. One thing, however, is completely clear in the Mauryan corpus: the aniconic depictions of the Buddha's presence encompass a systematic vocabulary of symbols specifically designed to avoid literal representation of the transcendent divine body.

Shakyamuni's Story: Creating the Historical Buddha

It was only under the Kushana Empire (30–375 CE), both in Gandhara and Mathura, that the Buddha first attained physical representation—that he first "got a body," so to speak. The reasons for this dramatic change remain obscure. There are, however, some clues, for it was during this time that Indian Buddhists began to interact with fellow monks from an international community. Traveling during the dry season, they journeyed from the plains of Bihar, south through Amaravati in Andhra, and up through the Silk Road in the west. In the process, they exchanged ideas, imagery, and interpretations, combining and collating the materials they shared. This process produced the story of the Buddha's life, which then coalesced into a series of key scenes, each one relating to a particularly instructive or memorable incident in his career—and each one associated with a specific pilgrimage center. One might think of this process as the expansion of the Buddha's career onto the body of the earth.

Then, as the story of Shakyamuni's career became more familiar and codified around the turn of the millennium, a selection of the most salient episodes also began to appear in the art corpuses of Gandhara and Mathura. These episodes include the birth, renunciation, enlightenment, first sermon, and death of the historical Buddha Shakyamuni. Now the essence of the divine Buddha's story could be condensed into a package as small as an *angadu*, or portable shrine. Capable of contraction to a singularity as well as expansion over the surface of the earth, the Buddha's story thus becomes as magically malleable—and as extraordinarily adaptable—as the tradition itself.

The Mahayana Multiverse

In the centuries around the start of the Common Era, learned Indian monks began compiling a new body of texts pertaining to the Mahayana, or "Great Vehicle" tradition of Buddhism. These new books proclaimed a veritable revolution in Buddhist thought. Philosophically, they championed a new conception of ultimate reality as emptiness (*shunyata*). At the same time, they set forth a new vision of the cosmos as a multiverse in which infinite numbers of "cosmic" buddhas preside over infinite numbers of worlds. These myriad "cosmic" buddhas, as a result of their vows to attain enlightenment for the sake of all beings, now preside over their own paradisiacal worlds. Some of these buddhas, like red Amitabha of the west, are so powerful that merely to hear their name results in rebirth in their Pure Land, no matter how wickedly a human sinner may have acted in his or her previous life. Other buddhas, such as blue Akshobhya of the east, specialize in the elimination of specific negative tendencies—anger in Akshobhya's case. Along with three additional buddhas, they constitute a five-member initiatory team capable of overcoming all obstacles to enlightenment "in this very life," according to the traditional Tibetan saying. Then, as if to complete the process, five "cosmic" buddhas were in due course assimilated to five key episodes in the life of the historical Buddha Shakyamuni, grounding the ostensible accidents of historical bodies in universal processes overseen by divine bodies.

Meditators access the obstacle-destroying power of each cosmic buddha by visualizing his body and its various adornments in precise detail, while simultaneously analyzing the aspect of Buddhist philosophy each symbolic element encodes. Under these conditions, such visualized buddhas can then become antidotes to specific psychological poisons that generate suffering and inhibit enlightenment.

Innovations such as the above meditation procedure were developed in the great monastic universities of northern India, especially Nalanda. Here, experiments into new meditative methods and philosophical approaches continued apace, resulting in an ever-expanding toolbox of techniques to transcend the ordinary world. But as more teachers initiated more students into the visualization of yet more buddhas, the institution faced a problem: How were they to account for this vast and growing plethora of buddhas? They responded with two powerful tools: tantra and mandala.

The Adamantine Vajrayana Body: Tantra and Mandalas

During the ninth century, the great monasteries of Bihar began trying to discern the integral order behind what was by now a proliferating profusion of buddhas, bodhisattvas, and other enlightened beings of myriad type. To do so, they compiled texts called tantras and images called mandalas. Designed to narratively integrate a number of teachings and deities into a single tableau for ritual memorization, initiation, and meditation, the tantras discussed visualizations and philosophies centered around specific groupings of Buddhist deities and symbols.

For their part, mandalas were designed to visually integrate Buddhist imagery found in the tantras into a geometrical series of nested circles and squares representing a three-dimensional palace from above, in ground plan. Making a visualized journey through the mandala, the meditator arrives at the body of the central deity. At this point, one visualizes the deity's body as one's own, all the while remembering that as it appears, it is nonetheless quite empty of substance. Indeed, to fully access this insight is to gain an entirely new conception of a body: one that is visualized rather than material, and on that very basis—when it is recognized—one that is more real than a material body, an adamantine body immune to death. Here, then, we see the ancient immortality project of humanity realized consciously as such.

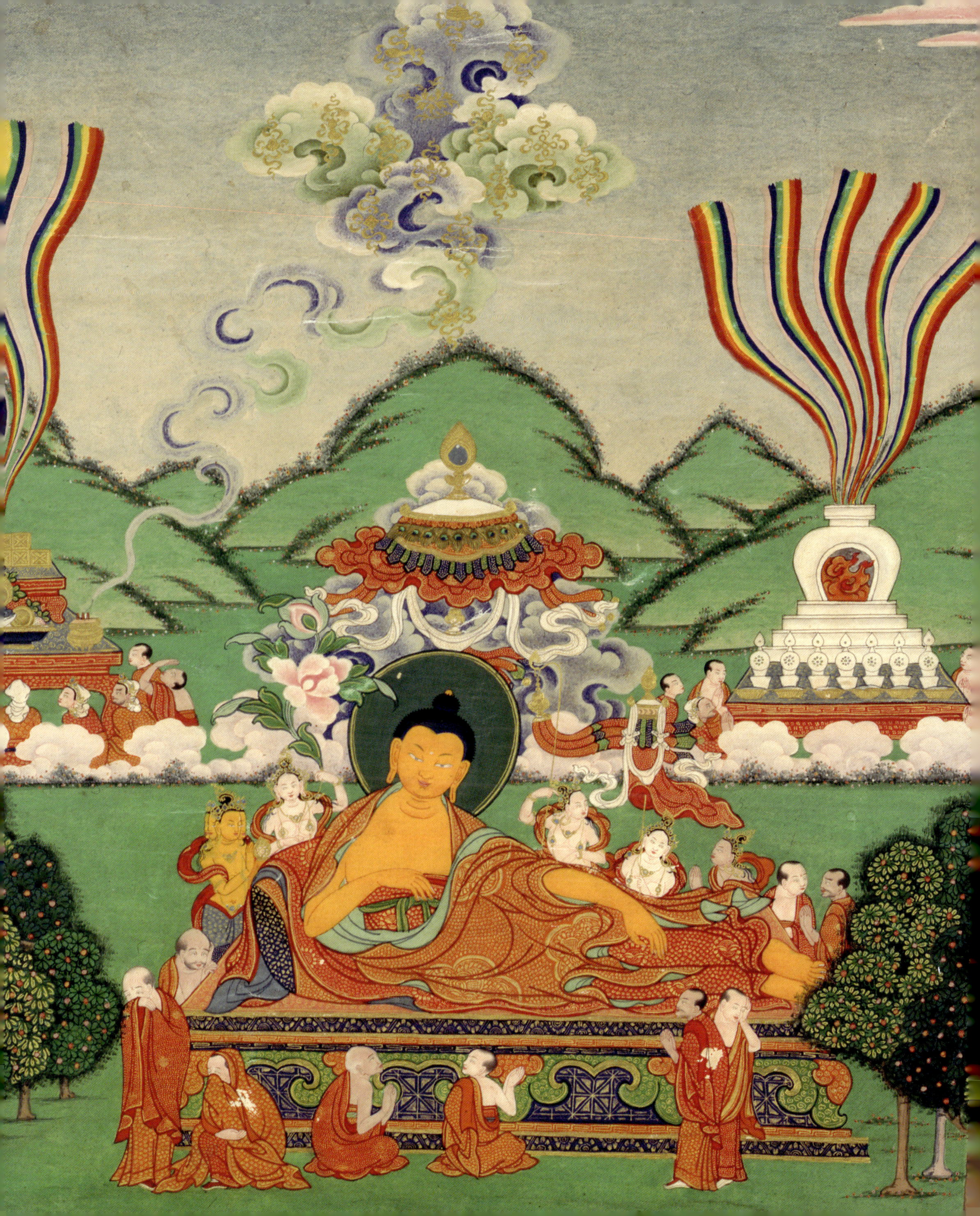

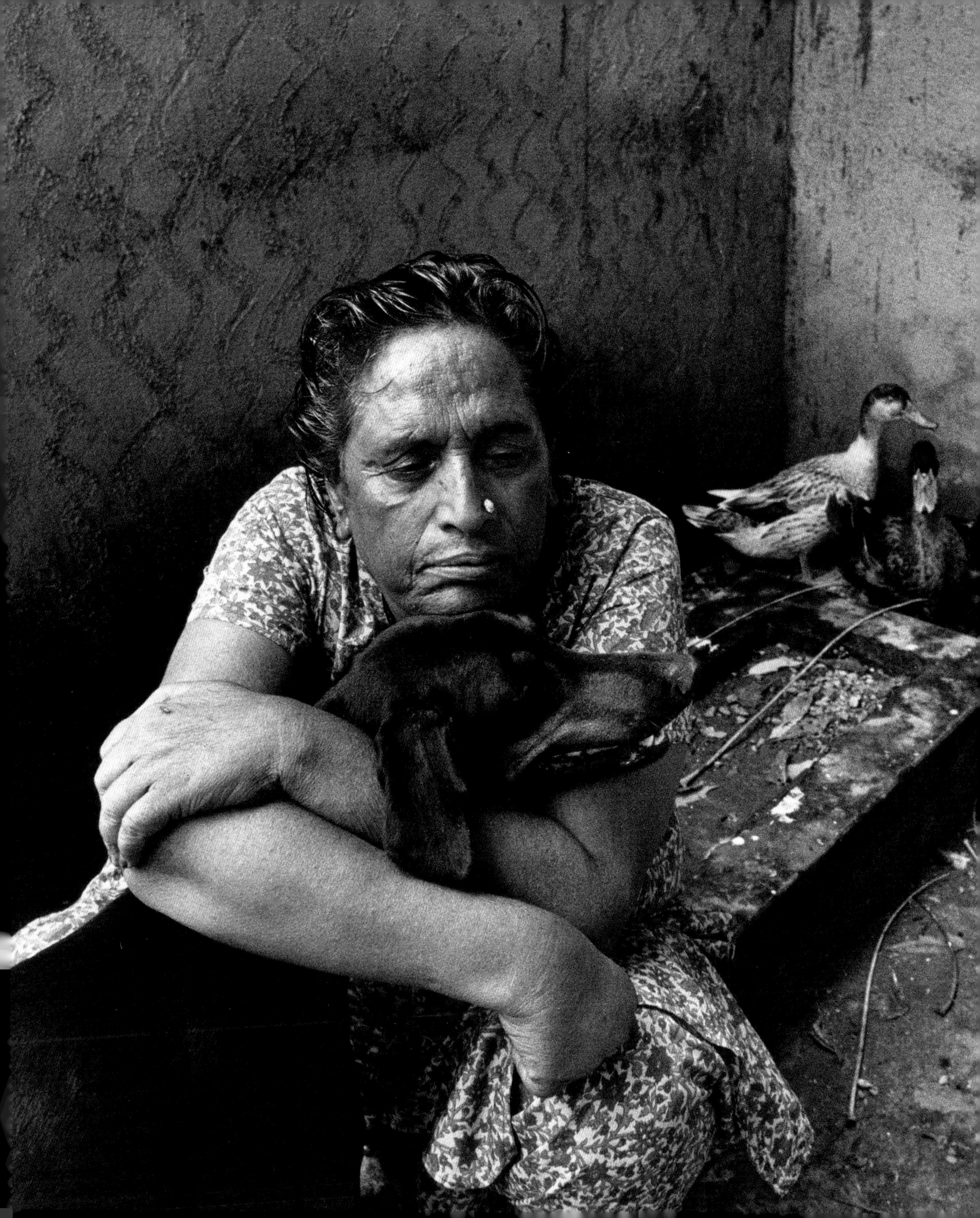

BODIES OF WORK

EXPLORING THE HUMAN AND THE DIVINE IN SERIES

KARIN G. OEN

If anything is sacred,

the human body is sacred.

—Walt Whitman, American poet (1819–1892)[28]

The history of art abounds with intersections between the human and the divine, the physical and the ethereal. A diminutive Paleolithic sculpture known as the Venus of Willendorf (24,000–22,000 BCE), discovered in present-day Austria and assumed to be a fertility totem, is an example of magnificently exaggerated female physicality worthy of worship for its symbolic reproductive power—power that still holds currency today for contemporary artists like Jeff Koons.[29] Michelangelo's *David*, a larger-than-life Florentine Renaissance sculpture (1501–1504), is praised as a masterpiece for its skillful portrayal of the perfection of the male form, rendered with easy grace and harmonic proportions.[30] It depicts a biblical king of Israel as heroic while profoundly human, preparing to do battle with the giant Goliath and armed with little more than intelligence, concentration, and faith. In these two radically different examples we can see the impulse across cultures and time periods to elevate the human figure into the realm of the divine. But what does this mean for the modern world and its largely secular culture? Is there still a relationship involving the human form, its imperfection, and the aspiration to make meaning? The humanist, egalitarian, and democratic values espoused by Walt Whitman in the nineteenth century are representative of the secular and agnostic views of the body and the divine that continue to the present day. In "I Sing the Body Electric," Whitman posed an essential question: "And if the Body were not the Soul, what is the Soul?"

This project examines a group of powerful sacred images—beautiful works of art that relate to the human form and visual manifestations of the divine associated with Hindu and Buddhist practice. It asks us to consider the relationship between the physical body and metaphysical concepts—that which is human and that which is divine—and the difference, if any, between the two. As is illustrated by the Venus of Willendorf and Michelangelo's *David*, these concepts and questions are not limited to the realm of Hindu and Buddhist art and are not exclusive to Asia. Their universality makes them the territory of a much broader inquiry. As such, the diverse historical works in this book converse with four series by contemporary artists. This is not an attempt to draw straight lines between works of art from different times and places; rather, it is to see what happens when we look at art with a relationship to the body and divine aspects of humanness across time, place, and medium.

Just as the Venus of Willendorf was one of many such female figurines carved in late Stone Age Europe and Michelangelo's *David* was one of many biblical sculptures commissioned to complete the niches of the cathedral of Florence, so the images of divine beings included in this exhibition are none of them completely unique in terms of subject matter or style. They are examined together as examples of similar subjects and as variations on the themes of the embodied divine and the intangible made visible. The contemporary works in *Divine Bodies* similarly aim to connect the worlds of the human and the divine, the mundane and the otherworldly. Although these are not the only lenses through which to view these works, it is illuminating to consider the following themes and their relationship to the series and individual works under consideration: the duality of presence and absence in the works of Gauri Gill and Pamela Singh; the fluid spectrum of beauty, sensuality, identity, and transformation inhabited by Dayanita Singh's subject, Mona Ahmed; and the use of humor as an avenue connecting sacred and secular figures and historical and contemporary contexts in the work of Vivan Sundaram.

Presence and Absence

In Gauri Gill's *Traces* series, large black-and-white photographs depict low mounds that function as desert graves for nomads and inhabitants of remote villages in the Thar Desert in Western Rajasthan, part of the natural geographic border between India and Pakistan. A humble counterpoint to India's iconic funerary architectural monuments like the Taj Mahal, these graves are not constructed to last for eternity but are impermanent and remain human in scale. Perhaps surprising to those familiar with Hindu funerals based around cremation, the practice of using such burial mounds is followed by both Muslims and Hindus in this northwestern Indian region, showing how environment affects traditions across faiths. The Bishnoi faith community, one of the groups whose graves are pictured in this series, is located mostly in the Thar Desert and in India's northern states. The Bishnoi strictly observe environmental conservation, and to this end, their mounded graves are minimally intrusive on the landscape, constructed without wood or stone. They will eventually erode and be swallowed up by the shifting desert sands; they have their own life cycle, as did the bodies they house, and are part of the continuum of natural growth and decomposition.

The subjects of these photos—the individuals buried in the graves—are absent while their decaying bodies remain, delineated by the simple mounded rocks, household objects, and other offerings. These humble markers are profound reminders of the sacred treatment our bodies inspire and the respect for that which is divine in all of us, but they are also reminders of the relative impermanence of human life. While the individual subject remains anonymous to viewers, the subjectivity—the personhood in question—takes on a more universal significance. Captured in minute detail on traditional film and developed as gelatin silver prints, Gill's photographs show us the inescapable materiality of the body and how it is treated after death as well as the textures and visuality of the environment in which these graves are found. In an interesting inversion, photographs—works far less permanent than most architecture or sculpture—become the enduring records of graves that are designed to reintegrate into the desert landscape.

The Presence of the Artist and Attributes of the Self

In a different way, Pamela Singh addresses notions of presence and absence in her *Tantric Self-Portraits in Jaipur*. With a simple series of compositional shifts, she removes herself—or key aspects of herself—from what she still considers self-portraits. This work reconfigures self-portraiture as a component of environmental portraiture, with the artist's own image included as an incomplete or ghostly presence rather than as the primary subject of the composition. The artist undertook this series from 2000 to 2003, after many years spent in photojournalism and art photography. Each day she would walk the streets of Jaipur and other cities in India, capturing the unstaged diversity of life on view. In order to incorporate herself into these works, she fitted the camera with a mirror so she could see the image she was taking from in front of the device. Her impulse was not to use the street as a backdrop for a self-portrait but rather to truly integrate herself into the scenes and with the people she photographed—and to have them be part of her life, separated by caste, class, and cosmopolitanism though they were. This daily fieldwork was her way of suturing together her world and theirs.

The relative presence and absence of the artist in each image are made more complicated by their composite nature. The photographs are overlaid with colors and symbolic drawings, making the artist felt more through these indices of authorship than in her physical representation. With these gestures, she offers her artistic and perhaps spiritual presence to viewers. She positions the images as mundane, casual, or accidental snapshots of everyday scenes that are then elevated to include a mystical component by virtue of her keen eye and subtle embellishments. The spiritual and the quotidian are intertwined in these photographs, as the artist's own identity is intertwined with the environment, people, buildings, and animals that fill her frame. In no way straightforward self-portraits, this body of work addresses the subject of self-representation and the impulse to balance outward- and inward-facing components of the self.

In addition to teasing out intersections between the human, the divine, and the body, Pamela Singh's use of vintage pigments in the *Tantric Self-Portraits in Jaipur* recalls photographic practices of the past. The legacy of nineteenth-century British photography is strongly felt in these images, as the colonial project of cataloguing India through its people and monuments—some of the earliest subjects of photography books published as early as 1847—was itself an exercise in portraiture. By incorporating the visual language of this era into her work, the artist reclaims these elements and alters the viewer's point of view from that of the colonial surveyor to the postcolonial subject. She replaces the foreign ethnographer's scrutinizing eye with an artist's inclusive vision of the city.

Beauty, Sensuality, Identity, and Transformation

The work of Dayanita Singh chronicles the life of Mona Ahmed, a eunuch and member of the hijra community in Delhi. An art photographer with a background in photojournalism, the artist first encountered her captivating subject on an assignment in 1989, when the two struck up a friendship that has underpinned their working relationship ever since. On the surface, this long-term project—seen in photographs, books, and moving-image work—is documentary in nature, showing the life of Mona Ahmed in private and public over the years. As specific and intimate as these images are, they are also studies in the interrelationship of beauty, gender, and identity in society—works that chart the cultural currency of beauty and sensuality as feminized commodities.

In South Asian cultural contexts, the hijra are considered a third sex, born male, self-identified as female, and evidence of the fluidity of gender as a product of culture and individual personality more than biology. In the case of the hijra—an Urdu word with Arabic origins that literally means "to leave one's tribe"—the members of the community traditionally live apart from mainstream society, forming social networks and supporting elders in the community who can no longer support themselves. In contemporary communities, such as the one in Delhi where Mona Ahmed makes her home, it is common for Hindu and Muslim hijras to live together. They traditionally support themselves through tips earned from dancing and singing as well as from monetary offerings received for performing blessings at auspicious events like weddings or the birth of children. These blessings are often unsolicited and paid for out of a mix of obligation and fear of the retaliation or curses that might result from failure to comply. The hijra are considered to be spiritually elevated, closer to the sacred or divine than "ordinary" people, but are simultaneously looked down upon and forced to live on the fringes of society.

This contradiction between godliness and the raucousness of bawdy entertainment defines the world of the hijra and is a source of some of the personal pain and strife that Dayanita Singh shows viewers in the life of Mona Ahmed. Once a larger-than-life personality who proclaimed herself the empress of Turkmen Gate, Mona Ahmed in her later years retreated from the public eye and the hijra community after being separated from her adopted daughter, choosing instead to make her home in a house built in the graveyard of her ancestors. This photographic project presents the subject in her full physicality while also providing windows into her thoughts and feelings through correspondence in which she conveys her life story to her publisher. These texts accompany the images when presented in book form, and her expressive features are magnified when shown as moving images in the video portrait *Mona and Myself* (2013). This project is essentially portraiture of long duration—over the course of decades—where the subject remains visually present and her identity evolves over time. Dayanita Singh gives her subject the space and time to evolve from the one-dimensional label of "eunuch" to the more expansive adjective "unique"—a word that she has long used to describe Ahmed. The power of transformation, be it physical, emotional, or spiritual, comes through brilliantly in this expansive series that incorporates time as one of its most powerful components.

Humor

As a coda to this enquiry into the nexus of the human and the divine, it is worth looking at the role that humor and postmodern irreverence can play in the relationship between the two. Divine beings can embody fierceness and kindness among many other fundamentally human characteristics, and the visual manifestation of these qualities often includes playfulness. The beauty embedded in a fierce growl or the ease of downturned eyes and a slight smile rendered in finely carved materials are evidence of the lightness that pervades much sacred sculpture. In Vivan Sundaram's *Khajuraho* series, this playfulness of gesture and composition is amplified to the level of outright humor.

As a young artist not long out of school in the 1960s,[31] Sundaram took published images of Indian temple sculpture as the basis for works that trace a palimpsestic transition from medieval stone deity to glamorous modern individual. Keenly aware of contemporary art trends and postmodern practices, Sundaram was also interested in mining the history of Indian art and architecture. The artist found classical foils to his contemporary drawings in the intricately carved erotic sculpture of Khajuraho, a Hindu and Jain temple complex dating to the tenth and eleventh centuries in Madhya Pradesh, as well as other sculptures from important monuments such as Ajanta, Ellora, and Elephanta. His cartoon-like additions of sunglasses, hats, clothing, and speech balloons to these revered subjects offer a new way of seeing these images while humanizing them. The gendered interactions of the gods, the monumental archetypes carved in stone, and the glib pen drawings of a youthful and mischievous artist come together in artworks that are thought provoking in themselves but even more so in the context of the divine bodies with which they keep company here. Self-perpetuating and self-renewing—like the Venus of Willendorf or the ubiquitous *David*—these reworked images speak not just to the global nature of contemporary art but also to the universal concerns of artists throughout history. To address the human in art is to address the divine, and to attempt an image of the divine opens the eyes to humanity.

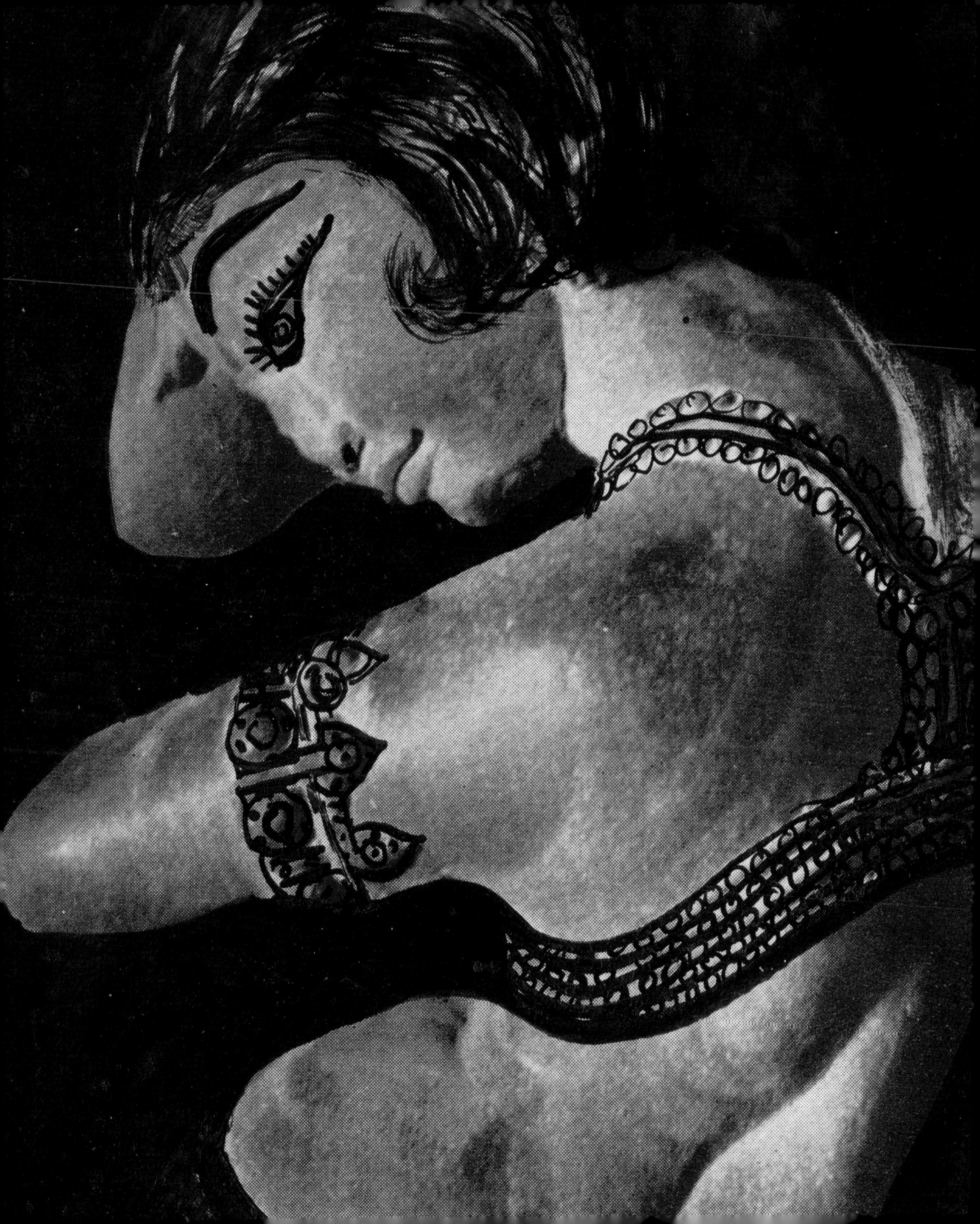

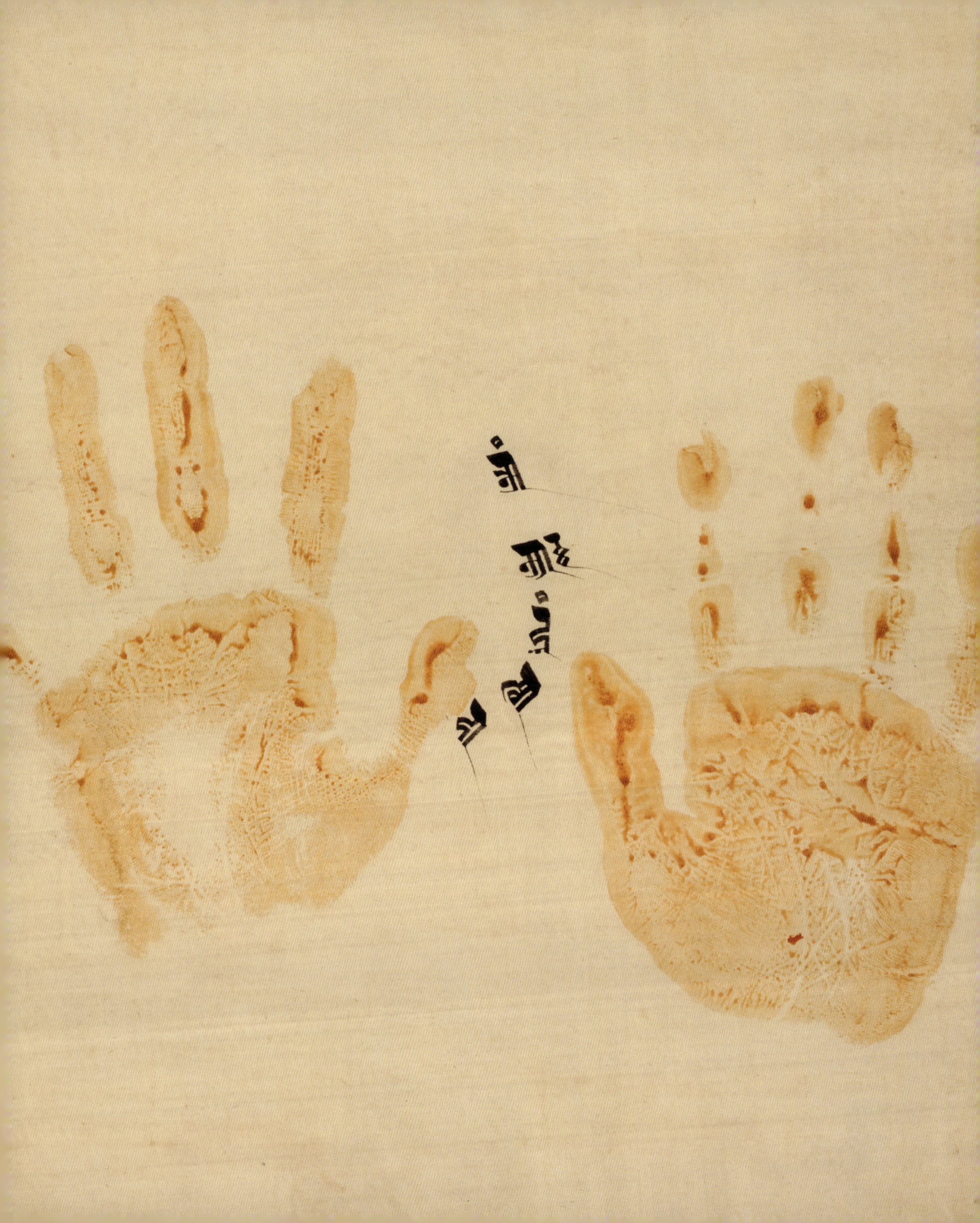

There are no endings. If you think so you are deceived as to their nature. They are all beginnings.

—Hilary Mantel, English writer (b. 1952)

Transience and Transcendence

The boundaries which divide Life from Death are at best shadowy and vague. Who shall say where the one ends, and where the other begins?

—Edgar Allan Poe, American writer (1809–1849)

Life and death are one, even as the river and sea are one.

—Kahlil Gibran, Lebanese American poet (1883–1931)

CRUCIFIED CHRIST

CAT.

1

APPROX. 1650–1750
Philippines
Wood with colors
H. 88 cm x W. 84 cm x D. 19 cm
Acquisition made possible by the San Francisco-Manila Sister City Committee, 2016.163

Take, eat; this is my body which is broken for you: do this in remembrance of me. —I Corinthians 11:24

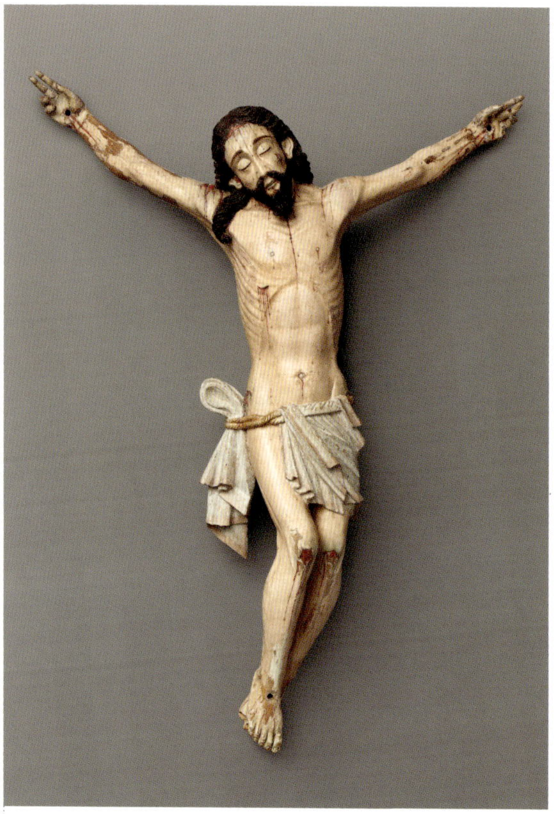

This naturalistic depiction of the crucified Christ was crafted in the Philippines. As was the custom in Catholic imagery from the period, Christ's body bears various wounds mentioned in the Bible. Along with them, however, appear numerous smaller wounds that both reveal the humanity of the embodied Christ and emphasize the compassion required to endure physical torture for the sake of others. The crucifixion of Christ's physical body set the stage for his resurrection into a divine body not subject to death. By symbolically consuming the flesh and blood of the crucified Christ during communion, believers assimilate divinity within their own bodies, thus enabling them to participate in Christ's transcendence of death, regardless of spatial, temporal, or cultural distance from the event itself. The physical assimilation of divine bodies is one of the most ancient themes in religious literature and can be traced back to the Egyptian Pyramid Texts of approximately 2500 BCE. | JD

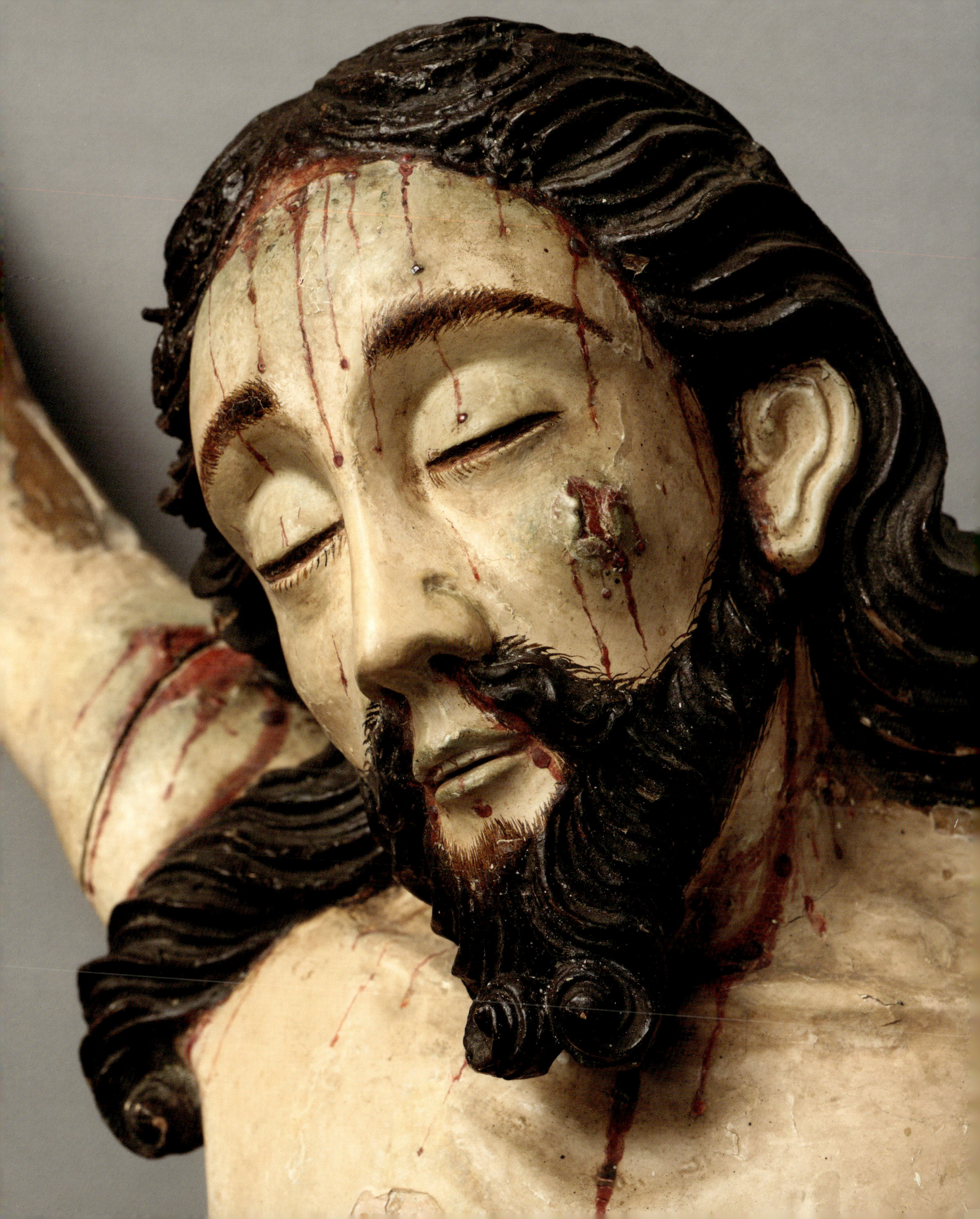

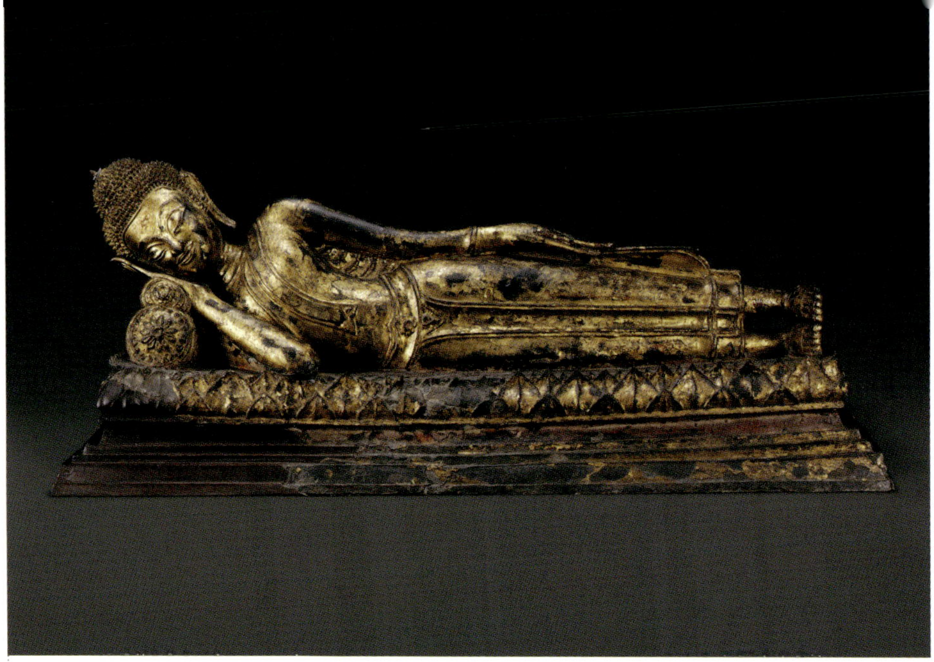

CAT.

2

RECLINING BUDDHA

1600–1700

Thailand; former kingdom of Ayutthaya
Brass with traces of lacquer and gilding
H. 36.8 cm x W. 94 cm x D. 27.9 cm
The Avery Brundage Collection, B60S109

One might think that the Buddha's death was the end of his career, but it most certainly was not. Indeed, it is a supreme irony that the death of the founder has often coincided with the beginning of a religion. This Thai sculpture commemorates the moment when the founder of Buddhism, the Indian prince Shakyamuni, died—a passage that gave birth to a tradition destined to last for millennia.

Here, the Buddha adopts the posture that represents the occasion of the death, or "final nirvana" (*parinirvana*), of his physical body. Since the Buddha did indeed have a physical body, his death was in many ways similar to any other. According to early Buddhist philosophy, the body's atomic constituents dissolve back into primordial nature, the source from whence they originally evolved during the process of birth and growth. These elements have three qualities: they are impermanent (*anitya*), have no essence (*anatma*), and involve suffering (*duhkha*). The question for the living seeker of enlightenment is: How to transcend the incessant activity of these elements, which results in the ordinary world of cyclical misery we call *samsara*?

The answer lies in something called dharma, the Buddhist way of life as described in the Buddhist scriptures. Sustained application of this system of thought and action allows meditators to go beyond the impermanence of the material world's elements. Dharma, indeed, was to be the Buddha's successor; after his demise, he appointed no person as his successor but instead set down the rule, "Let the dharma be your guide."

The importance of the dharma is such that it is counted one among the "Three Jewels" of Buddhism, coequal with the community of monks (*samgha*) and the Buddha himself. Indeed, it is likely that the importance of the dharma led directly to the notion that the Buddha possessed a "body of dharma" (*dharma-kaya*) transcending his material body and thus comprising his ultimate source. | JD

DEATH OF THE BUDDHA SHAKYAMUNI

APPROX. 1700–1800
Tibet
Colors on cotton
H. 45.4 cm x W. 31.8 cm (image);
H. 100.3 cm x W. 59.4 cm (overall)
The Avery Brundage Collection, B66D23

CAT.
3

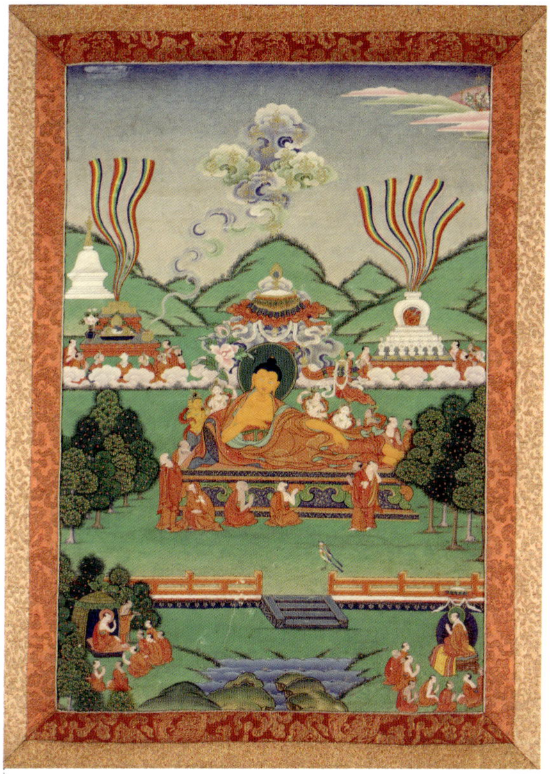

This *thangka* is the culminating work in an important series of eastern Tibetan paintings that depict key events in the life of the historical Buddha Shakyamuni. It preserves two interconnected moments in time. The first and most prominent is that of the Buddha's death, which dominates the center of the painting. He lies on his right side in preparation for his final nirvana, and although his own expression is beatific and heavenly wonders appear in the sky above, the atmosphere from the human perspective seems one of quite understandable grief.

The second moment, however, reveals that grief is not the end and, at least in the spiritual world of this painting, neither is death itself for the Buddha, the "Blessed One" (Bhagavan). Just behind and to the right of the dying Buddha appears a magical scene that postdates his bodily death: the occasion of his cremation. Inside a white furnace, the funereal fire can be seen burning bright red. From the white urn there pours forth a miraculous rainbow of light whose appearance is, in Tibetan Buddhist thought, linked with a given being's attainment of immortality and enlightenment, one intermingling with the other to an indeterminable extent. Indeed, according to narrative sources regarding the previous lives of the Buddha, relics do indeed radiate residual blessings. At the upper left of the painting, what appears to be Shakyamuni's stupa (a Buddhist reliquary; see cats. 4 and 5) also emits a rainbow of lights that mark it as a manifestation of the miraculous.

The reverse of this painting reveals another avenue through which the spiritual power of Shakyamuni becomes present. Between the centuries-old handprints of the consecrating lama are a series of Sanskrit syllables carefully executed in the ritual *landza* script: *Om ah hum sva ha*. The first three syllables follow the contour of the dying Buddha's body as it is painted on the reverse of the *thangka*, appearing at his brow, throat, and heart. These syllables are understood to seal (mudra) the body, speech, and mind of the Buddha into the painting. *Sva ha* is an ancient Sanskrit phrase dating back to the Vedic scriptures, written as early as 1700 BCE; for millennia it has filled ritual actions with spiritual power. This *thangka*, then, is the key to a technique created to ritualistically render the body, speech, and mind of the Buddha Shakyamuni present. | JD

MINIATURE STUPA (BUDDHIST RELIQUARY)

APPROX. 100–150
Pakistan; former kingdom of Gandhara
Stone (schist)
H. 18 cm x Diam. 9.8 cm
Gift of Milla L. Handley and Raymond G. Handley, 1999.49.a-.c

CAT.
4

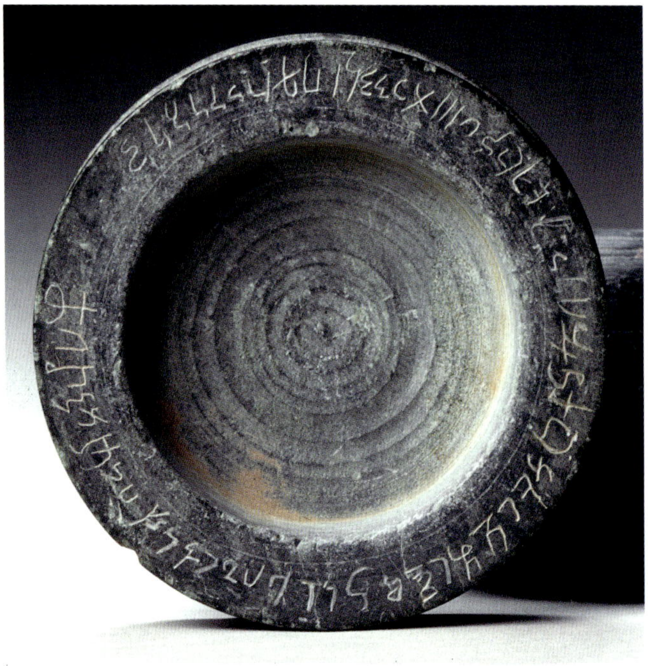

After the death of the Buddha, his body was cremated. Being divine, however, only his bones remained after the pyre was extinguished; according to legend, everything else was consumed in the fire—something that would not take place with an ordinary body. Shakyamuni's bodily remnants, however, were not ordinary but were saturated with the spiritual power (*punya*) of the Buddha.[32] The problem, of course, would be to locate and contain this power so that it might be accessed reliably and repeatedly over time. It would fall to the monumental reliquary known as a stupa to perform this function. Properly sealed and consecrated, such reliquaries were thought to last until the entire manifest cosmos—*samsara* itself—came to an end. In other words, stupas are hieroglyphs of negentropy (the opposite of entropy); in Buddhist thought, they stop time. The monarchs of ancient north India sought to capture and preserve Shakyamuni's time-stopping spiritual power by enshrining their share of his relics in large stupas. Over time, more and more stupas appeared, and by the turn of the millennium, the body of the Buddha, in the form of stupas containing his power-saturated relics, was projecting itself across the South Asian subcontinent.

Stupas do not, however, have to be monumental in order to perform their function. Moreover, they need not contain only the relics of a buddha or other person who had "touched nirvana with the body," as the texts state. Indeed, especially in the northwestern regions of the subcontinent known as Gandhara (now in Afghanistan and Pakistan), the stupa could be used in a funereal context to help deceased persons gain better rebirths. An inscription on this stupa reveals how the process worked. The dedication was made by a nun, one Utaraya, on behalf of her parents—a standard procedure in early Buddhism. Why would she seal items she understood as relics of the Buddha in a stupa and then dedicate the collocation of materials to her parents? The inscription states that Utaraya "established a relic of the lord" inside the stupa, an inherently meritorious activity. However, she did so "for the merit of her father and mother." In so doing, Utaraya's parents receive the karmic virtue of making such an endowment, which, because it is sealed inside a stupa, will last in perpetuity. The result is an unending flow of positive karma for Utaraya's parents—a perpetual good-karma engine, one might say. | JD

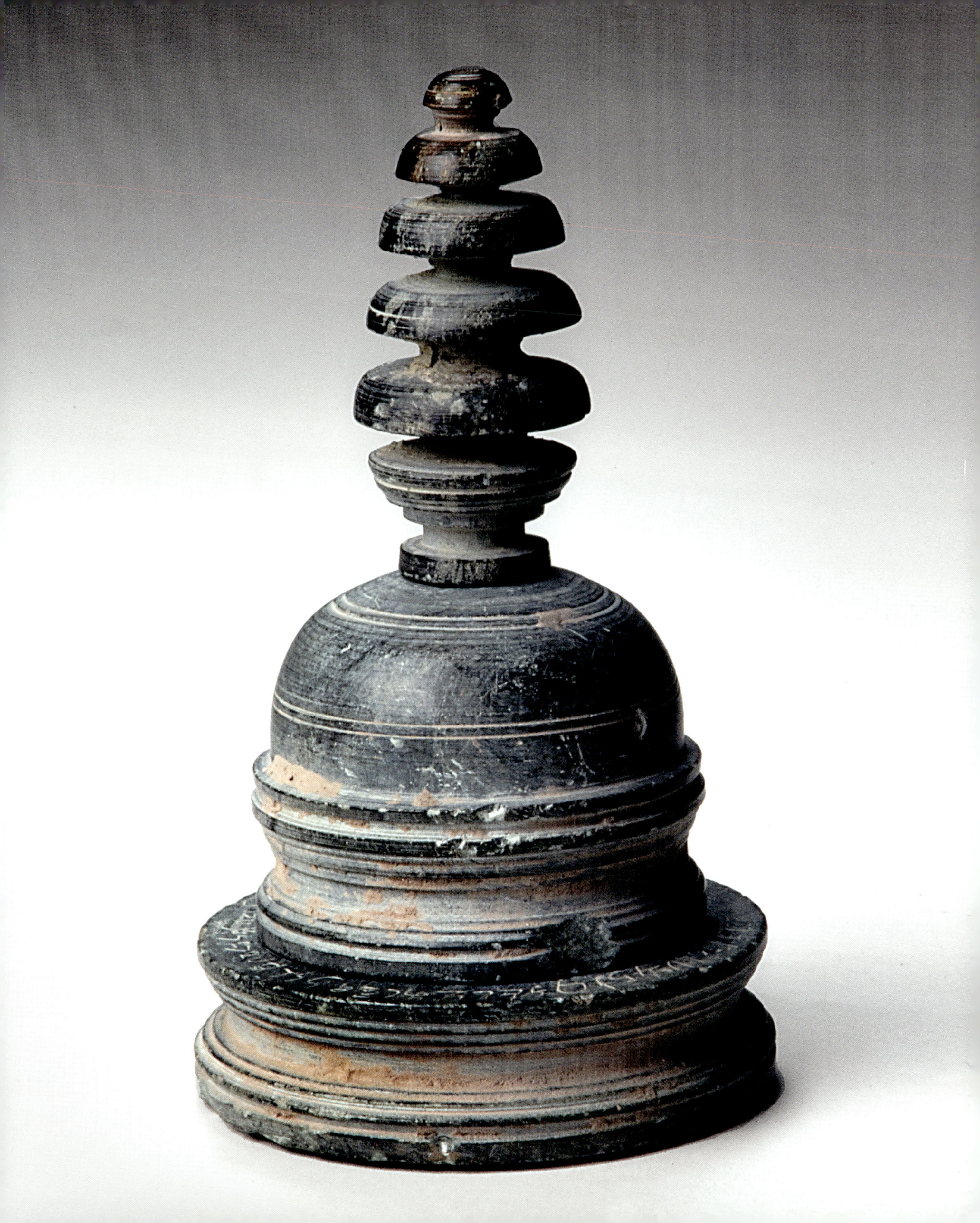

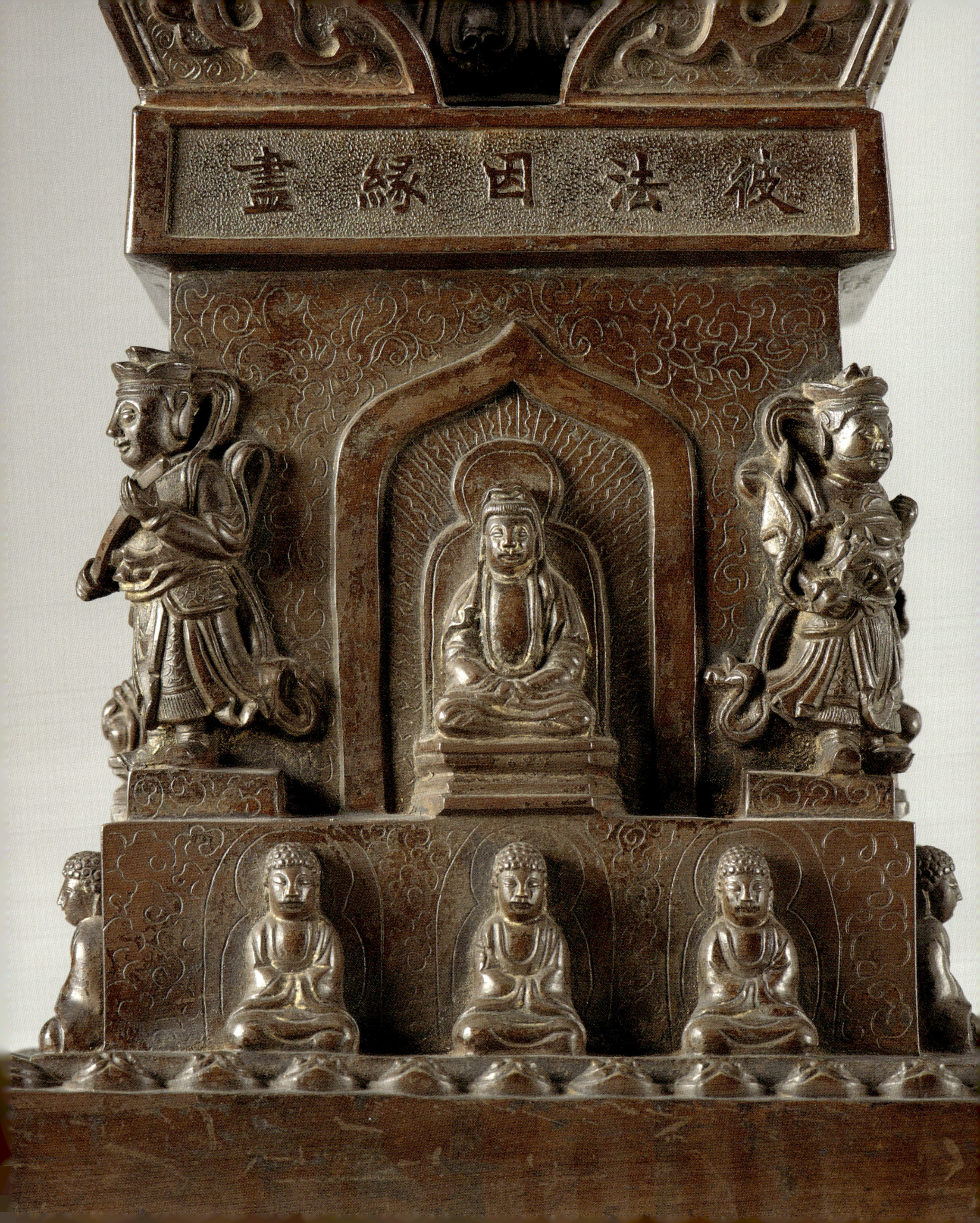
彼法因緣盡

MINIATURE STUPA (BUDDHIST RELIQUARY)

APPROX. 1700–1800
China
Qing dynasty (1644–1911)
Bronze with traces of gilding
H. 41 cm x W. 18.4 cm x D. 18.4 cm
The Avery Brundage Collection, B61B13+

CAT.
5

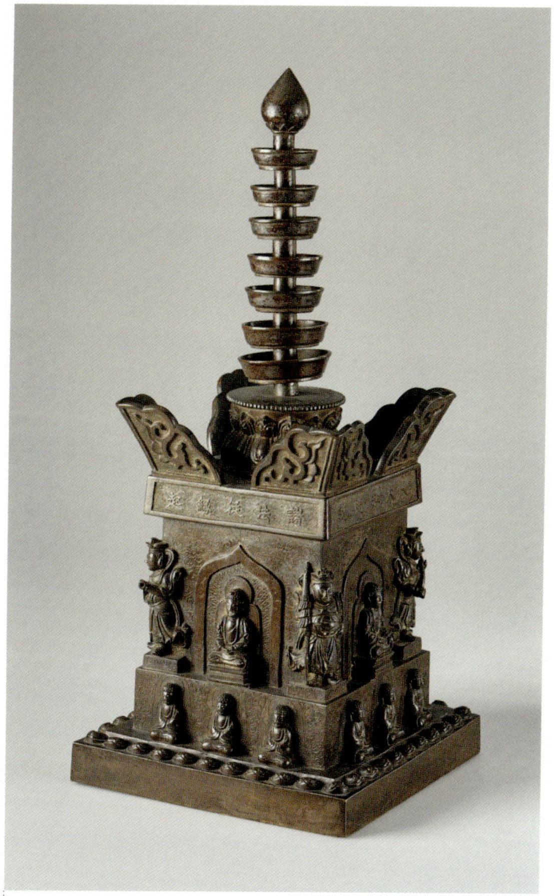

Whatever its size and whatever its age, the stupa is the monumental center of the Buddhist tradition. In its most ancient Indian form, the stupa was a reliquary mound designed as a receptacle for the cremated remains of deceased holy men. In early Buddhist thought, the stupa was a reliquary understood to be "saturated with the merit" of the person enshrined therein.

This stupa differs in many ways from those produced in South Asia. In India, for example, the most ancient monumental stupas typically consist of a domed superstructure surmounted by a cube-like box. In these cases, the symbolism is generative, as the dome both visually and linguistically recalls an egg (the Sanskrit term for egg is *anda*, the word also used to refer to the dome). This much later Chinese stupa exhibits a very different morphology. The central dome has been replaced by a cubic structure that would have appeared on top of the *anda* in earlier examples. Moreover, four important figures appear at each side of the stupa: Akshobhya, Ratnasambhava, Amitabha, and Amoghasiddhi—the four buddhas. Together with invisible Vairochana at the center, they comprise a cosmogram, or model of the universe. The Guardian Kings of the Four Directions occupy the intermediate sectors of the stupa—a configuration that marks the stupa as a mandala (a geometric meditation diagram) as well as the center and summit of the cosmos.

This imagery was derived from a crucial text—the *Sarva-tathagata-tattva-samgraha Tantra (The Collection of the Qualities of All the Buddhas)*—that transmitted Esoteric Buddhism to East Asia in the seventh century. The stupa also bears the so-called Buddhist Creed, rendered in Chinese characters, which is thought to transmute that upon which it is properly inscribed into a functional stupa. It is also understood as a very brief summary of the train of thought that led to the Buddha's enlightenment: "Of those things that arise from causes, / The Tathagata [Buddha] has taught those causes, / And also what their cessation is: / This is the doctrine of the Great Sage." Perhaps it is for this reason that the stupa is regarded as a visual epitome of the Buddha's mind. | JD

TRACES SERIES, 1999–
BIRTH SERIES, 2005

CAT.
6

BY GAURI GILL (INDIAN, B. 1970)
Lent by the artist and Nature Morte Gallery, Delhi

Untitled works from *Traces* nos. 1, 2, 4, 6, 8, 33, 35, 45: gelatin silver prints, H. 33 x W. 22.9 cm
Untitled works from *Traces* nos. 3, 5, 7: inkjet prints, H. 218.4 x W. 147.3 cm
Untitled works from *Birth* nos. 1–8: gelatin silver prints, H. 22.9 x W. 33 cm

Gill lives with and photographs people and landscapes over long periods of time, capturing embedded time as well as natural and human life cycles. She gets to know her subjects intimately and photographs them to respectfully document this intimacy, granting in turn a privileged access to her viewers. Her *Traces* and *Birth* series are parts of a larger body of work entitled *Notes from the Desert*, set in Western Rajasthan along the border between Pakistan and India. These particular photographs show the calm that follows the drama of birth and death, bringing to mind the continuum of bodily experiences that need not be considered sacred to be recognized as a powerful connection among all of humanity. Through Gill's lens, we see the highs and the lows of life with straightforward simplicity. The people of these diverse desert villages are socially and economically marginalized, but they maintain important ties to tradition, marking life's milestones in ways that might otherwise be lost to history or conformity with contemporary culture.

Over time Gill's photographs have come to comprise an archive of the people who live in this region. Many of these works address their imprint on the land, which is minimal, ephemeral, and humble. Her *Traces* series takes as its subject their simple, low, mounded graves made from natural materials and personal offerings and in various states of erosion and decay. These impermanent markers of the end of life for people from both Muslim and Hindu communities paint a picture of customs and rituals in India more complicated than one based on simplistic divisions between these two major faith groups. Gill's *Birth* series from 2005 shows a midwife, Kasumbi Dai, delivering her granddaughter in Motasar, Ghafan, a remote village near the border of Pakistan. Gill spent many days living with Dai, who died in 2010, and assisted with the baby's delivery on the sandy floor of the modest desert home. The birthing mother is veiled, and her arms are mostly covered in ivory bangles, markers of the customs and identity of her caste. Despite these visible indicators of difference and distance from the modern, urban world, the physicality, the pain, the support offered, and the emotions associated with birth are universal. | KGO

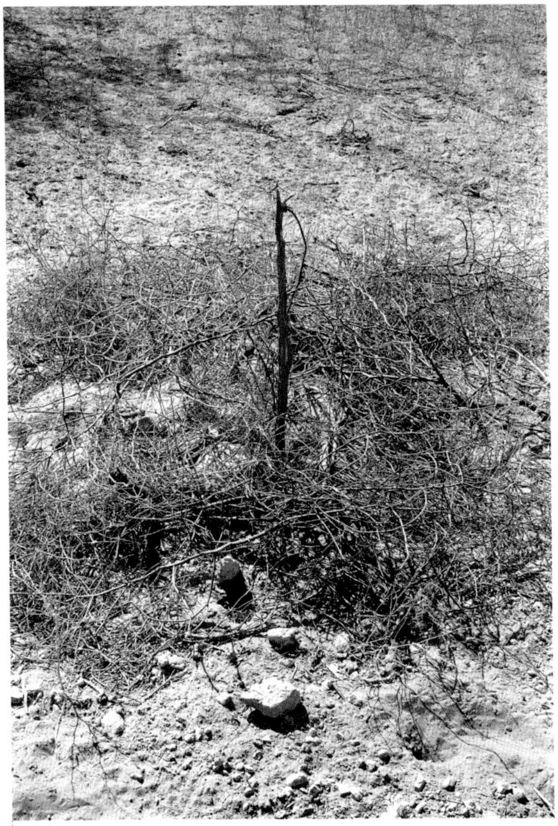

1

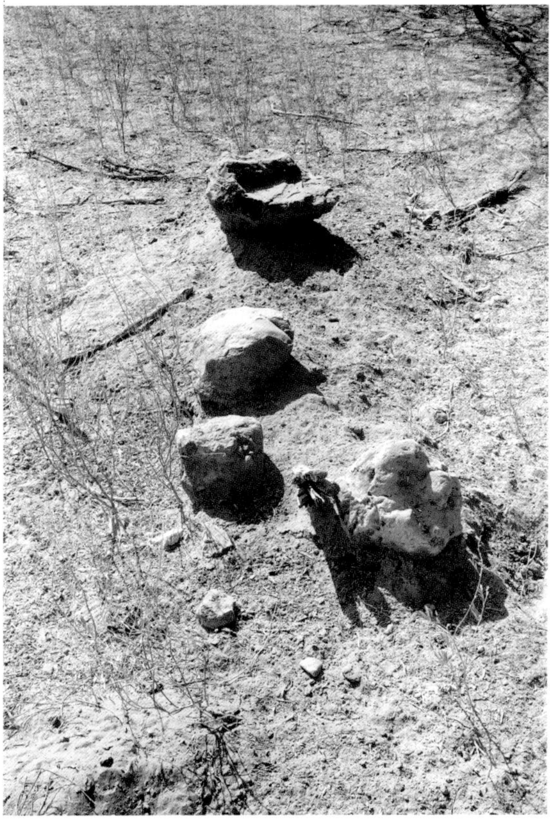

2

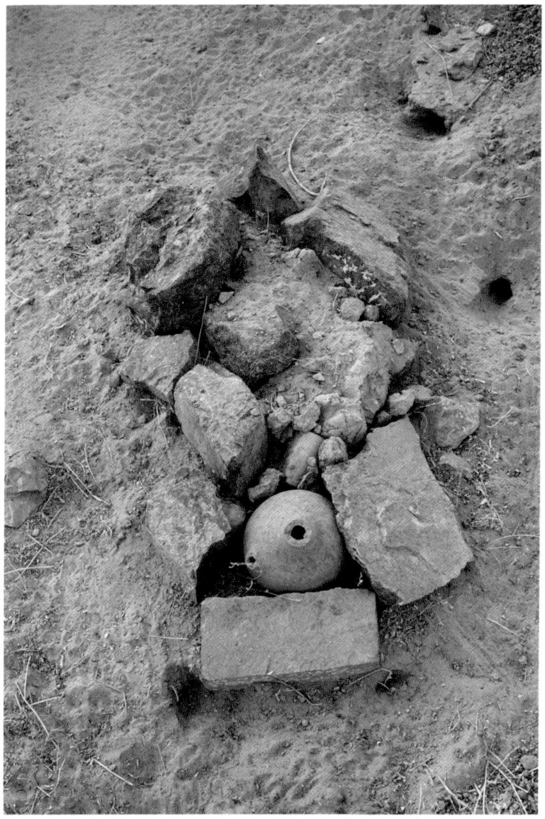

3

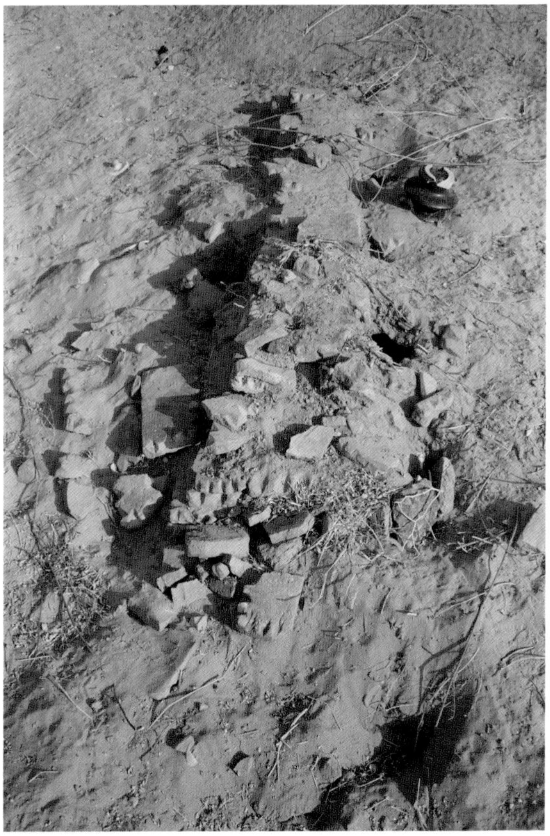

4

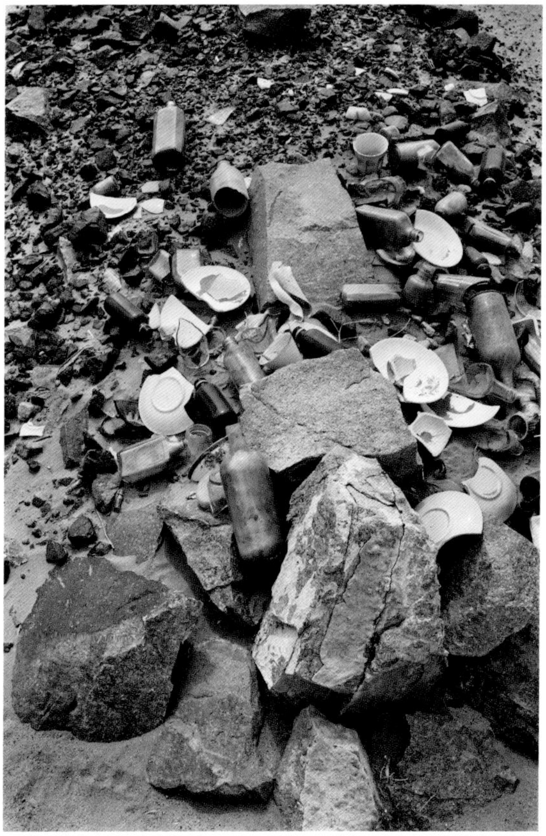

5

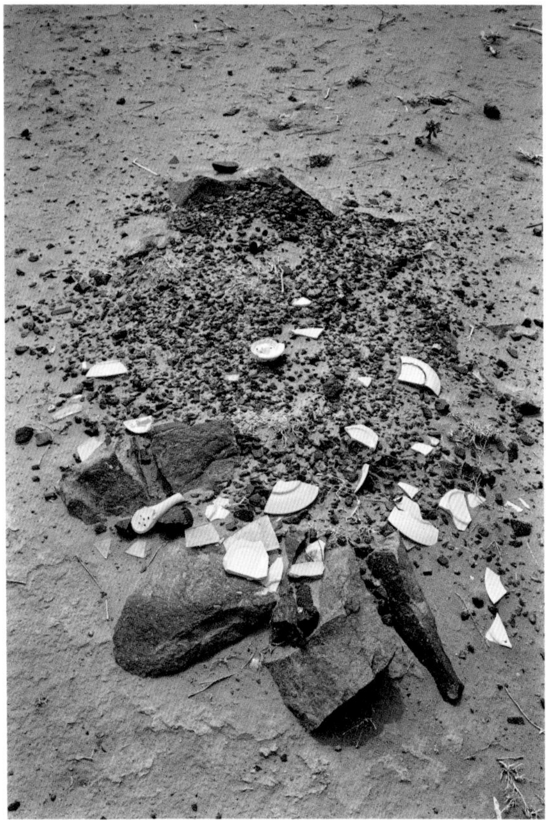

6

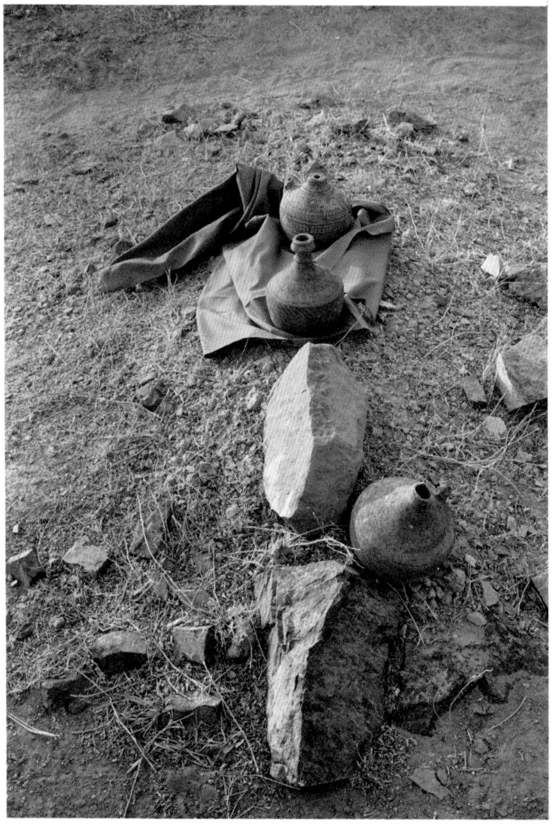

7

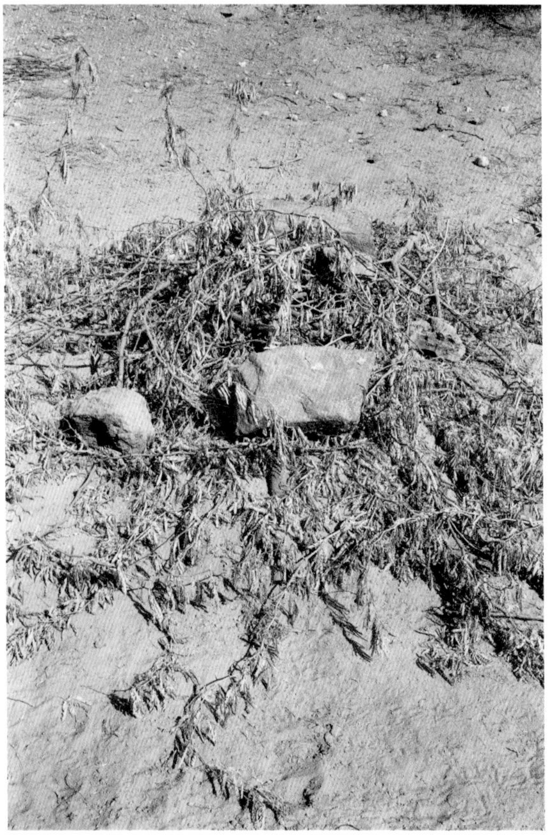

8

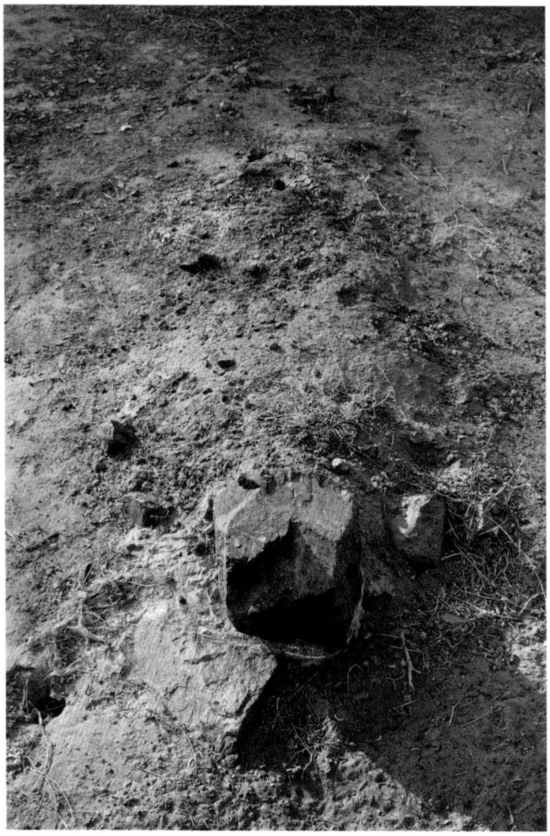

33

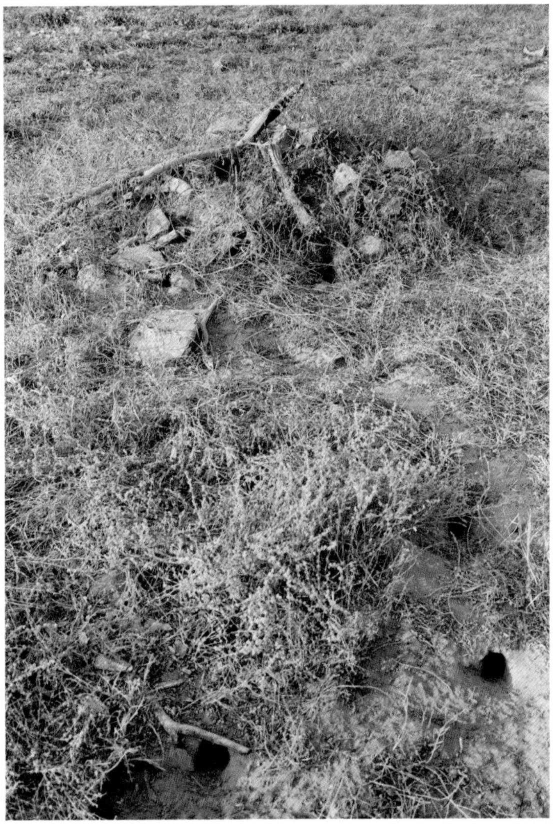

35

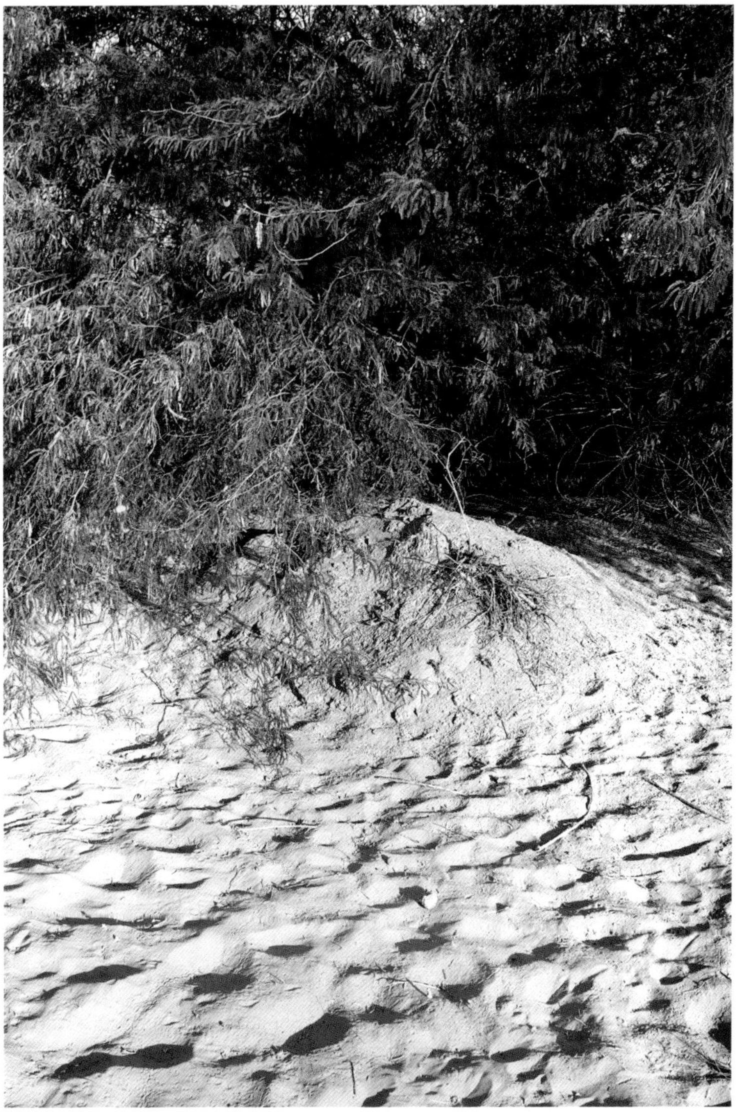

45

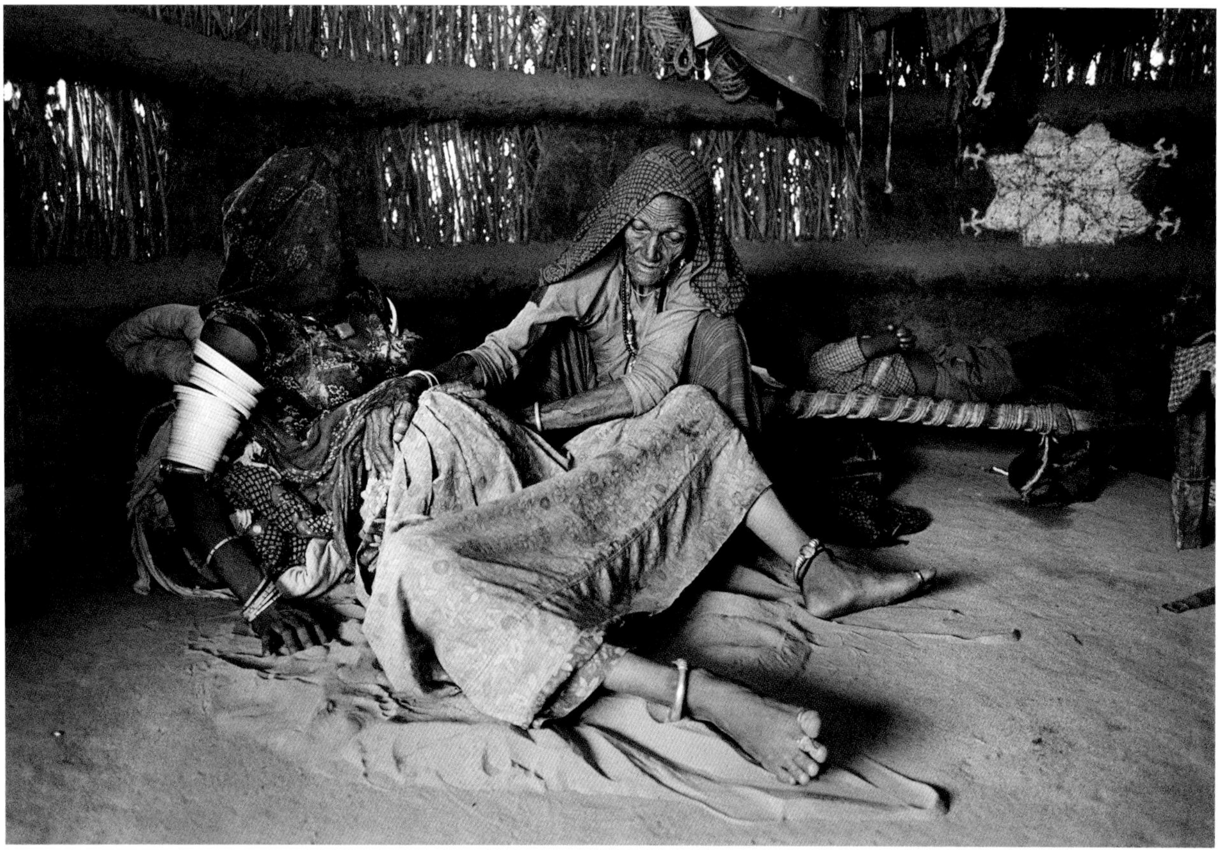

1

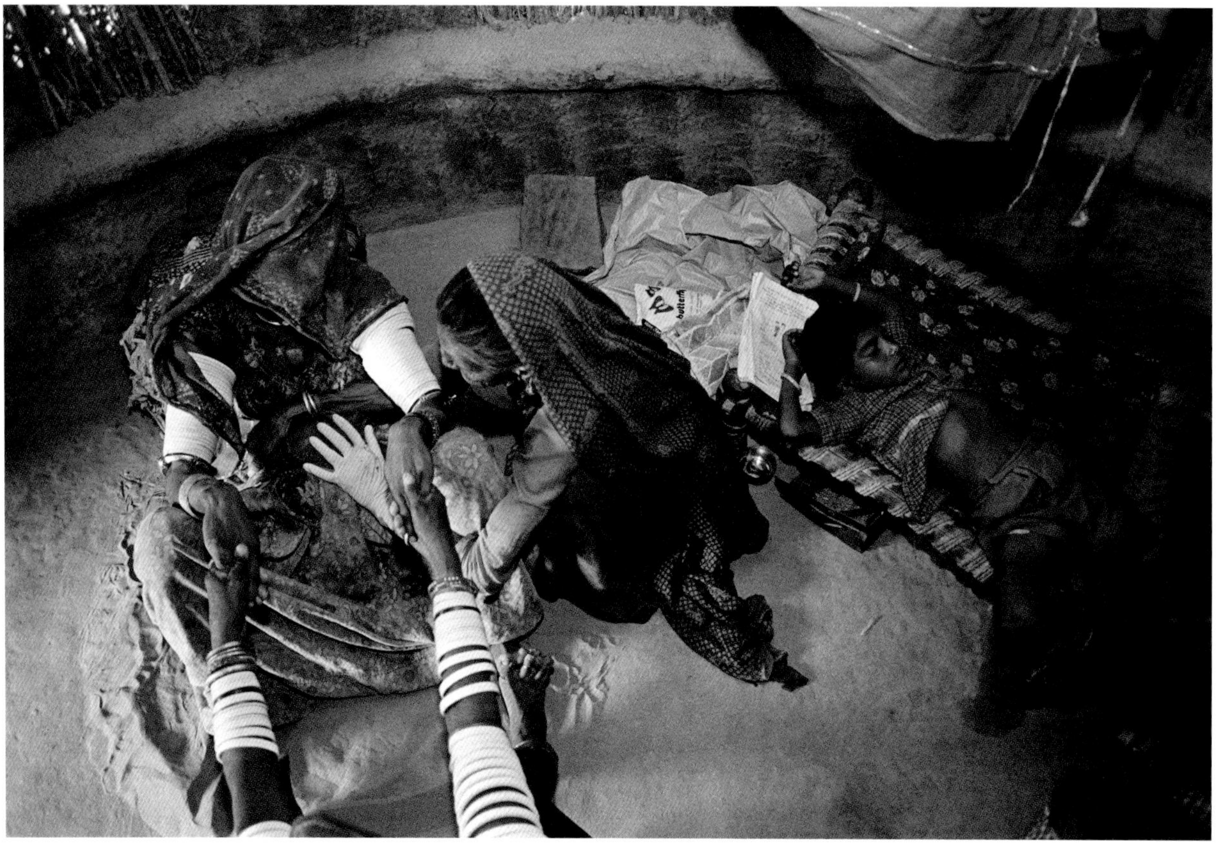

2

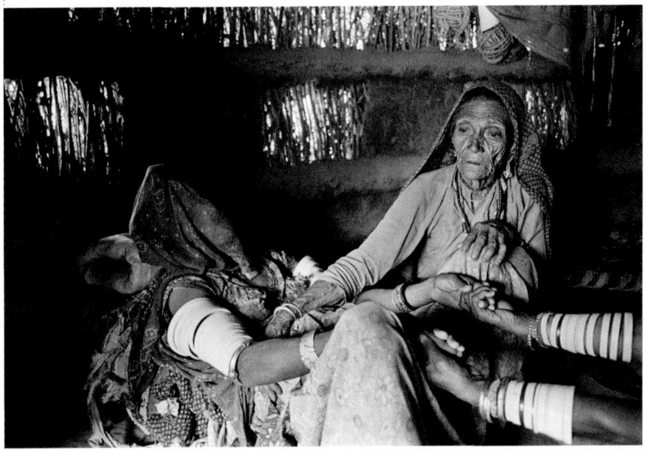

3

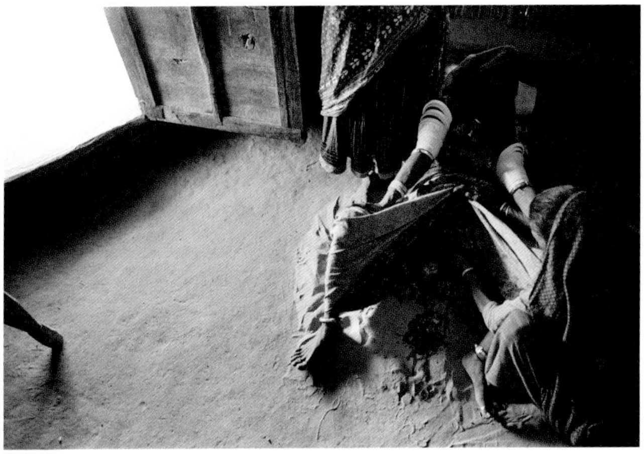

4

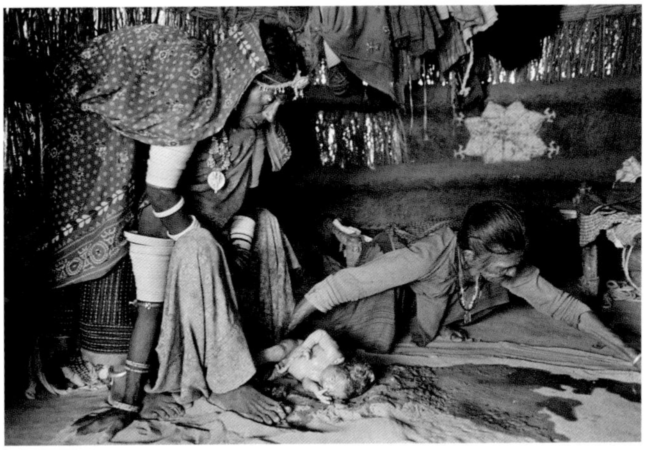

5

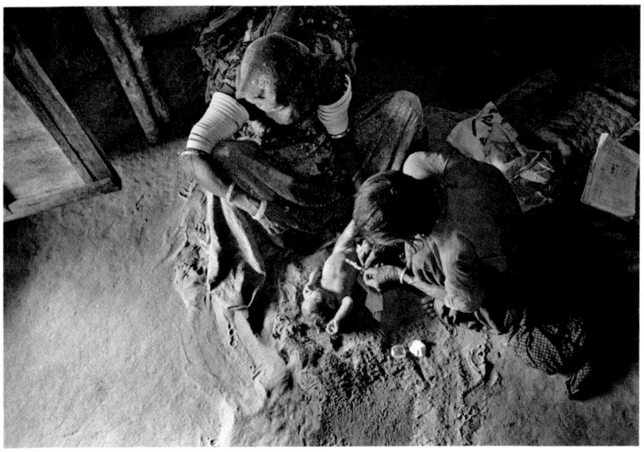

6

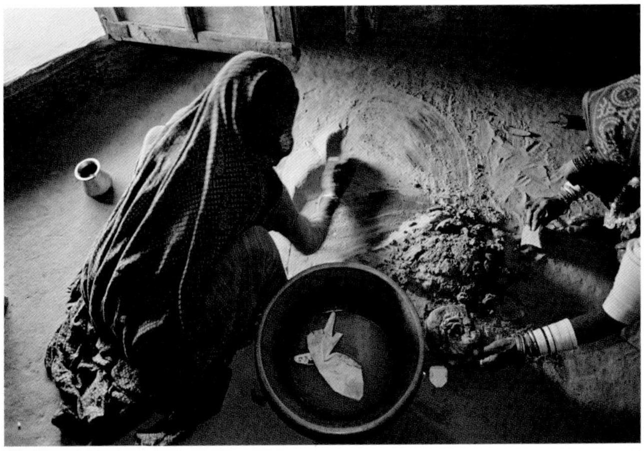

7

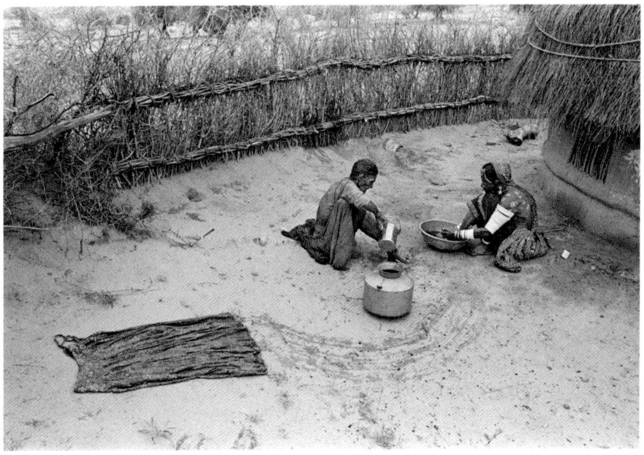

8

IMPERMANENCE: THE TIME OF MAN, 2006/2017

BY DAVID HODGE (AMERICAN, B. 1955) AND HI-JIN KANG HODGE (SWEDISH AND AMERICAN, B. SOUTH KOREA, 1974)
Multichannel video installation with sound, 23 minutes
Lent by the artists

CAT.
7

David and Hi-Jin Hodge's video work helps us explore the universality of impermanence and how human lives can nonetheless have meaning. The artists invite us to reconsider the evident, but often ignored, relationship between existence and the end of life. The 122 interviewees, ranging from philosophers to gardeners, economists, spiritual leaders, doctors, and patients, eloquently reflect on topics such as death and change and their impact on everyday lives. The participants' moving responses emphasize that just as impermanence (*anitya*) is a central concept in Buddhism, it is also a universal concern. | QA

This project began as an installation for a 2006 exhibition that called on artists to pick one of a number of Buddhist themes, and we chose impermanence.

The reasons for our choice were many, but at that moment in time we were most affected by the death of a dear friend. This experience led us to wonder if others had similar stories about impermanence in its most extreme form: death.

It only took one interview to learn that we had struck a chord. While few people talk openly with one another about impermanence, we learned that many had thought deeply about the subject. It wasn't merely the religious and spiritual thinkers who proved the most interesting. It was a question we all talk about with ourselves.[33] | DAVID HODGE AND HI-JIN KANG HODGE

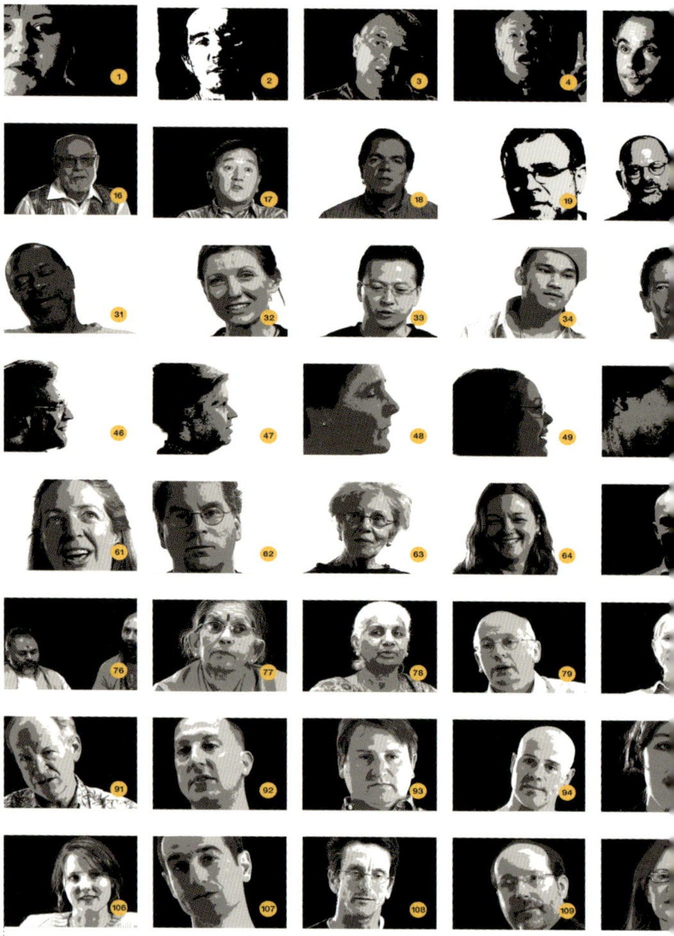

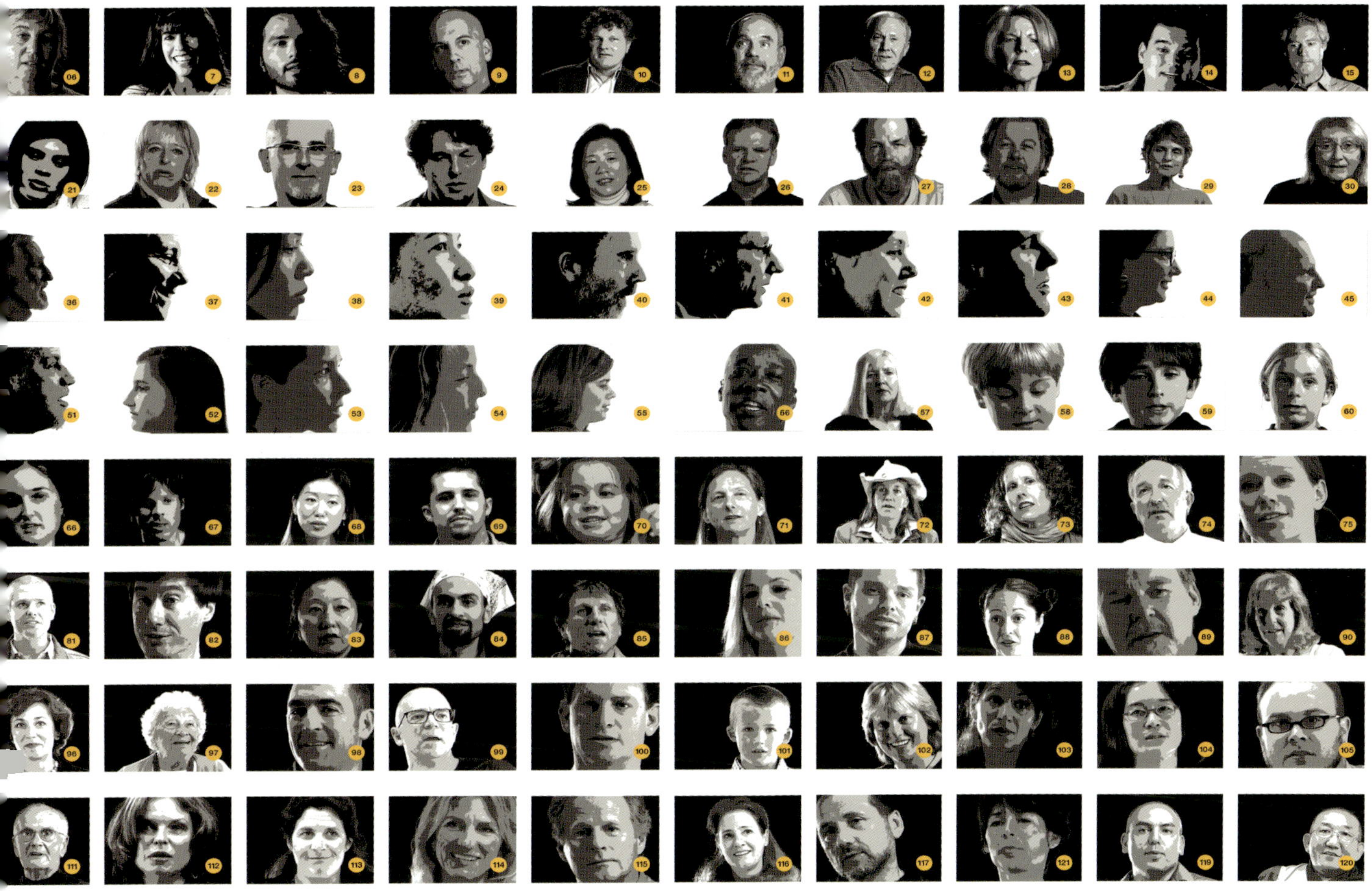
06
7
8
9
10
11
12
13
14
15
21
22
23
24
25
26
27
28
29
30
36
37
38
39
40
41
42
43
44
45
51
52
53
54
55
56
57
58
59
60
66
67
68
69
70
71
72
73
74
75
81
82
83
84
85
86
87
88
89
90
96
97
98
99
100
101
102
103
104
105
111
112
113
114
115
116
117
121
119
120

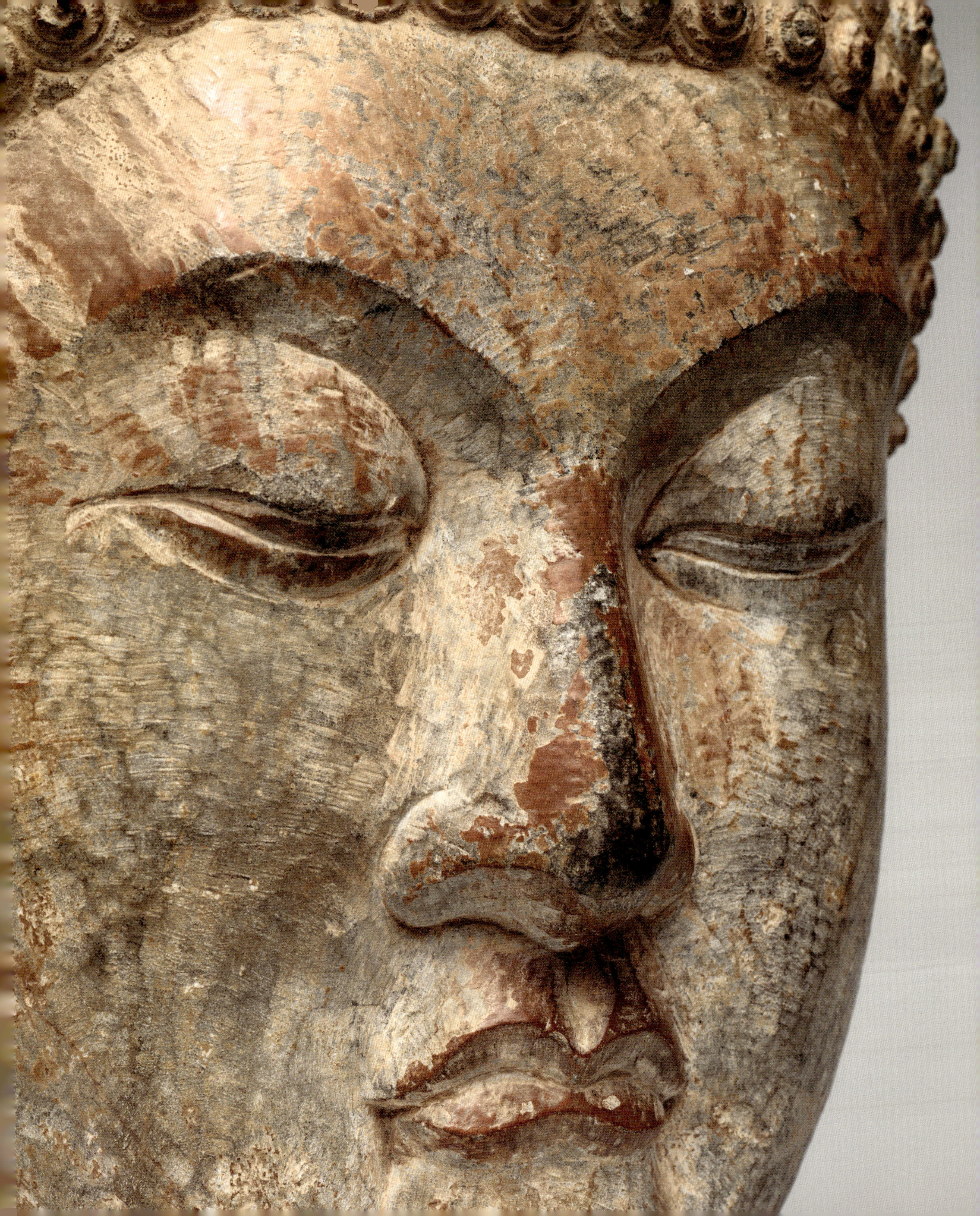

Man has no body distinct from his soul, for that called body is a portion of soul discerned by the five senses.

—William Blake, English poet and artist (1757–1827)

Embodying the Sacred

Every man is a divinity in disguise, a god playing the fool.

—Ralph Waldo Emerson, American poet and essayist (1803–1882)

HEADS OF BUDDHA IMAGES

CAT.

8

Most scholars date the earliest images of the Buddha to the first century CE, several hundred years after his death. While no likeness of the Buddha is known from his lifetime, there remains a remarkable overall consistency in artistic representations from later centuries, as seen in this sampling of the heads of Buddha sculptures produced in different Asian cultures over many centuries. They all look similar, and one may ask why. The features that make the face of the Buddha distinct from any other Asian sacred figure are: eyes downcast in meditation or inward reflection, a gentle smile of compassion, a circle between the eyebrows (*urna*) sometimes thought to denote his ability to see beyond material surfaces, a protrusion on the crown of his head (*ushnisha*) signaling his enhanced wisdom, individual hairs denoted as tight curls, and elongated earlobes signifying his renunciation of the material world.[34] Many images of the Buddha were also originally gilded.

These marks (*lakshana* in Sanskrit) on the Buddha's face and body visually express what many texts describe as the thirty-two major marks that are characteristic of a "great man" (*mahapurusha*).[35] The arrival of the Buddha into this world as a Universal Ruler (*chakravartin*) had been predicted by sages who were able to recognize him by the marks on his body, several of which were visible on the newborn Prince Siddhartha (Shakyamuni). These qualities were symbolic of the Buddha's character and served as indicators of his past and future actions. By inscribing internal states onto the body's surface, they give manifest form to the close links between beauty and perfection of character that is both the result and a sign of a dharmic way of life. The Buddha's perfect face expresses his inner perfection. What distinguishes the various cultural representations of the Buddha is that artists seem to have drawn upon local features in imagining the ideal. This accounts for the differences in the shape of the face, individual facial features, and details of ornament in these heads. In many instances, however, there are striking resemblances between images made across vast geographical distances, commonalities that reflect patterns of circulation for texts and images.

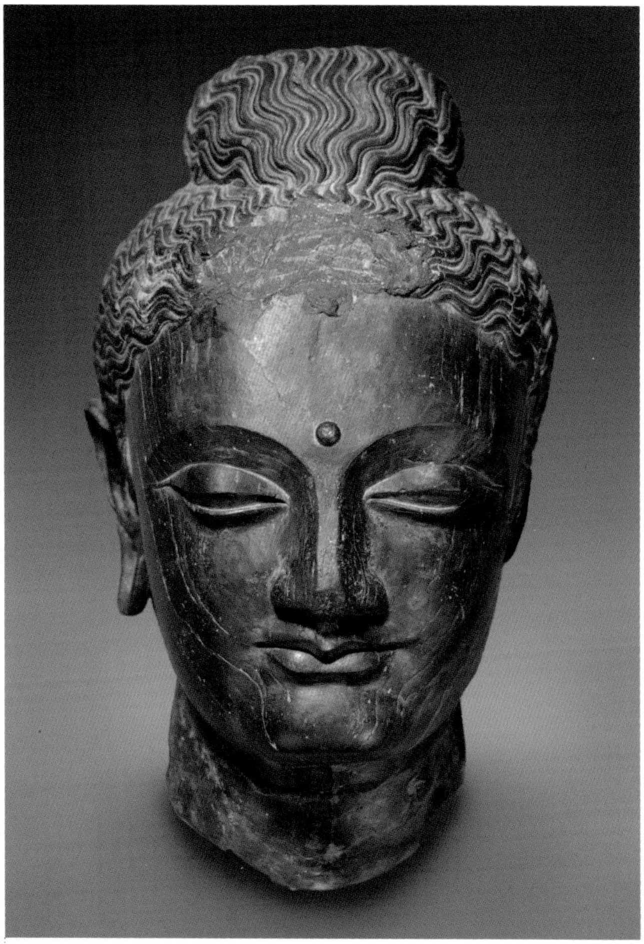

HEAD OF A BUDDHA IMAGE
APPROX. 300–500
Pakistan; Peshawar valley, former kingdom of Gandhara
Stone (schist)
H. 61 cm x W. 30.5 cm x D. 27.9 cm
The Avery Brundage Collection, B60S419

CAT.

9

Scholarly debate continues about where the first buddha images were produced—whether in the northwestern region of Gandhara (present-day Pakistan and Afghanistan; cat. 8) or the Mathura region in India (modern Uttar Pradesh state). Questions also remain about the movement of actual objects and the related transmission of ideas. The Buddha's teachings spread from India to other parts of Asia, including Sri Lanka, China, Tibet, and Southeast Asia. At least from the early centuries of the Common Era, monks traveled great distances to India in order to visit major pilgrimage sites associated with the life of the Buddha and to study at monasteries at places such as Bodhgaya (in Bihar province, India), where the Buddha himself attained enlightenment. It is probable that monks and other travelers took back with them portable devotional images and/or illustrated manuscripts that became a source of inspiration for local artists.[36] | QA

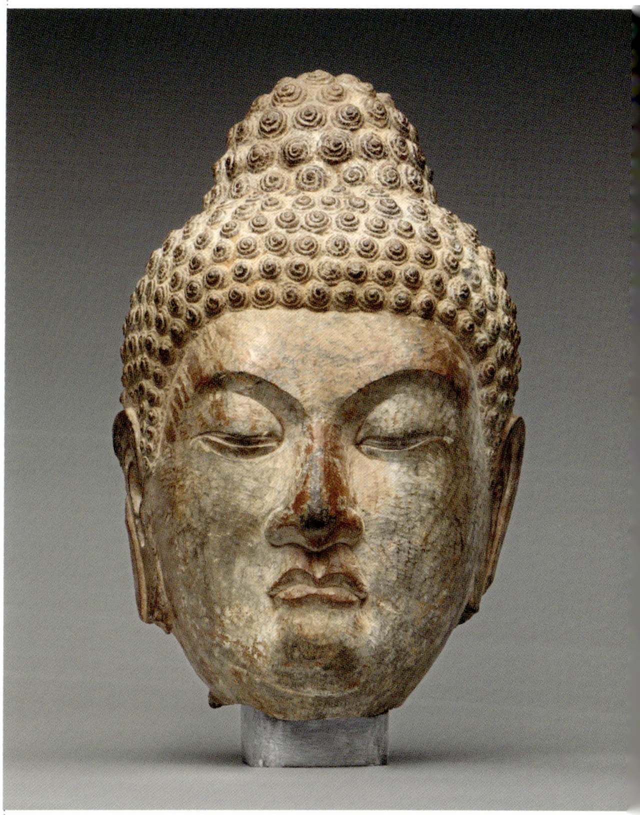

HEAD OF A BUDDHA IMAGE
PROBABLY 618–800
China
Tang dynasty (618–907)
Limestone
H. 40.6 cm x W. 25.4 cm x D. 26.7 cm
The Avery Brundage Collection, B60S31+

CATS.

10 and 11

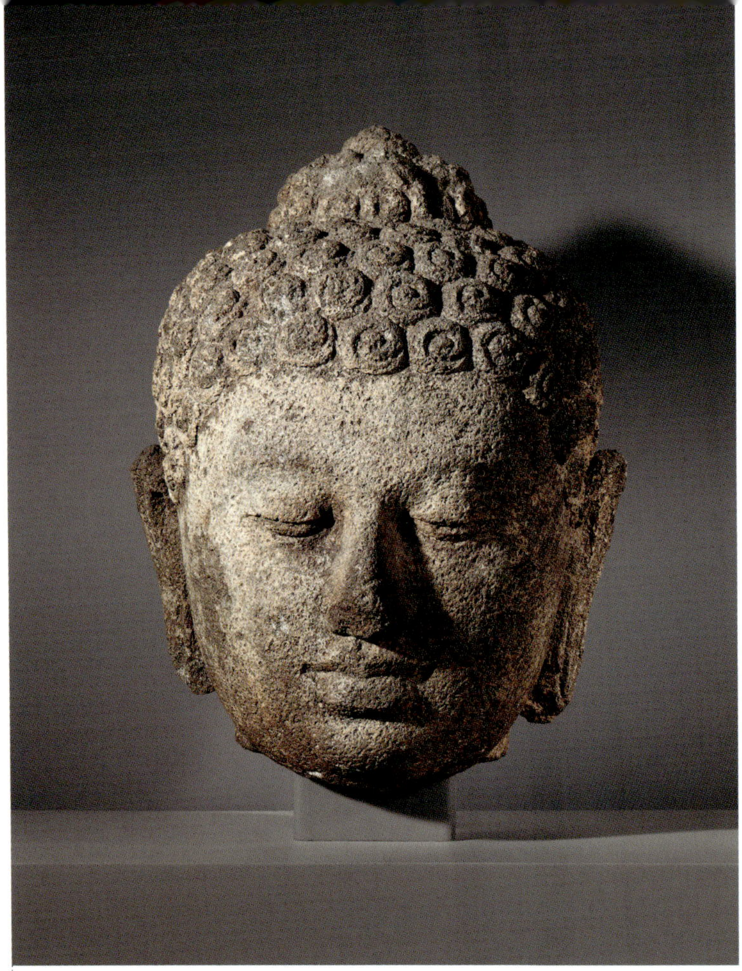

HEAD OF A BUDDHA IMAGE
APPROX. 800–850
Indonesia; Borobudur, Central Java
Stone
H. 31.8 cm x W. 25.4 cm x D. 22.9 cm
The Avery Brundage Collection, B60S379

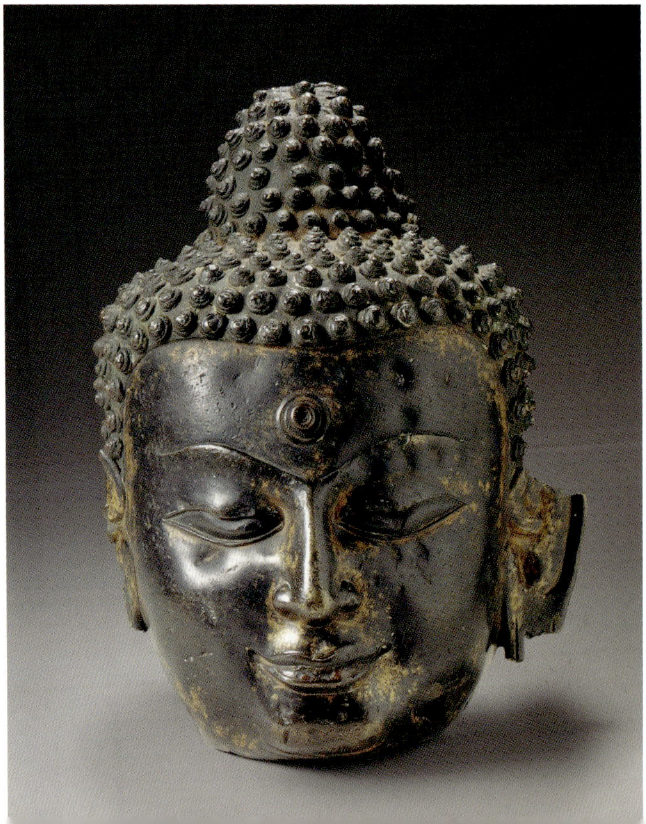

HEAD OF A BUDDHA IMAGE
APPROX. 900–1100
India; Bihar state
Brass with traces of inlaid copper and gilding
H. 40 cm x W. 29.2 cm x D. 21.6 cm
Acquisition in memory of Stuart Harvey made possible by Forrest Mortimer with assistance from friends of Mr. Harvey's, 2001.30

CAT.
12

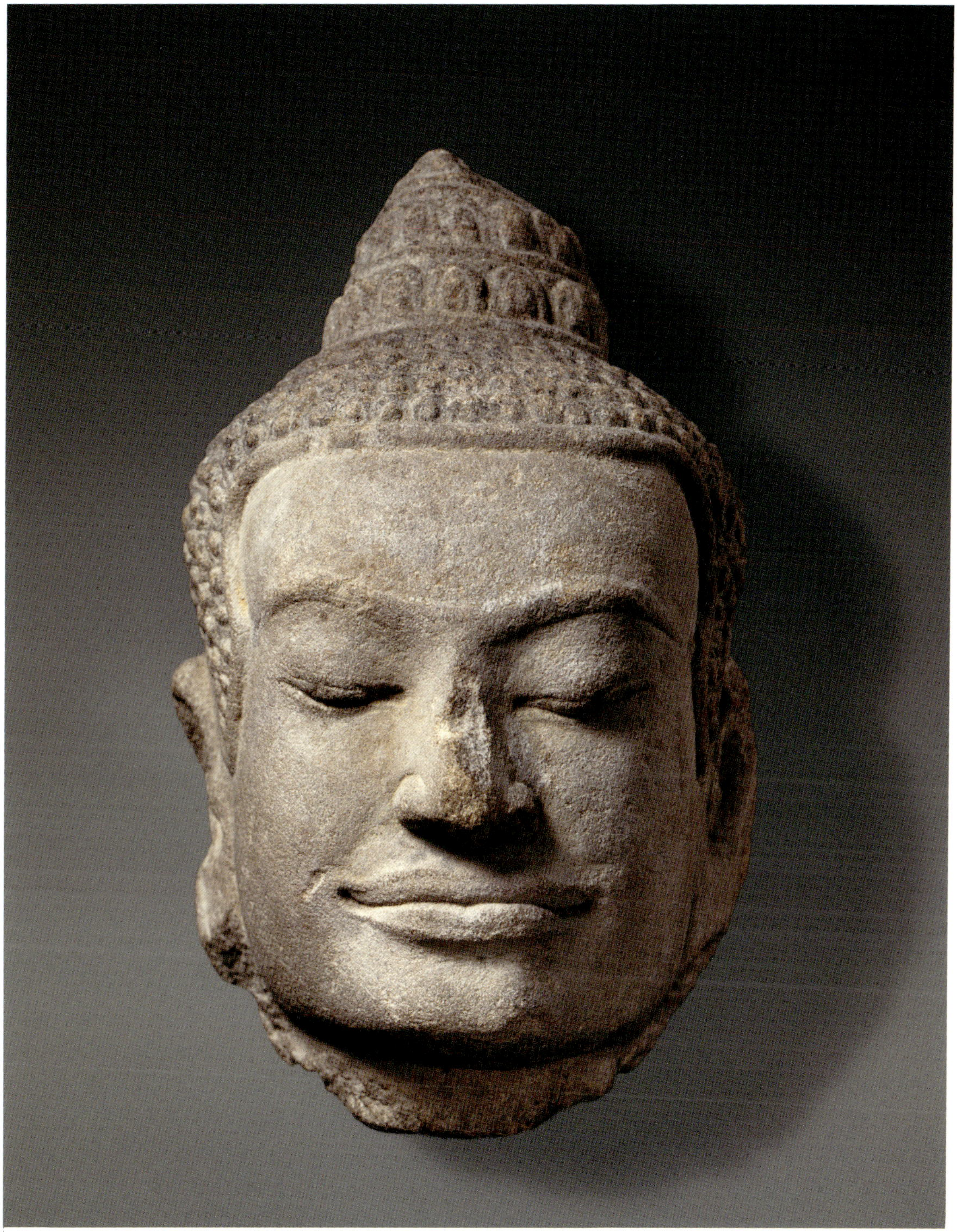

HEAD OF A BUDDHA IMAGE
1200–1250
Thailand
Sandstone
H. 28.3 cm x W. 15.2 cm x D. 18.4 cm
Transfer from the Fine Arts Museums of San Francisco, 1999.8

CATS.

13 and 14

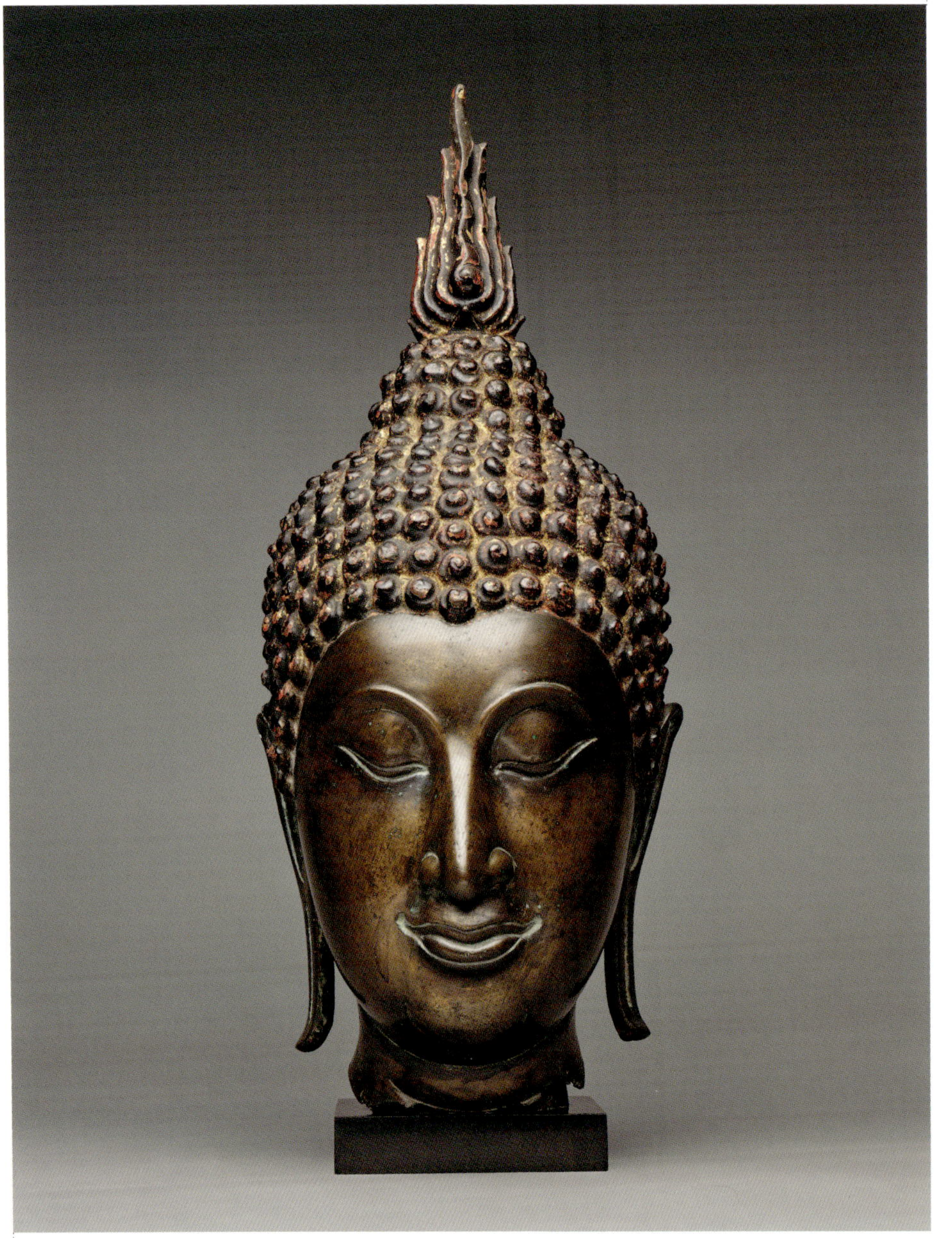

HEAD OF A BUDDHA IMAGE
APPROX. 1350–1450
Thailand; former kingdom of Sukhothai
Leaded bronze with traces of lacquer and gilding
H. 48.3 cm x W. 17.8 cm x D. 21 cm
The Avery Brundage Collection, B60S197

HEAD OF A BUDDHA IMAGE
APPROX. 1500–1600
Thailand; former kingdom of Ayutthaya
Bronze
H. 27.9 cm x W. 16.5 cm x D. 15.2 cm
The Avery Brundage Collection, B60S13

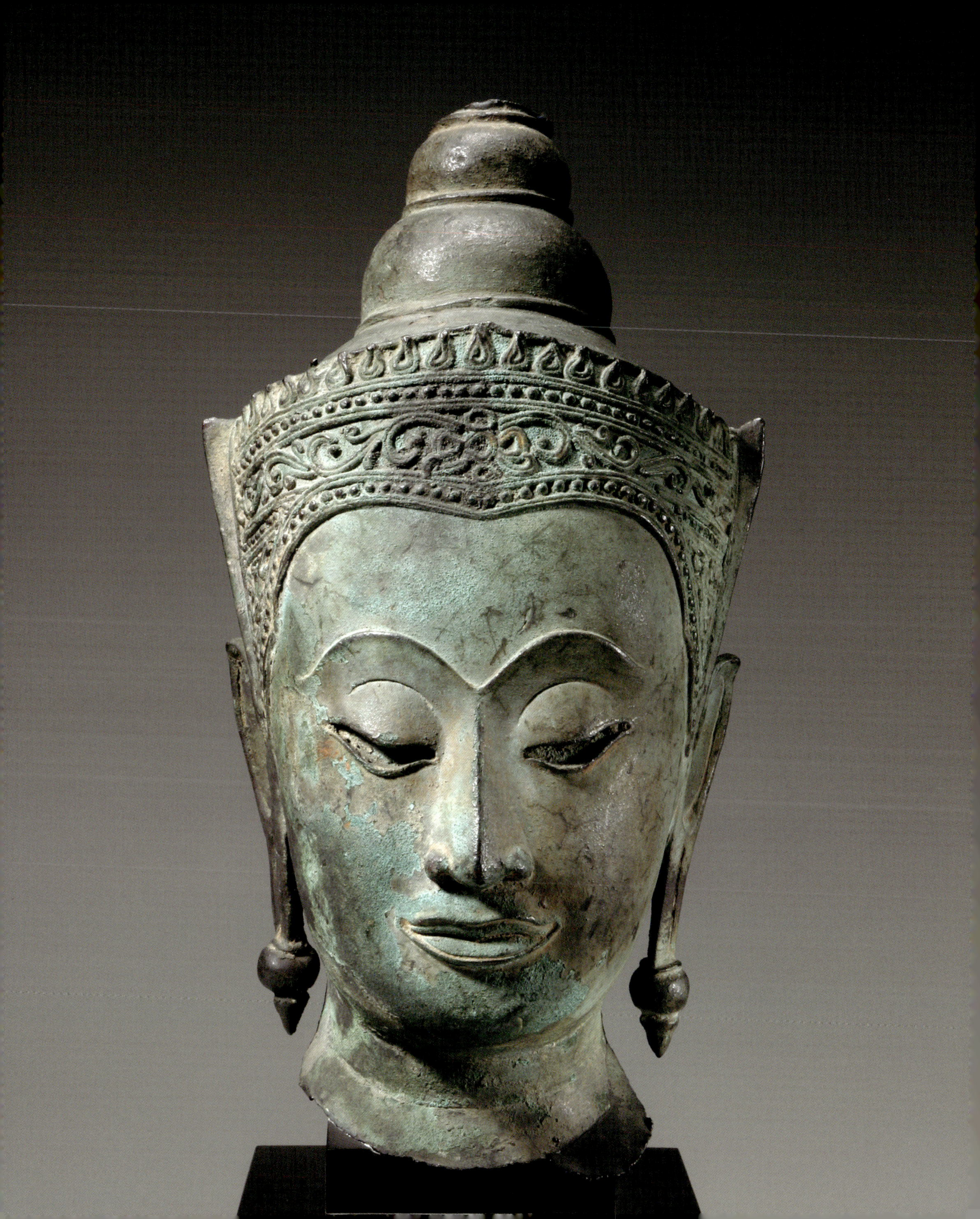

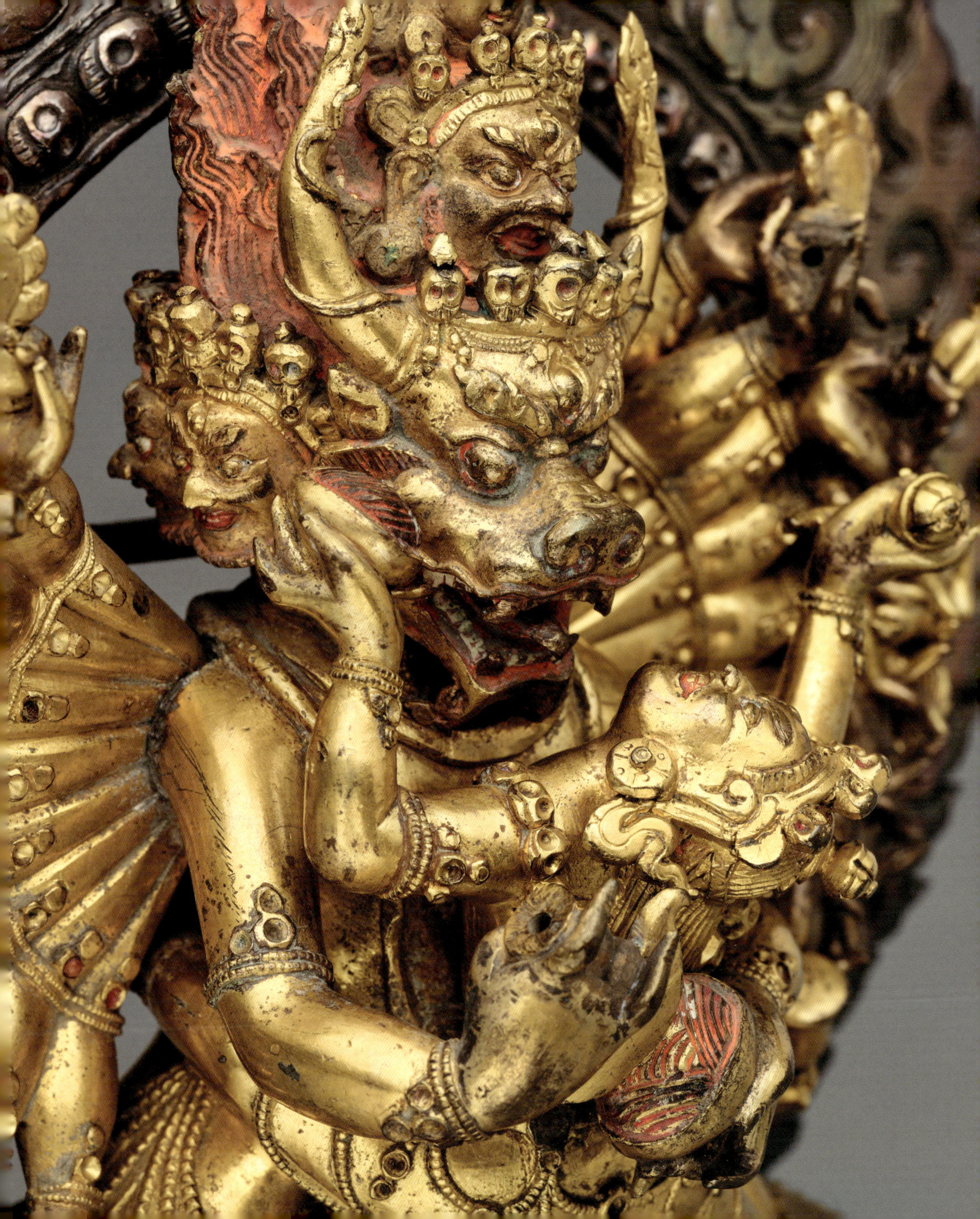

God is one, but with internal differences, represented as the souls and the material creation. God has qualities. He is an ocean of Divine knowledge, bliss, compassion and other unlimited attributes.

—Ramanuja, Indian philosopher (1017–1137)

The Many Aspects of Divinity

I am in love with every church
And mosque
And temple
And any kind of shrine
Because I know it is there
That people say the different names
Of the One God.

—Hafez, Persian poet (1315–1390)

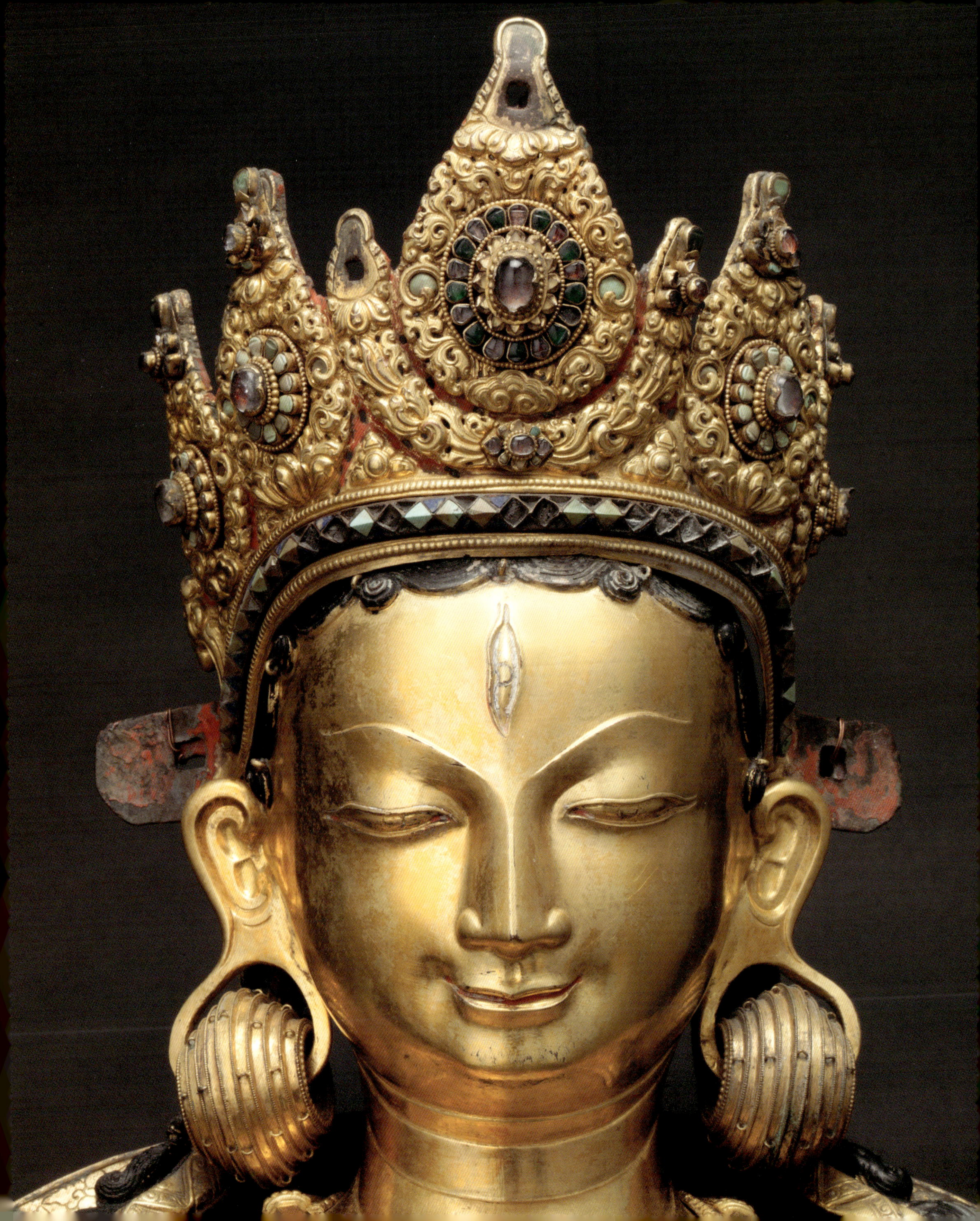

THE BUDDHIST DEITY WHITE TARA

CAT.
15

APPROX. 1400–1500
Nepal
Copper with gilding, turquoise, lapis lazuli, other gemstones, and glass
H. 54.6 cm x W. 43.2 cm x D. 31.8 cm
The Avery Brundage Collection, B60S22+

The body of White Tara is radiant with gilding and stunning aesthetic touches that reflect her divine nature, and she is laden with symbolism that further emphasizes her sacred qualities. Her right hand, posed in the gift-giving gesture (mudra), bestows spiritual attainments on those who meditate upon her. Her left hand displays the fear-dispelling gesture, showing that she protects devotees from all dangers and disasters. She can do so because the eyes on her palms and the soles of her feet allow her to survey all such dangers. They also symbolize the "doors of liberation" through which she frees beings from misery. But there is more than formal Buddhist symbolism in this sculpture: she is an image of divinity itself, where the sacred is represented by aesthetic excellence. Her flawless facial features, voluptuous body, and sensuous ornaments—the way the formal symmetry of her floating scarves and crossed legs contrasts with the sway of her torso and neck—seem to radiate the perfection of divinity.

Mythologically, White Tara is closely related to the bodhisattva Avalokiteshvara; she is said to have sprung from one of his tears as he witnessed the infinite sufferings of sentient beings. Historically, she became an important bodhisattva in the seventh century, when a queen of the Tibetan monarch Songtsen Gampo was deified after her death as White Tara. From a religious perspective, she comprises the wisdom, compassion, and enlightened activity of all the Buddhas arising in the form of a beautiful goddess. | JD

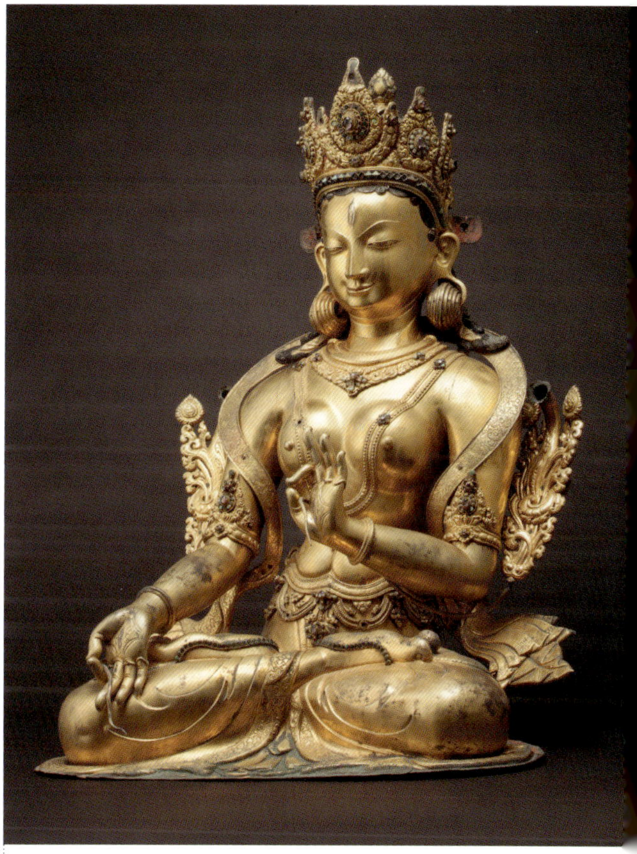

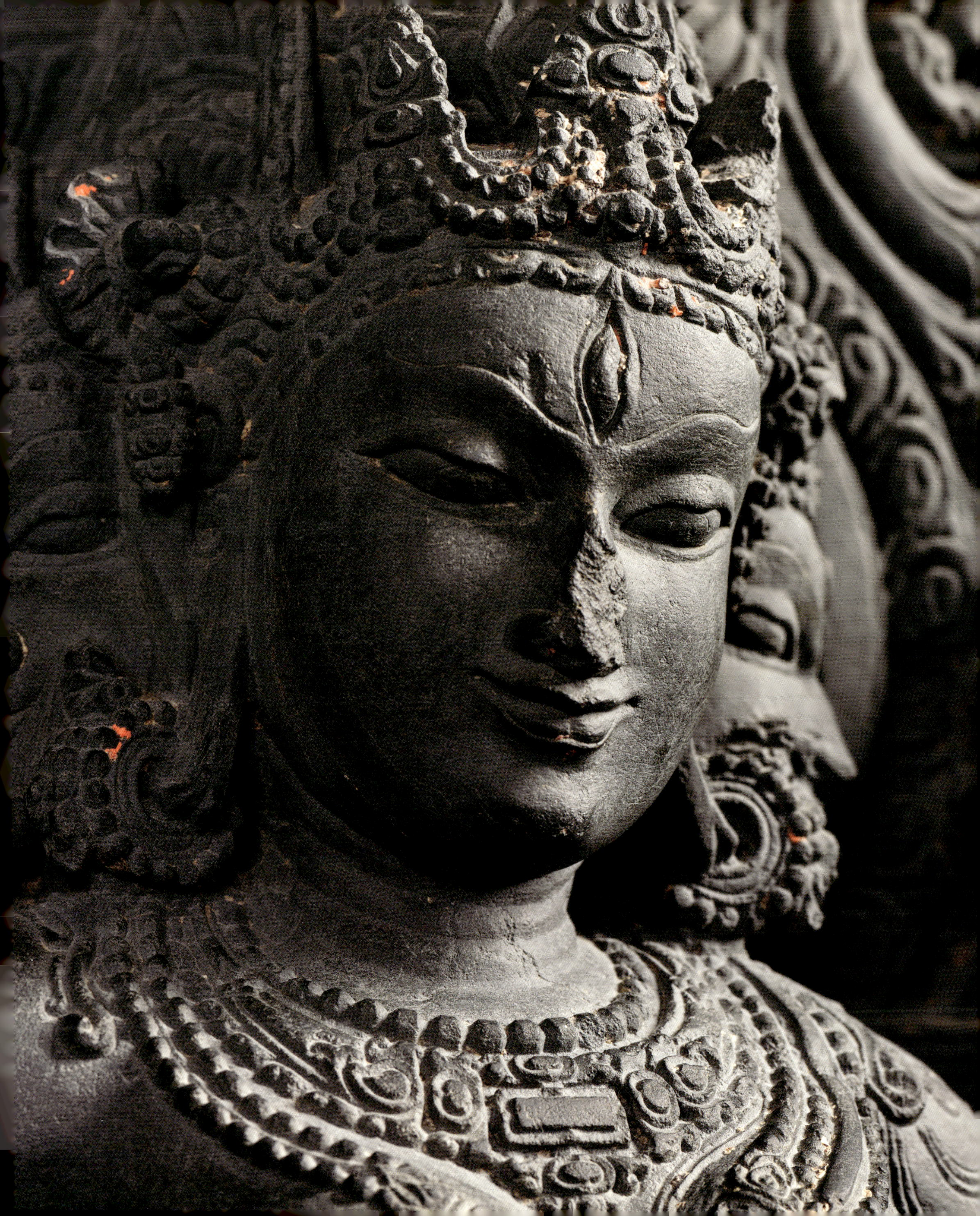

THE BUDDHIST DEITY VAJRA TARA

1075–1200
India; perhaps Nalanda, Bihar state, Magadha region
Basalt
H. 100.3 cm x W. 59.7 cm x D. 22.9 cm
The Avery Brundage Collection, B63S20+

CAT.
16

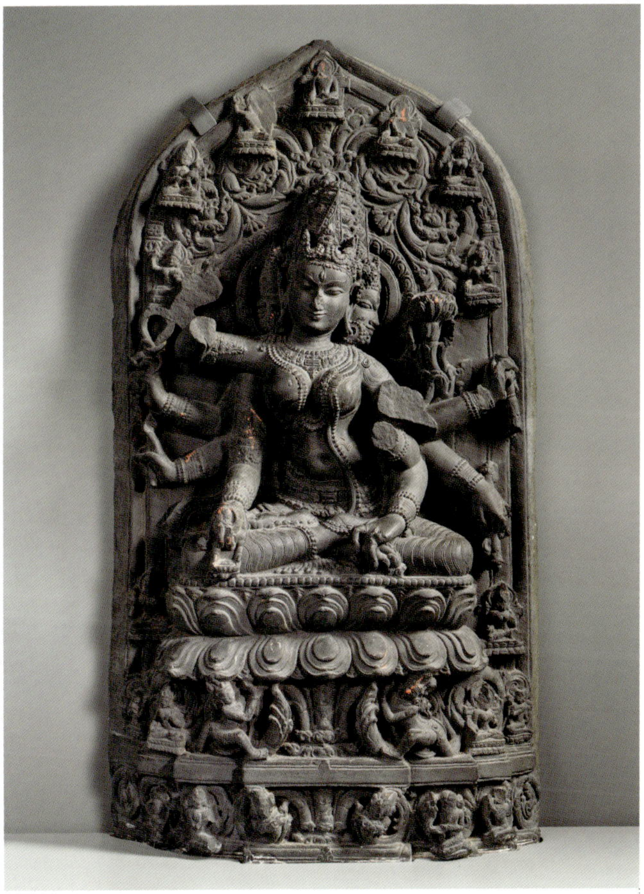

Tara—whose name translates as "the star"—is a manifestation of Avalokiteshvara, the bodhisattva of compassion. In her ordinary two-armed form, she smiles kindly and, through the eyes on her hands and feet, witnesses the sufferings of beings caught in the cycle of existence (*samsara*). This fierce form of the deity can be explained in part by her name: in Sanskrit *vajra* means both "thunderbolt" and "diamond," and it is also the name of a legendary weapon that combines the hardness, strength, and swiftness of those things. She is described in the literature of Vajrayana ("Thunderbolt Vehicle") Buddhism, also known as Esoteric Buddhism. According to Vajrayana teachers, the speed and power of this approach emulates that of the *vajra*, making it possible to achieve enlightenment "in this very life."

Here, each of Vajra Tara's arms bears a symbolic implement with which she vigorously, even violently, removes obstacles to enlightenment: the noose holds the mind in check, the elephant goad guides action along correct paths, and the lotus expresses the compassion that underlies even such highly directive activities. Esoteric Buddhism employs mandalas—geometric meditation maps—to organize and guide the visualization of divine bodies such as that of Vajra Tara. Indeed, the five smaller images above Vajra Tara here mark the four cardinal directions of the cosmos along with its axial center; since this configuration is that of a mandala, it becomes clear that the body of Vajra Tara is itself part of a larger body—that of the mandala-palace in which her meditation takes place. | JD

THE BODHISATTVA AVALOKITESHVARA (SHO KANNON)

APPROX. 1100–1150
Japan, Heian period (794–1185)
Wood with traces of lacquer and gilding
H. 167.6 cm x W. 58.4 cm x D. 57.2 cm
The Avery Brundage Collection, B60S420

CAT.
17

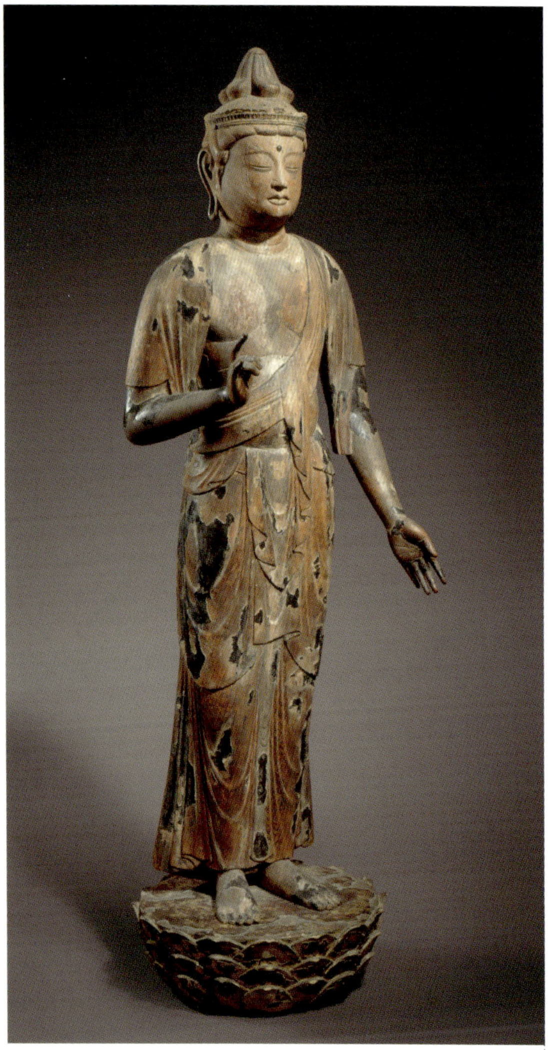

Sho Kannon is one of the most popular deities in the Japanese Buddhist pantheon, nearly matching Amitabha of the Pure Land teaching. As an agent of the buddha Amitabha, Sho Kannon watches over humankind and extends his limitless compassion to all sufferers. The peaceful appearance of this figure—it once held a lotus in its extended right hand—offers quietude and hope, and its original gilding would have been a symbol of the deity's luminous consciousness and inner beauty. Sho Kannon is immediately recognizable as a Buddhist deity through such features as bodhisattva's garments (dhoti, shawl, and scarf), downcast eyes, gentle smile, the circle between his eyebrows, and hands posed in benevolent gestures (mudra; see, for example, cats. 15, 37, and 46). | QA

THE JAIN TEACHER PARSHVANATHA

1000–1100
Bangladesh; perhaps Dhaka District
Stone
H. 61 cm x W. 27.9 cm x D. 7.6 cm
The Avery Brundage Collection, B63S21+

CAT.
18

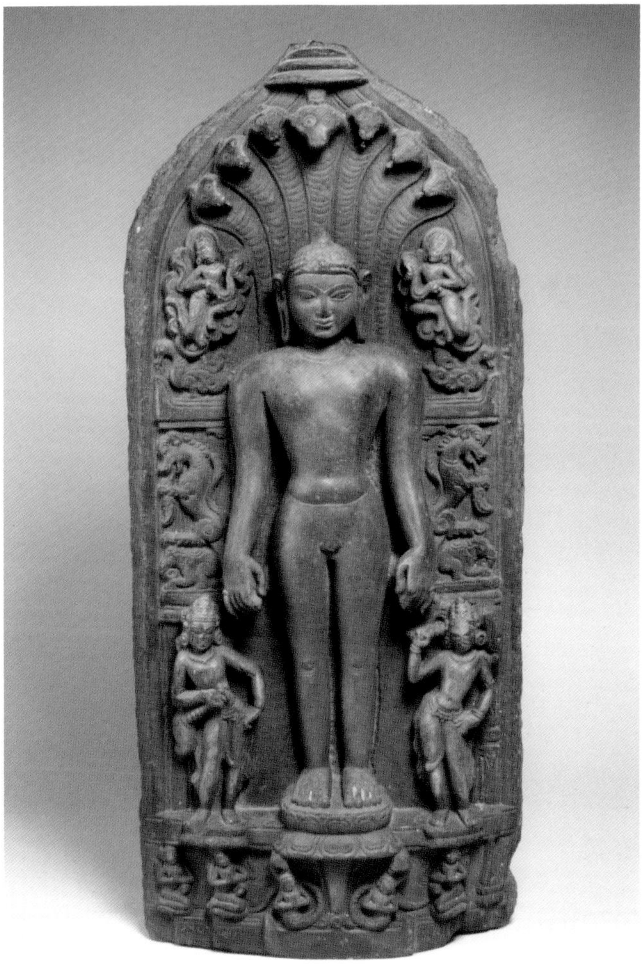

In the Jain faith, the focus of devotion is on twenty-four revered teachers, or *jinas* (spiritual victors). Also known as *tirthankaras* ("those who make the ford"—that is, the passage across the sea of births and deaths, or *samsara*), these beings are seen as perfect men and not cosmic divinities. Their qualities of purity, enlightenment, and asceticism are symbolically inscribed on their bodies. Parshvanatha is the twenty-third of these spiritual teachers. He is shown in the typical representation of a *jina*: a perfectly balanced figure standing with his feet firmly planted and arms not touching the body, a still pose that captures an immense amount of alertness and controlled energy. Like other images of *jinas*, Parshvanatha is here unadorned by jewelry or garments, with his eyes open to indicate the eternal consciousness associated with the enlightened and purified soul. It is mainly through the practice of nonviolence, asceticism, and meditation that a *jina* achieves his status of perfection. In this form, he is free of karma ("action"), which in the Jain context is understood as a material, colored, sticky substance that clings to the body and coats the soul, preventing it from manifesting the positive qualities that would eventually lead to the release from the cycle of birth and rebirth. A soul free from karma appears bright and light, and typical images of Jain sacred beings are made of white marble or luminous metals to express this attribute. Here, Parshvanatha's smooth, polished, and unornamented body is indicative of his purity.[37] | QA

THE HINDU DEITY PARVATI

APPROX. 1050–1100
India; Bihar state
Basalt
H. 111.8 cm x W. 63.5 cm x D. 26.7 cm
Museum purchase, B67S2

CAT.
19

Parvati, wife of Shiva, is one of the most powerful goddesses of Hinduism, and as Devi (Goddess), she represents the female power of the universe. Frequently seen as Shiva's companion (see cat. 42), she also appears as an independent figure in all her majesty. Lush, full-breasted, narrow-waisted, and beautifully adorned with jewelry and fine garments, Parvati (and other images of great goddesses) embodies feminine abundance as the source of life and fulfiller of devotees' desires. Here, a partial figure of Shiva's son, Skanda, appears seated on Parvati's knee, reinforcing her nurturing aspect. Imagery associated with life, fertility, and purity—such as water (poured in homage by the elephants above her head) and lotus flowers—fulfill a similar iconographic function, while the lion throne on which she sits underscores her cosmic power.

Parvati holds a round mirror in her raised hand. Goddesses are often portrayed holding mirrors, objects traditionally associated with women. In the Indian context, however, it is not an expression of vanity but, rather, has philosophical meaning: the mirror reflects the material world and reminds the devotee that the phenomenal world is an illusion (maya). Yet, while the mirror helps question the validity and truth of the world that we know, suggesting its falseness, it also enables one to see—and, through seeing, to discern that which is ultimately real. Thus, the being and the likeness of the goddess are images of the "real" nature of the universe. | QA

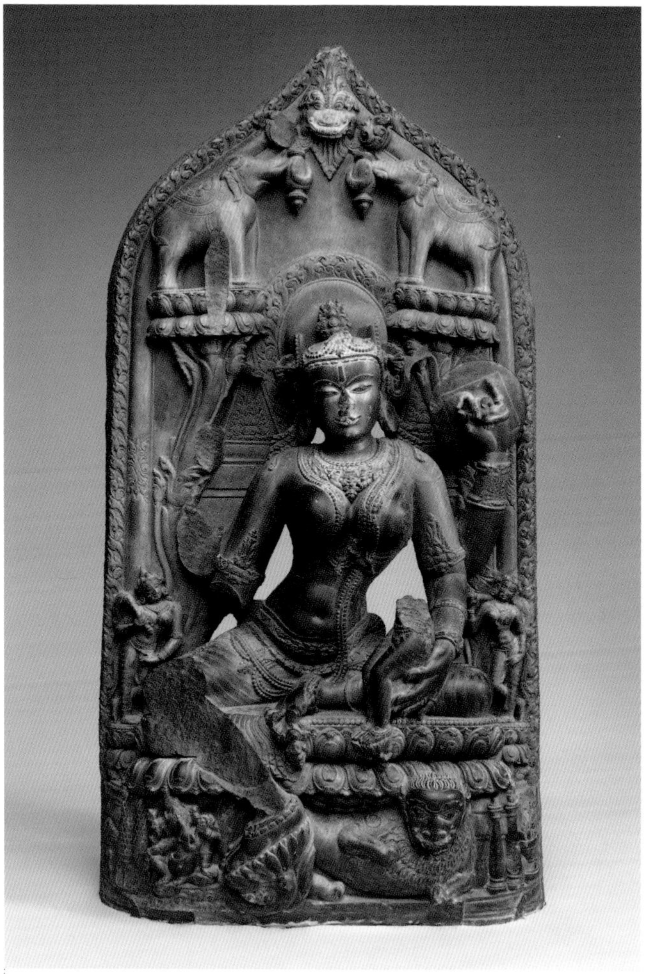

NATURE DIVINITY

APPROX. 100–200
India; Uttar Pradesh state, Mathura region
Sandstone
H. 69.2 cm x W. 16.5 cm x D. 15.9 cm
Gift of the Atholl McBean Foundation, B69S13

CAT.
20

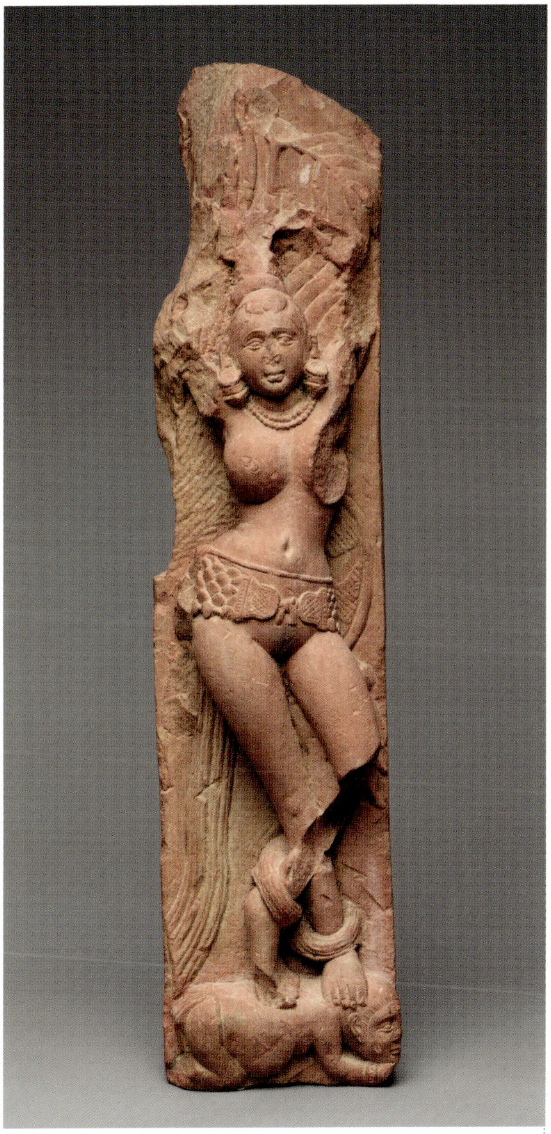

In textual and oral sources across India's religious traditions, moral perfection and inner beauty are frequently equated with splendid bodies, both female and male. Nature's fertility and abundance are often artistically represented in terms of the beautiful human body. Here a full-breasted young woman with wide hips strikes an elegant, dance-like pose; she is elaborately adorned with coiffed hair and wears heavy ear ornaments, a beaded necklace, armbands, and a jeweled belt. Her breasts and pudenda are visible beneath her clothing, the transparent folds of which wrap around her ankles and drape down behind her. The damage to this sculpture does not diminish it as an ideal of feminine splendor.

The woman's semidivine status as an ancient nature deity (*yakshi*) is suggested by the dwarflike figure on which she stands. Reinforcing the link between the sensuous female form and nature's fertility, she is shown holding a branch of the flowering *shala* tree. This woman-and-tree motif (*shalabhanjika*) has ancient roots in Indian culture and is repeatedly mentioned in literature, which frequently analogizes plants and the female body. It was believed that women, by their very presence and touch, could transfer their fertility, causing trees to bloom in springtime; at the same time, their own fecundity could be enhanced by "pregnant" nature.[38]

These literary and visual tropes were incorporated at a fairly early date into Buddhist contexts. This figure, originally part of a railing surrounding a Buddhist stupa, is one such example. Inscriptions on several related figures record that these were gifts from monks, nuns, and laypersons. Such images, then, were featured prominently on religious architecture as symbols of auspiciousness. In narrative scenes of the Buddha's birth, for example, his mother, Queen Maya, is almost always depicted standing in a pose similar to this figure, elaborately adorned, and holding a tree branch as the infant Buddha emerges in miraculous birth from her waist. | QA

THE HINDU DEITY SHIVA

APPROX. 1300-1500
India; Tamil Nadu state
Bronze
H. 95.2 cm x W. 29.8 cm x D. 25.4 cm
The Avery Brundage Collection, B69S14

CAT.
21

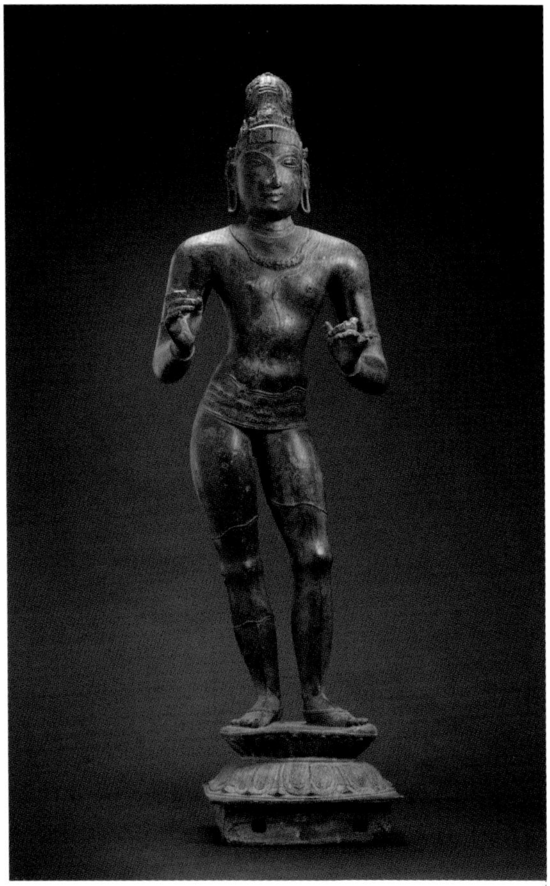

The perfection of a god's physical body was understood in Hindu traditions to be emblematic of his inner beauty and spiritual supremacy. In the concept of bhakti, which can be described as intense devotion to one's personal god, worship of the formless divine can be expressed through meditation, songs, ritual worship (*puja*), and other means. *Puja* requires that images of deities become a focus of the devotee's thoughts and attention. Such communion with the divine can take place in a variety of settings: in home shrines, temples, open roadside shrines, or ritual processions.

This image of Shiva was used in processions, when the sculpture would have been dressed in fine garments, jewelry, and garlands and anointed with sandalwood and other aromatic substances in order to celebrate the god's perfect beauty. But even "unclothed," as seen here, Shiva is sensuously portrayed. He has wide shoulders, a slender torso and arms, firm and rounded buttocks, and supple toes and fingers. His matted hair is piled crown-like on his head, and he wears a necklace, armbands and anklets, and a sheer lower garment whose delicate folds are articulated on his legs. Shiva's pose is pliant, as if arrested in the swaying motion of his gait; one can almost see the *prana* (life breath) rise in the gentle slope of his belly. Viewers of such images would be moved to adore the splendor of the divine. Many poet-saints composed hymns extolling the physical aspects of the gods and often described the divinity's overwhelming beauty with erotic overtones and in the voice of a lovesick woman, as in the seventh-century poet Sambandar's ode to Shiva:

"O god with matted hair!" she cries,
"You are my sole refuge!" she cries,
"Bull rider!" she cries, and faints in awe.
O lord of Marukal
Where the blue lily blooms in field water,
Is it fair
To make this woman waste from love's disease?[39] | QA

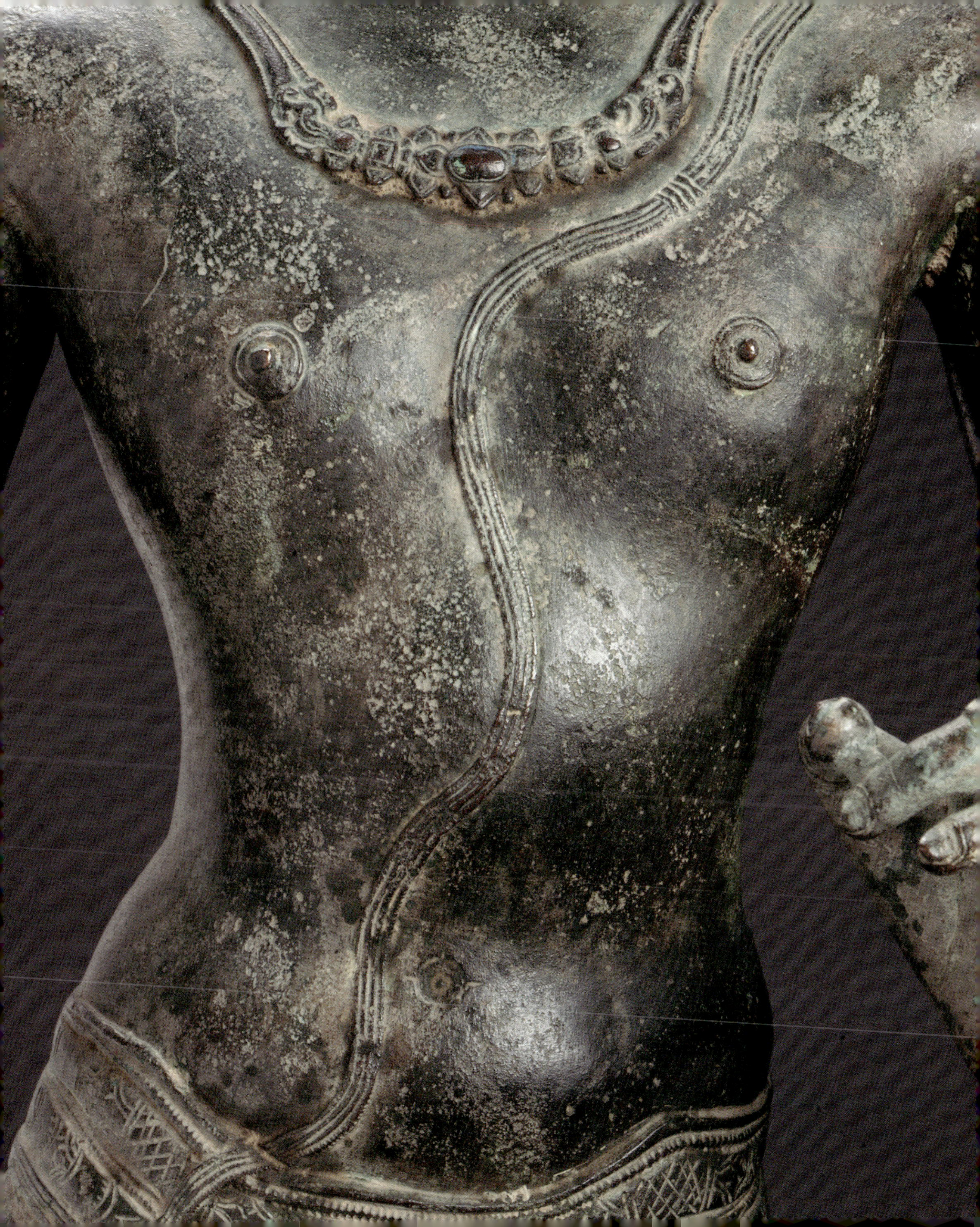

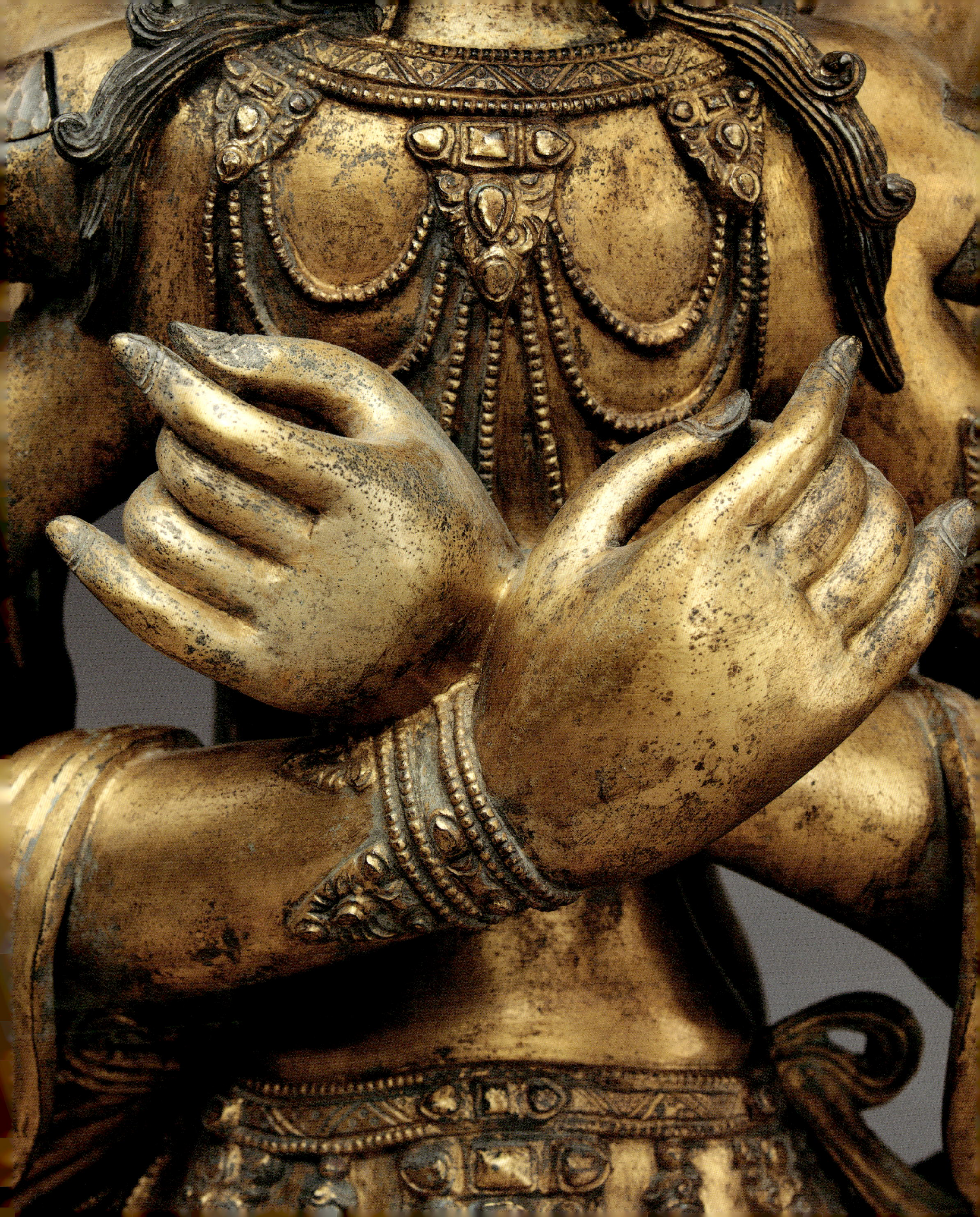

THE BUDDHIST DEITY GUHYASAMAJA

APPROX. 1400–1500
China; Beijing
Ming dynasty (1368–1644)
Bronze with gilding
H. 66 cm x W. 45.7 cm x D. 31.7 cm
The Avery Brundage Collection, B64B23

CAT. 22

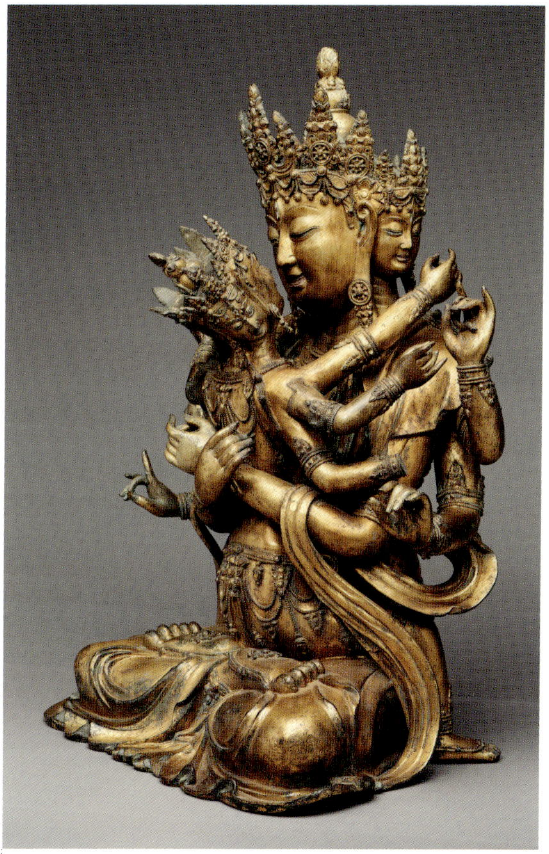

If you imagine a single, iconic image of what the divine body of the Buddha might have looked like, it would probably not resemble this stunning bronze sculpture. Yet in Himalayan Buddhism, this is the ultimate image of an enlightened being fully on the level of a buddha: Guhyasamaja, whose name means "hidden union." How are we to understand a depiction of enlightenment in the form of beings with multiple arms, legs, and heads joined in sexual congress? In the words of the text giving this figure its name, the *Guhyasamaja Tantra*, this image depicts a "hidden union" between apparent opposites—male and female, of course, but also of mind and body, or in Buddhist philosophy, wisdom (*prajna*) and the spiritual technique of acquiring it (*upaya*).

To describe the details of this process, the *Guhyasamaja Tantra* employs what is called "twilight language," a coding system that features a series of interwoven correspondences between concrete imagery and abstract philosophy. At its broadest level, the text uses the "twilight language" of sexual union (*mithuna*) to symbolize the mystical unity of opposites that occurs in meditation—precisely what is happening in this sculpture. But the symbolic code goes much deeper. In his two central hands Guhyasamaja would have held the bell and ritual weapon (*vajra*; see cat. 16) of the cosmic buddha Akshobhya. In his other hands, he would have held the symbols of the four other cosmic buddhas: the wheel of white Vairochana and the lotus of red Amitabha in his two right hands, and the gem of yellow Ratnasambhava and sword of green Amoghasiddhi in his two left hands. Taken together, these five buddhas are the fundamental inhabitants of the most basic meditation map of Vajrayana, or Esoteric Buddhism; accordingly, this sculpture comprises a dynamically embodied mandala. Indeed, the passion and dynamism of both Guhyasamaja and his female counterpart Sparshavajra are characteristic of sculpture created in China during the Ming dynasty, either as gifts for Tibetan lamas or as ritual equipment for Vajrayana temples within China. | JD

THE BUDDHIST DEITY RAGARAJA (AIZEN)

CAT.
23

Japan
Edo period (1615–1868)
Wood with gilding, colors, and crystal
H. 66 cm x W. 57.1 cm x D. 36.8 cm
The Avery Brundage Collection, B60S9+

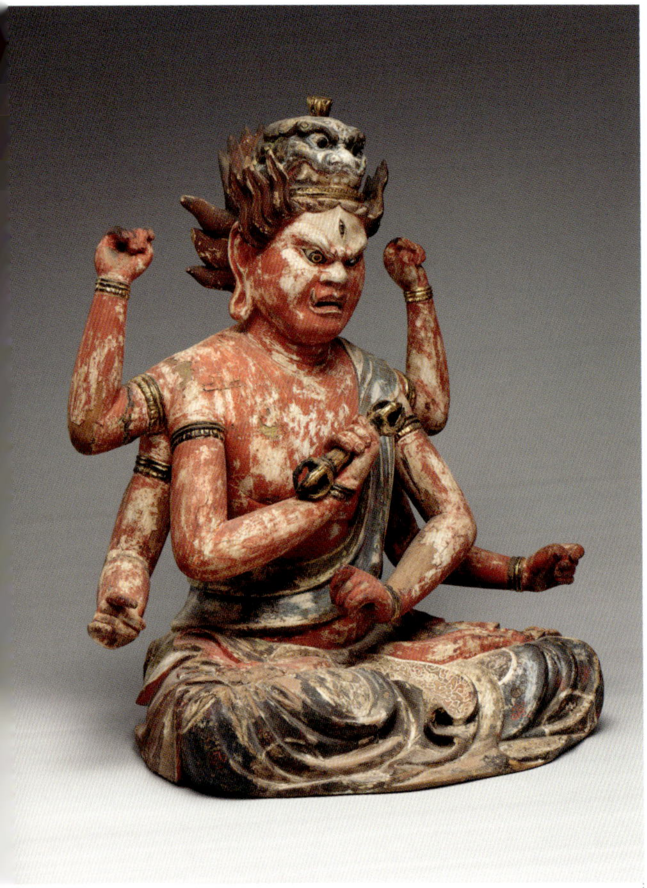

Vajrayana, the "Thunderbolt Vehicle" of Esoteric Buddhism (see cat. 16), offers its meditative practices as the most powerful antidotes for the various afflictions (*klesha*) that inhibit psychological health. These practices focus on visualizing divine bodies whose symbolic powers are "equal to what must be tamed": when mental obstacles are dangerous and uncompromising, the spiritual response will be correspondingly potent. Since one of the most turbulent emotional states in Buddhist thought is passion, the figure responsible for transmuting passion into wisdom must be as powerful as the emotional state he counters. This sculpture of Aizen, whose Japanese name is a translation of the Sanskrit designation Ragaraja ("King of Passion"), represents one of the most important of these harrowing, affliction-destroying divine bodies.

Among the most stunning of Aizen's features are his fanged mouth, flaming hair, and fiercely furrowed brow. Above his forehead looms the mien of an unknown animal, while just below is the open third eye with which Aizen sees through surface appearances. Aizen's six hands emphasize his ability to perform multiple spiritual tasks simultaneously. In its present form, however, only the *vajra*—a symbolic weapon combining the properties of diamonds and thunderbolts—remains as a symbol of spiritual techniques (*upaya*). Originally, Aizen would have held a bell in his lower left hand to symbolize wisdom (*prajna*), while a bow and arrow would have appeared in his upper left and right hands, respectively. The center pair of hands would also have held objects: an invisible implement (simply and mysteriously referred to as "that" in the texts) and, the key to his identity, a lotus flower. The lotus, along with his ruddy skin, associates Aizen symbolically with Amitabha, whose fierce form he constitutes. By visualizing Aizen, practitioners are empowered to quash the otherwise problematic force of sexual desire and sublimate it into more productive or creative endeavors.

Aizen may have once been part of a three-dimensional mandala constructed within an Esoteric Buddhist temple. Environments of this type would have been immersive, in that they were designed to collapse artistic representation with experienced reality so that, when combined with meditation, practitioners perceived their own physical bodies as occupying the visionary world of the mandala. | JD

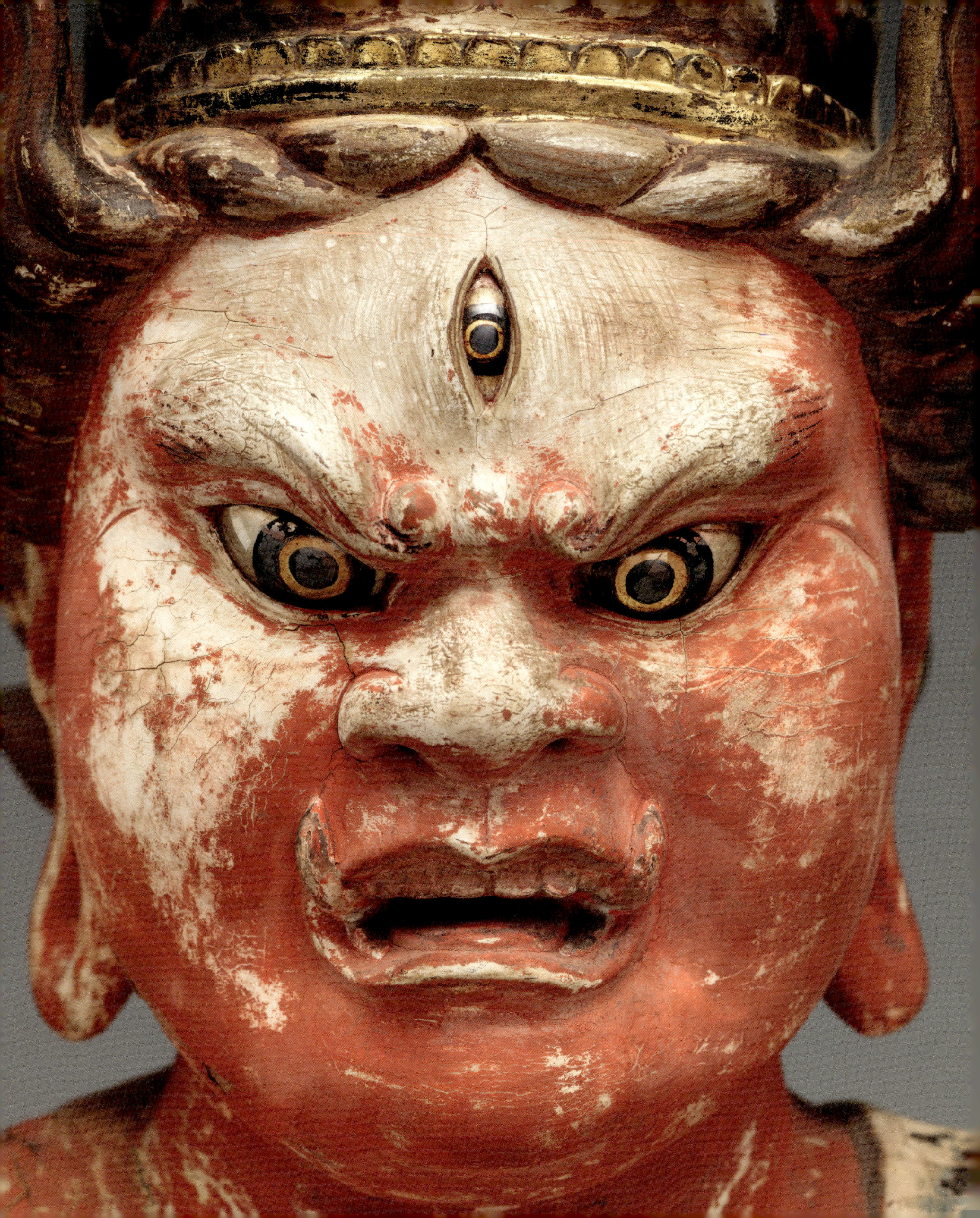

THE HINDU DEITY SHIVA

APPROX. 1300–1500
India; Karnataka state
Stone (chlorite schist)
H. 82.5 cm x W. 45.7 cm x D. 24.8 cm
Gift of the Connoisseurs' Council, 2000.6

CAT.
24

Bhairava ("horrific" in Sanskrit) is Shiva's ferocious form. Like Chamunda (cat. 25) and other fierce beings, he has bulging eyes, fangs, a garland of skulls, and a cobra wrapped around his body. He is naked and is seen with other inauspicious things, such as a carrion-eating dog who scavenges in cremation grounds. Worst of all, he holds a head of Brahma. Shiva had chopped off one of Brahma's five heads in a bitter dispute. In penance for this frightful sin, Shiva was compelled to wander the world as a naked beggar with the head of Brahma stuck to his hand "to destroy evil and benefit creation."[40] In this transgression of social codes, Bhairava inspires fear and awe but, as sinner, also holds the power of redemption.

Bhairava can be understood in a variety of ways, from fierce tantric deity to a powerful protector. Texts describing Shiva in this form emphasize both his horrifying qualities and his elegance and seductiveness. Here, what should be a repulsive image is, instead, shapely and sensual. The deep carving accentuates a gracefully swaying posture, and Bhairava's face appears rather gentle—despite his fangs. The artist has lavished careful attention on beautifying the sculpture's various parts, so that the whole is an eloquent testimony to the unsettling attractiveness of the dreadful and horrific. | QA

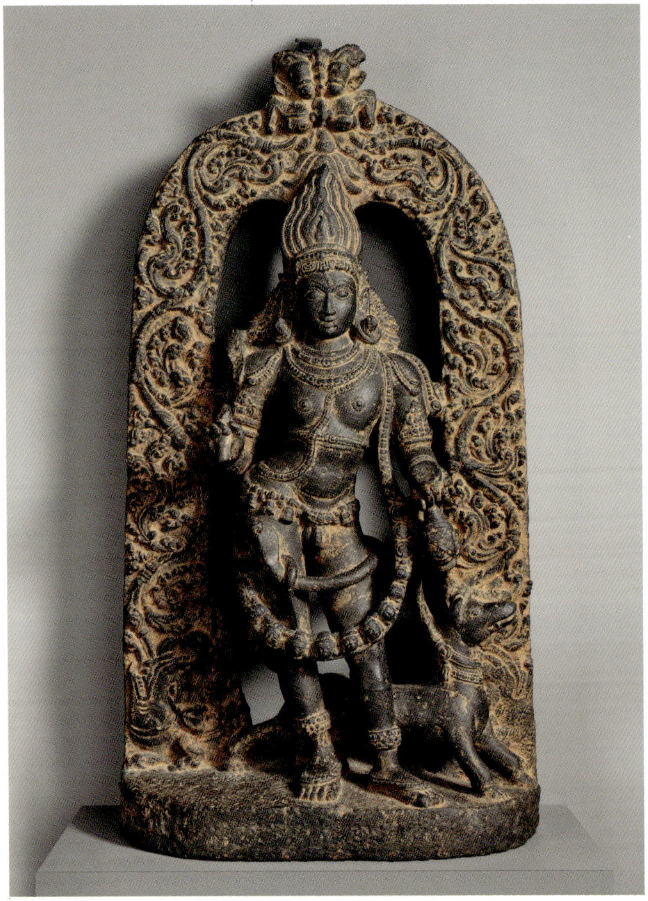

THE HINDU DEITY CHAMUNDA

800–1000
India; Rajasthan state
Sandstone
H. 58.4 cm x W. 38.1 cm x D. 17.8 cm
The Avery Brundage Collection, B62S39+

CAT.
25

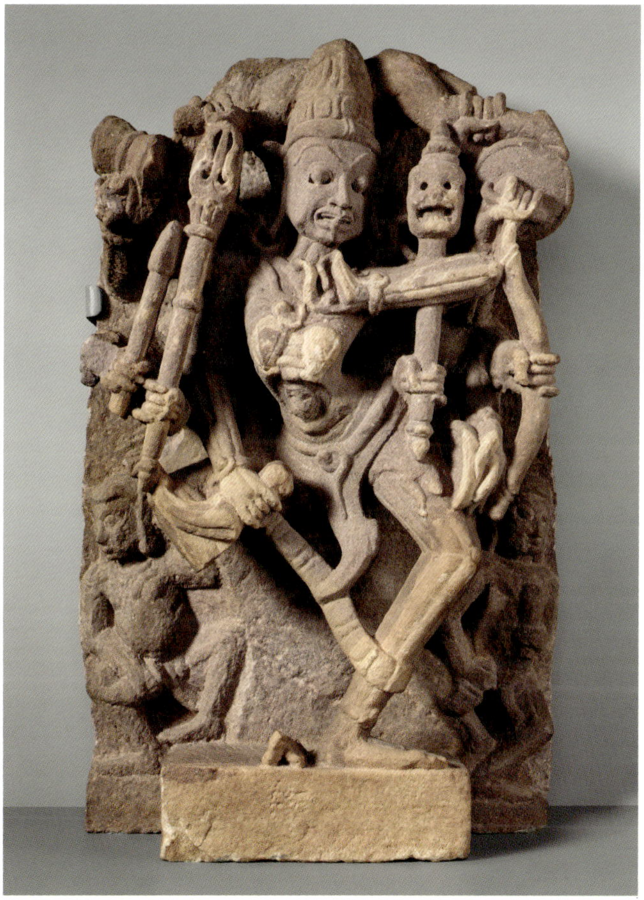

The terrifying Chamunda (also known as Kali, one of Hinduism's most familiar deities in popular culture) represents the power of unleashed ferocity. She is the force (*shakti*) of the goddess, the primordial energy that, along with the power of the male divine, brings the world into being. The *Devi Mahatmya (The Glories of the Goddess)* text describes the moment of Chamunda's creation when the warrior goddess Durga sets out to overcome two male demons (representative of egotism, ambition, and other obstacles that prevent an individual from spiritual achievement). When Durga saw them, "her face in anger became black as ink. From her knitted brows sprang forth Kali [Chamunda], with her dreadful face....She carried a strange skull-topped staff; she was shrouded in a tiger skin and looked utterly gruesome with her emaciated skin. Her mouth gaped widely, terrifying with its lolling tongue, and filled the directions with roars."[41]

Nothing stands in Chamunda's way in overcoming impediments, whether they come from the external world or from within; she transcends even time, which in human terms is denoted by death. Images of Chamunda communicate this intensity through her skeletal—though lithe—body, with sagging breasts, bulging eyes, and fanged mouth, her elephant-hide cape, tiger-skin skirt, and necklace of skulls. Some of these details are difficult to read on this sculpture's worn and damaged surface. The deity holds in her arms (clockwise from the top) a corpse, a shield, a skull-topped staff, a bow, a skull cup, a ritual knife, a trident, a spear, and a drum. Several of these attributes are associated with Shiva and Vishnu and here serve as visual reminders that Chamunda combines the great powers of the male gods.

When seen together, typical images of Parvati (cat. 19) and Chamunda represent two opposing aspects of the same force whose individual qualities are conveyed through their respective forms: where one is nurturing and benevolent, the other is ferocious and unyielding. According to Hindu thought, both aspects are necessary in one's spiritual life. | QA

THE DAOIST IMMORTAL LI TIEGUAI

CAT.
26

China; Fujian province
Qing dynasty, reign of the Qianlong emperor (1736–1795)
Porcelain
H. 31.8 cm x W. 12.7 cm x D. 10.2 cm
The Avery Brundage Collection, B60P25

Li Tieguai, one of the Eight Immortals of Chinese Daoist tradition, appears in this porcelain sculpture as an elderly beggar with bulging eyes, a deformed head, and elongated ears. But Li Tieguai's body had not always been that of an emaciated mendicant. Before he had overcome death and attained the status of an Immortal, his body had been both strong and handsome. What then happened to him that his now-immortal body appears in this all-too-human form?

According to traditional accounts, Li Tieguai had, during the course of his preparatory training, made a journey from earth to heaven. To do so, he arranged for his soul (*hun*)—here depicted as the roiling mass of clouds upon which he stands—to leave his physical body. After telling a disciple to cremate him if he did not return to reanimate his body in seven days, Li Tieguai departed earth for realms celestial. The disciple, however, cremated Li Tieguai's handsome body prematurely. Thus, when his soul returned to earth, Li Tieguai was obliged to enter the first body he could find—that of a sick and lame beggar who had just died.

At that point, Li Tieguai's master—none other than the founder of Daoism, the great Laozi—beheld his disciple's plight. Magically appearing on the scene, Laozi gave Li Tieguai a gourd of medicine that never emptied and an indestructible iron crutch. Now promoted to the status of a full Immortal, Li Tieguai would become the patron of both beggars and apothecaries; to this day, some of the latter use Li Tieguai's iron crutch as a sign of their vocation. | JD

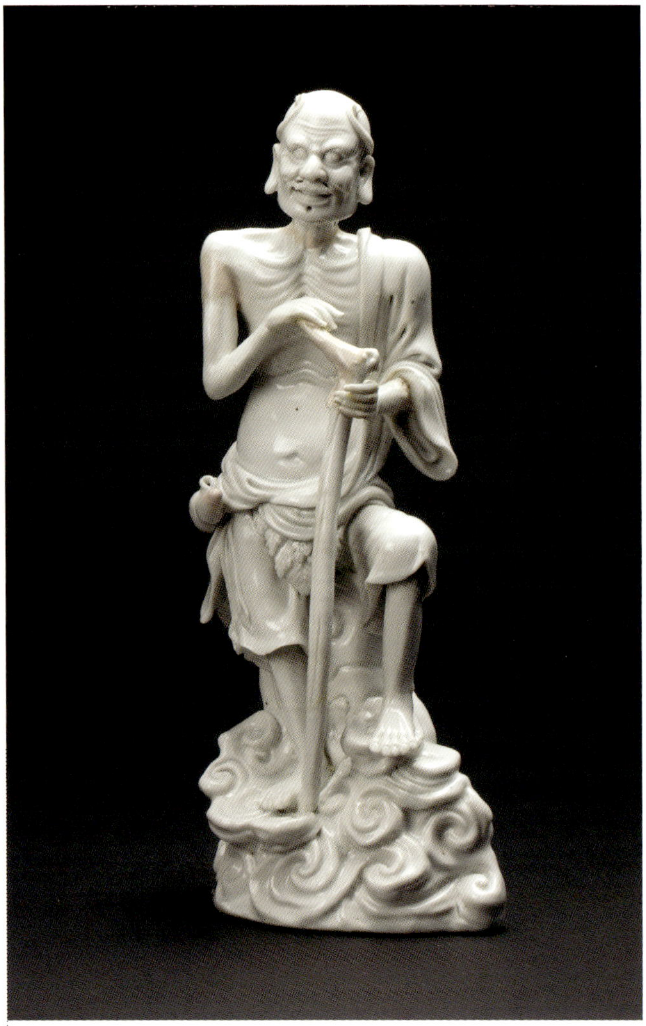

THE BUDDHIST DEITY VAJRABHAIRAVA

APPROX. 1700–1800
Tibet
Bronze with gilding
H. 24.1 cm x W. 19.1 cm x D. 9.2 cm
The Avery Brundage Collection, B60B139

CAT. 27

Vajrabhairava occupies what is perhaps the single most intimidating body-image in all of Himalayan Buddhism. Directly translated, his name means "the diamond terrifier." From his weapon-filled arms to his buffalo-demon head, he is a veritable vision of fear. Indeed, this makes sense because Vajrabhairava is closely tied to that most fearsome of phenomena: death. Despite his terrifying body, Vajrabhairava is not in fact death itself, whose name is Yama. Instead, Vajrabhairava's terrifying body is a divine countermeasure *against* death. How can this be?

The symbolic mythos of Vajrayana, or Esoteric Buddhism, provides the answer. One day, the story goes, the bull-headed god of death Yama was found indiscriminately consuming every being he could. First, he would snare them with his lasso and then draw them into his maw. With relentless efficiency the god of death was emptying the cosmos of sentient beings. Alarmed, the buddhas knew something had to be done or the universe would soon be completely depopulated. They summoned Manjushri, bodhisattva of wisdom and bearer of the fiery sword of discrimination, and asked him to intervene. Master of spiritual technique (*upaya*) that he is, Manjushri determined to stop the killing spree through a singularly ingenious method. Cleverly, he did not challenge death directly. Instead, he approached the infuriated Yama and transformed his body into a mirror. At that point Yama saw his own image. Duly terrified by his own gruesome reflection, Yama asked Manjushri to end the display, promising that if Manjushri did so, he would swear to serve the cause of Buddhism in the future. The deal having been struck, Manjushri assumed his normal form. For his part, Yama vowed to help Buddhist practitioners by reminding them how human life presents such a short and precious opportunity for meditation. | JD

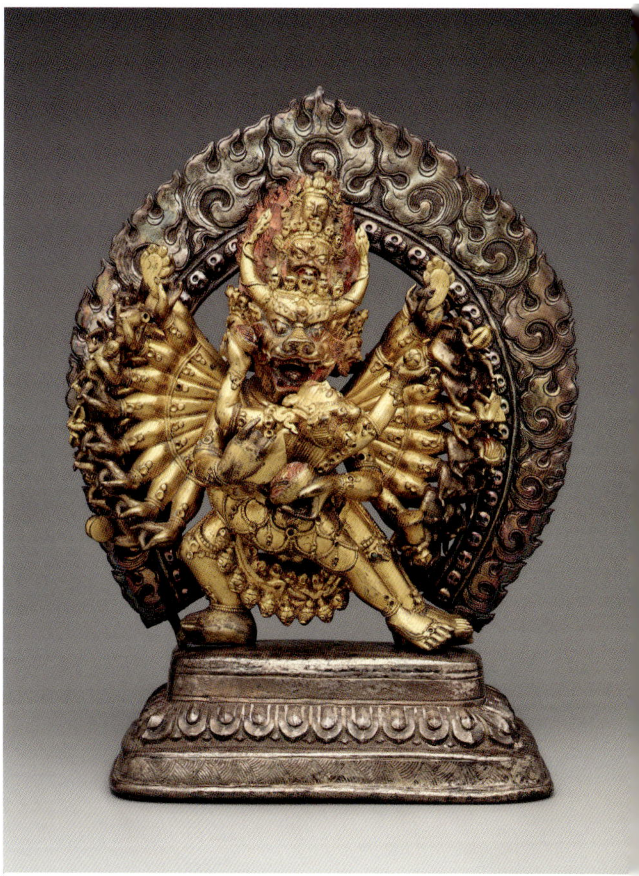

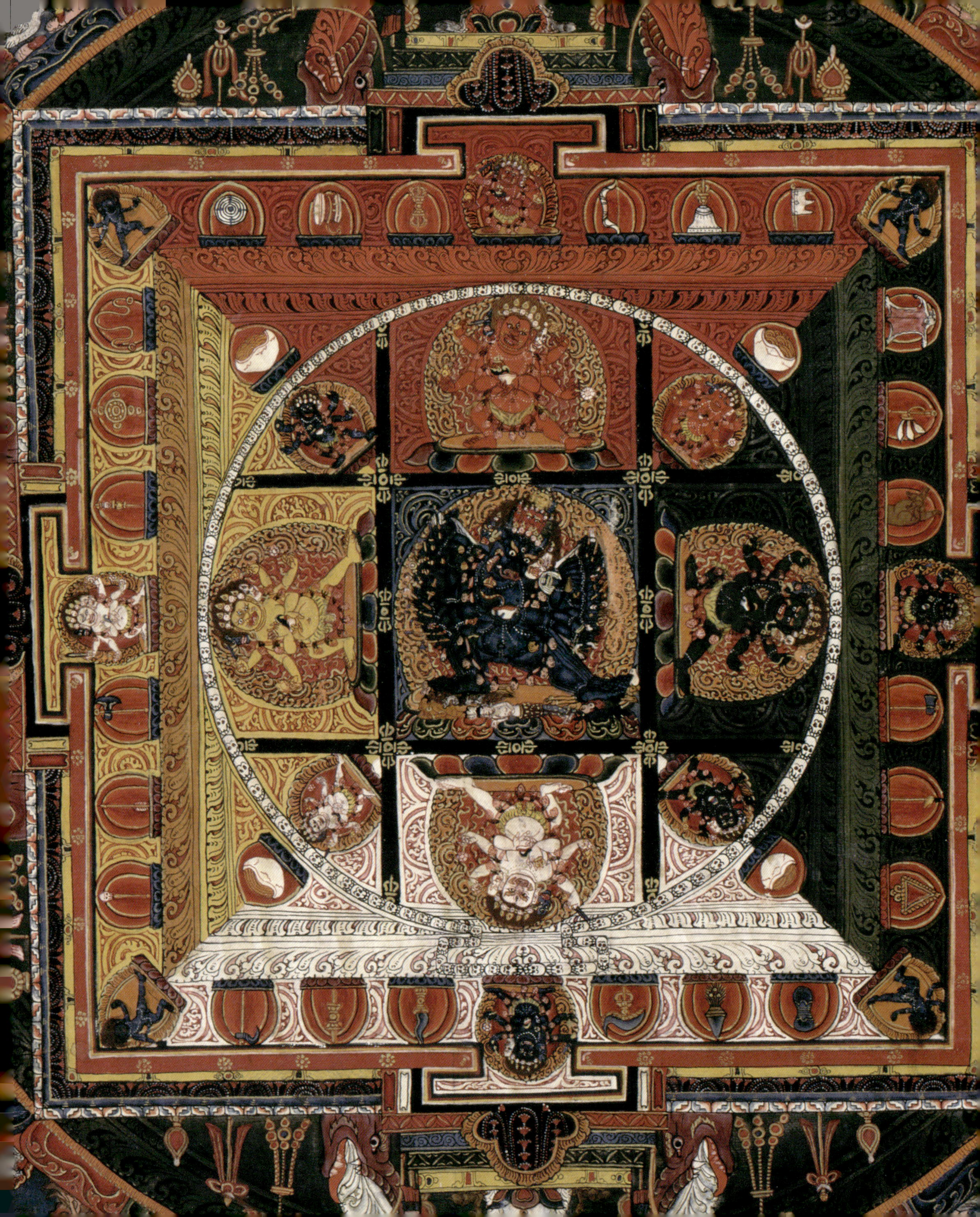

MANDALA OF THE BUDDHIST DEITY VAJRABHAIRAVA

1650–1750
Tibet; Ngor Monastery
Colors on cotton
H. 41.9 cm x W. 40 cm (image);
H. 86.4 cm x W. 50.8 cm (overall)
The Avery Brundage Collection, B63D5

CAT. 28

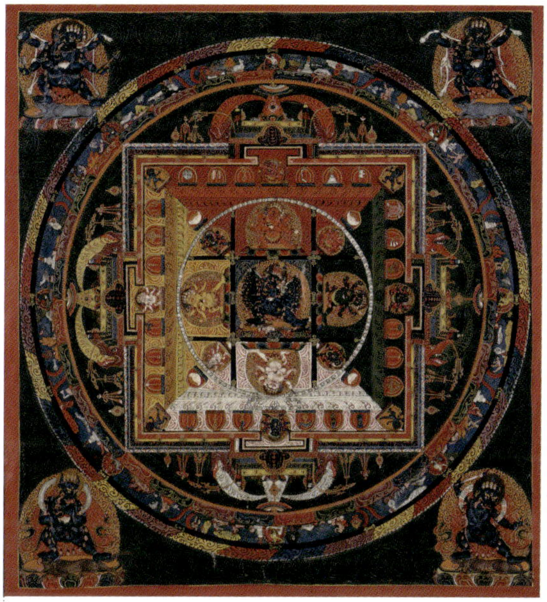

This Buddhist religious painting is called a *thangka*, or "flat body." Paintings of this type are models for meditative visualization. During such practices, the figures on the painting, having been previously committed to memory, are first re-created in the mind's eye through concentration. Then, the meditator imaginatively enters the visualized body of the divinity.

Thangka practice involves another sort of journey as well. When viewed from above, the painting comprises the ground plan of a visionary palace. Transforming it into three dimensions in the mind's eye, meditators travel through the mandala from the periphery to the center. The meditative voyage begins at the corners of this small painting. Here, we encounter four protectors of the dharma. Each is a manifestation of time or death and wears the semblance of a fierce buffalo demon, tongue lolling and hair flaming above a body as blue as empty space itself. Just beyond the four fearsome dharma protectors looms a barrier that must be crossed: a multicolored circle of flame that symbolically separates the ordinary world from the visionary world of meditation.

As the flames clear, the meditator sees the charnel grounds where yogis and yoginis practice violent and sexual rites around the stupas of the deceased. This symbolic complex stands not for some geographically conceived hell but rather for the transcendence of conventional norms of behavior and perception. Then, piercing a web of tiny *vajras* (ritual weapons embodying the hardness of diamonds and the force of thunderbolts), we arrive at the mandala palace sitting atop the pericarp of a gigantic lotus flower, visible here only at the tips of its petals. Above the lotus and at the foundation of the mandala palace lie two crossed *dorjes*, scepter-like implements that symbolize enlightenment. Like the lotus flower on which the palace sits, only the tips of these *dorjes* are visible.

At last, we enter the palace by the lower gate. From here, the meditation progresses clockwise and inward, past a series of guardian and offering deities, each assigned to its proper direction and color within the mandala. Ultimately, the meditator arrives at the figure of Vajrabhairava, "the diamond terrifier." Bull headed and indigo colored, Vajrabhairava reflects the form taken by the bodhisattva of wisdom, Manjushri, in his attempt to win death to the Buddhist cause (see cat. 27). By visualizing her own body in this form, a meditator absorbs the death-defeating qualities embodied by Vajrabhairava.

| JD

THE HINDU DEITY KRISHNA AS AN INFANT

CAT.

29

APPROX. 1860
India; Thanjavur, Tamil Nadu state
Opaque watercolors, gold, and colored glass on cloth, over wood
H. 61.5 cm x W. 47 cm
Bequest of Marjorie Walter Bissinger, 2011.27

The Hindu deity Krishna is worshiped in a number of forms. One of the most surprising appears in this painting, where he is depicted as an infant. At one level, the representation of the deity as a child emphasizes how adorable he is; at another, it reflects the young Krishna's notoriously mischievous nature. Perhaps most famously, Krishna stole butter from his mother, Yashodha, recruiting his friends in the venture. But there is more than mythology here, for the representation of Krishna as a child invokes the theological notion of play (*lila*). In this conception, the universe is understood not as a planned or serious phenomenon but rather as the result of the "play" of the divine. Thus does the whimsical body of the cosmic deity Krishna simultaneously evoke mythological narratives and philosophical ideas. | JD

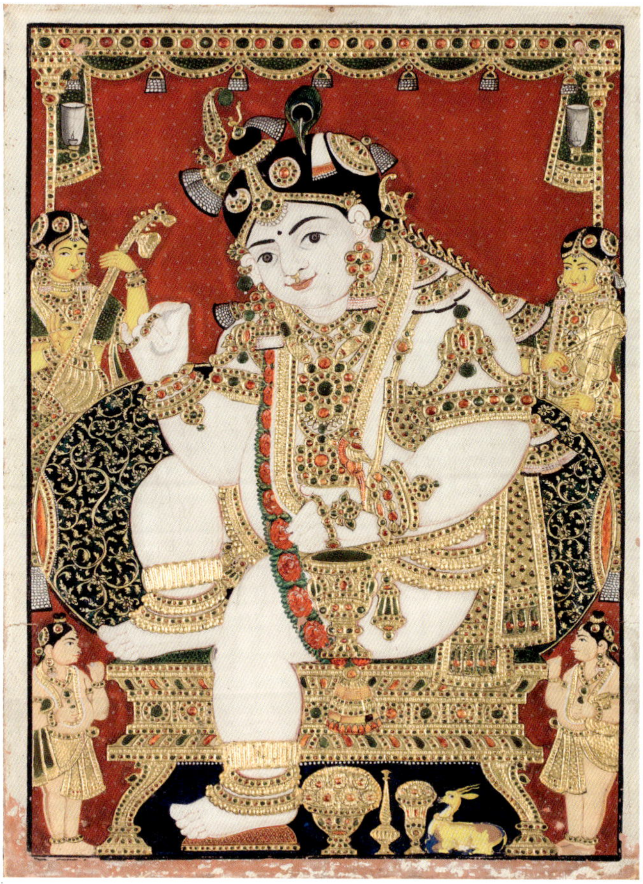

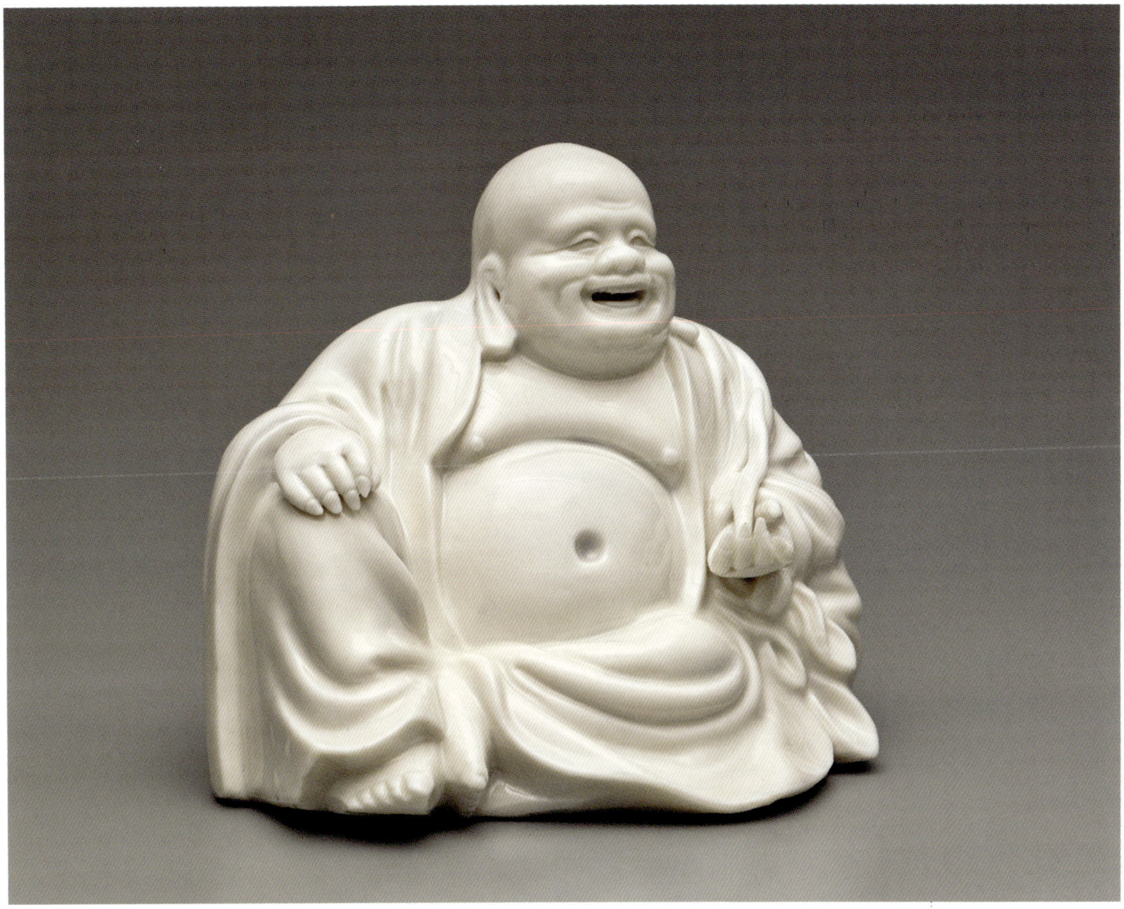

CAT.
30

THE BUDDHIST DEITY MAITREYA (BUDAI HESHANG)

China; Dehua, Fujian province
Qing dynasty (1644–1911)
Porcelain with glaze
H. 17.7 cm x W. 18.4 cm x D. 13.3 cm
The Avery Brundage Collection, B60P1788

The Buddhist deity Budai Heshang is an incarnation of Maitreya, the buddha of the future, whose name means "the friendly one." Indeed, this figure exudes joviality; it is as if the artist has captured his image just as Budai Heshang commences a belly laugh. His casual physical posture, as well as his prominent belly, encourages a relaxed attitude toward the quest for enlightenment. And he is indeed enlightened: elongated ear lobes like his are among the thirty-two marks that identify a buddha. Budai Heshang's relaxed demeanor highlights Maitreya's role in Buddhist mythology: his appearance will inaugurate a new world order in which liberating Buddhist teachings, forgotten for an interval, will be reintroduced. Beings born during Maitreya's time will find enlightenment very easy to achieve; accordingly, Budai Heshang has only two possessions to aid him in his quest: a rosary of meditation beads and a canvas bag that holds—nothing? | JD

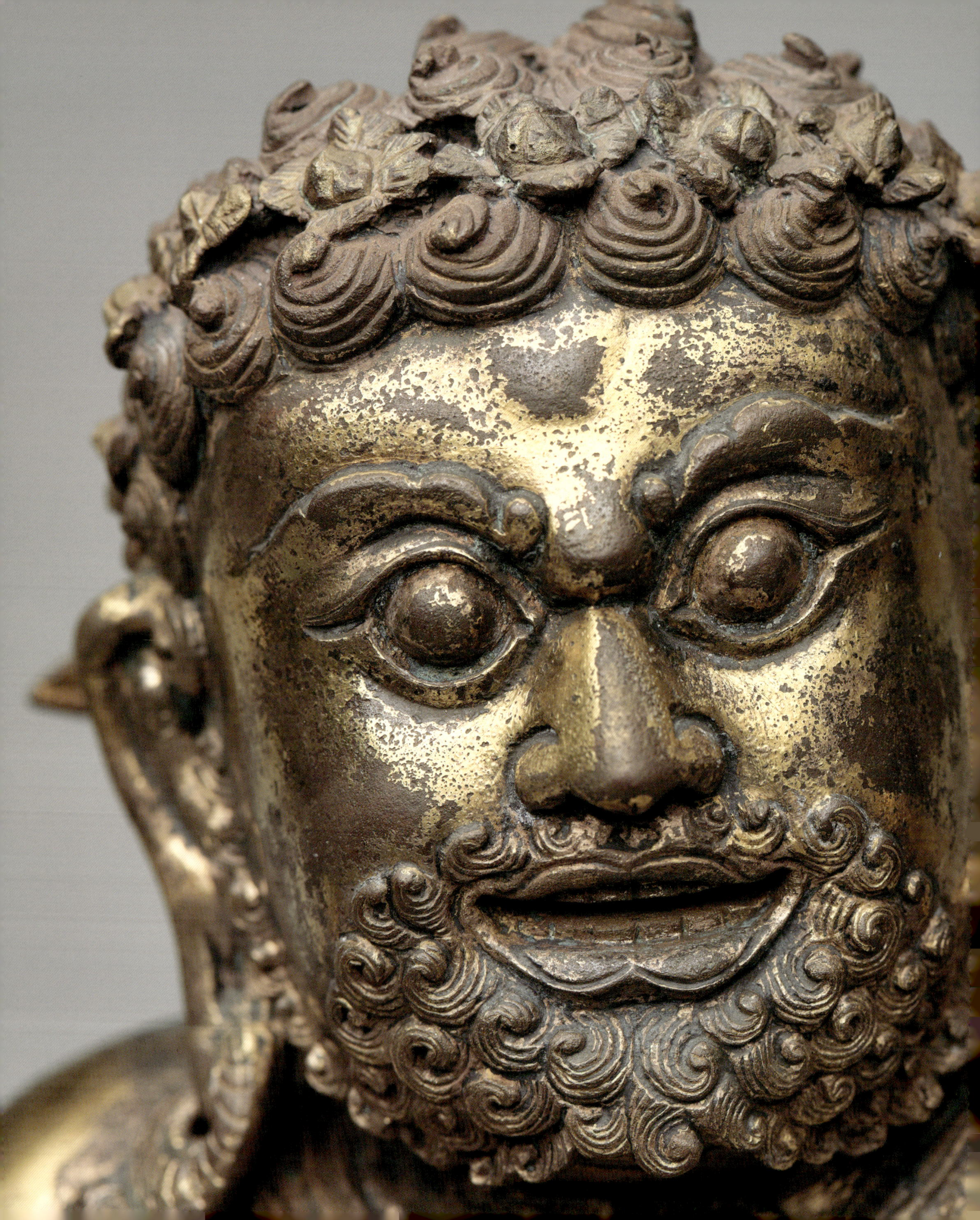

THE BUDDHIST ADEPT VIRUPA

APPROX. 1400–1450
China; Beijing
Ming dynasty (1368–1644)
Bronze with gilding
H. 26.7 cm x W. 25.4 cm x D. 16.5 cm
The Avery Brundage Collection, B62B20

CAT.
31

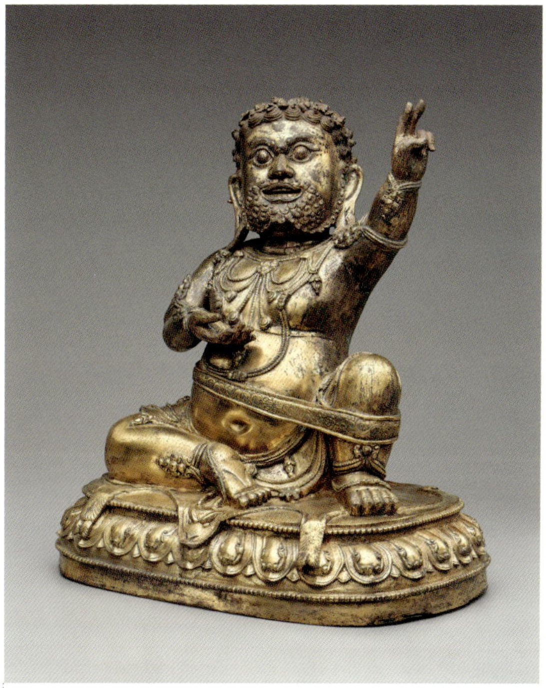

Translated directly from the Sanskrit, Virupa's name means "Mr. Repulsive." Indeed, his body conforms to very few South Asian conventions of beauty. His fleshy limbs accentuate Virupa's rather portly appearance, and his bulging eyes suggest both joy and a touch of the madman. As it turns out, this appearance is entirely appropriate, for Virupa is one who has confounded convention and in so doing has found freedom from the illusory bondage of worldly perspectives and practices. In the process, conventional society and its values become the stuff of hilarity—comical to think that we would take anything so foolish seriously or, in the language of Buddhism, that we would so thoroughly conflate appearance and reality.

But Virupa wasn't always this joyful. For many years he served as abbot, the administrative leader, at Nalanda Monastery, arguably the greatest Buddhist university ever created but hardly an adventuresome post. Unfortunately, Virupa had been unsuccessful spiritually, never once having a direct personal encounter with his chosen deity. Frustrated, he therefore determined to abandon his spiritual quest. Throwing his meditation beads in the latrine in disgust, Virupa retired for the evening. While asleep, his chosen deity, the fierce red Vajrayogini, appeared to him in a dream. She admonished Virupa, telling him that he would have been enlightened that very evening had he not thrown his beads away. She told him to recover them, and when he did so, Virupa was forthwith enlightened.

Overjoyed at his long-delayed liberation, Virupa resigned his monastic post, put flowers in his hair, and took to traveling and teaching across northern India. At one point, he found himself at a tavern and possessed of a mighty thirst. The bartender, amazed at Virupa's drinking capacity, told Virupa he could continue to drink until the sun went down. Virupa, using his meditative powers (*siddhi*), then stopped the sun until he had drunk his fill—much to the dismay of the hapless innkeeper. In this sculpture, Virupa's left hand halts the sun, while his right holds his (now missing) skull bowl. This legendary story, like so many Himalayan artworks, contains a crucial hidden message: by seeing all conventional categories, from language to behavior to professions, as just that, a person is liberated from the bondage of taking them seriously. Perhaps that is the reason for Virupa's big grin. | JD

TANTRIC SELF-PORTRAIT IN JAIPUR SERIES, 2000–2003

CAT.

32

BY PAMELA SINGH (INDIAN, B. 1962)
Gelatin silver print with oil, acrylic, gold, mud, and vermillion powder
Various sizes, H. 61 cm x W. 61 cm to H. 94 cm x W. 94 cm
Lent by the artist and SepiaEYE Gallery, New York

From 2000 to 2003 photographer Pamela Singh made daily excursions in the old city of Jaipur. Coming from a background in photojournalism, Singh approached this project with a genuine interest in the people she would encounter. Yet her goal was not to turn her objective lens on these people as conventional subjects but to highlight the intersection of her life with theirs. The results are enigmatic, almost dreamlike images that subvert the conventions of self-portraiture and reference modes of art making from the past. Overlaid with symbols, hand colored using obsolete vintage pigments, and displayed in artist-designed frames, these works recall nineteenth-century photography from India but lack the formality of those images, which catalogued architecture and people according to their proper name, title, location, and rank. Dismembered and anonymized, these fragmentary portraits of subjects and artist comingle and coexist across barriers of time, class, and caste. Singh is present in the work as an early twenty-first-century female flaneur, and viewers are offered these poetic, ambiguous compositions as windows onto a type of street life that has largely vanished fifteen years later.

Singh includes elements of herself in these images but does not follow any particular formula. In *Tantric Self-Portrait in Jaipur #1* we see the upper portion of her face, including her eyes, front and center. The viewer's focus alternates between her penetrating gaze and the target-like architectural feature that looms above her: an image that gives physical form to *bindu*, the object of focused meditative concentration. In *#2*, the original photographs are unfocused to the point of abstraction, and this earthly image is subsumed by the artist's overlay of what appears to be astronomical or astrological charts. *Tantric Self-Portrait in Jaipur #18* shows Singh from the shoulders down, standing on a processional staircase and attended by equally poised dogs facing in opposite directions. In *#13* and *#15* we see further examples of Singh's unusual take on the concept of the self-portrait. These are ostensibly images of bodybuilders, men who engage in a spiritual practice that involves weightlifting as a form of devotion and discipline. Their sculpted bodies are very rarely seen outside their small circle, as they practice early in the morning, before most city dwellers wake and dress in

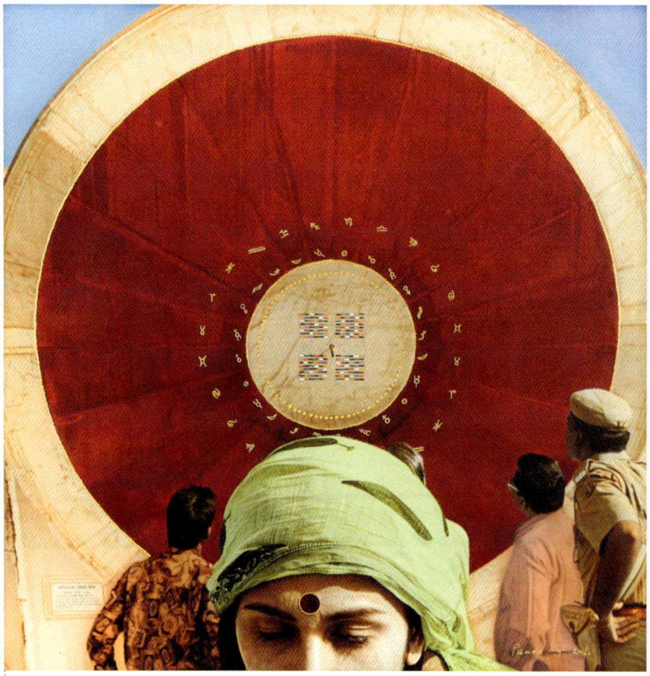

1

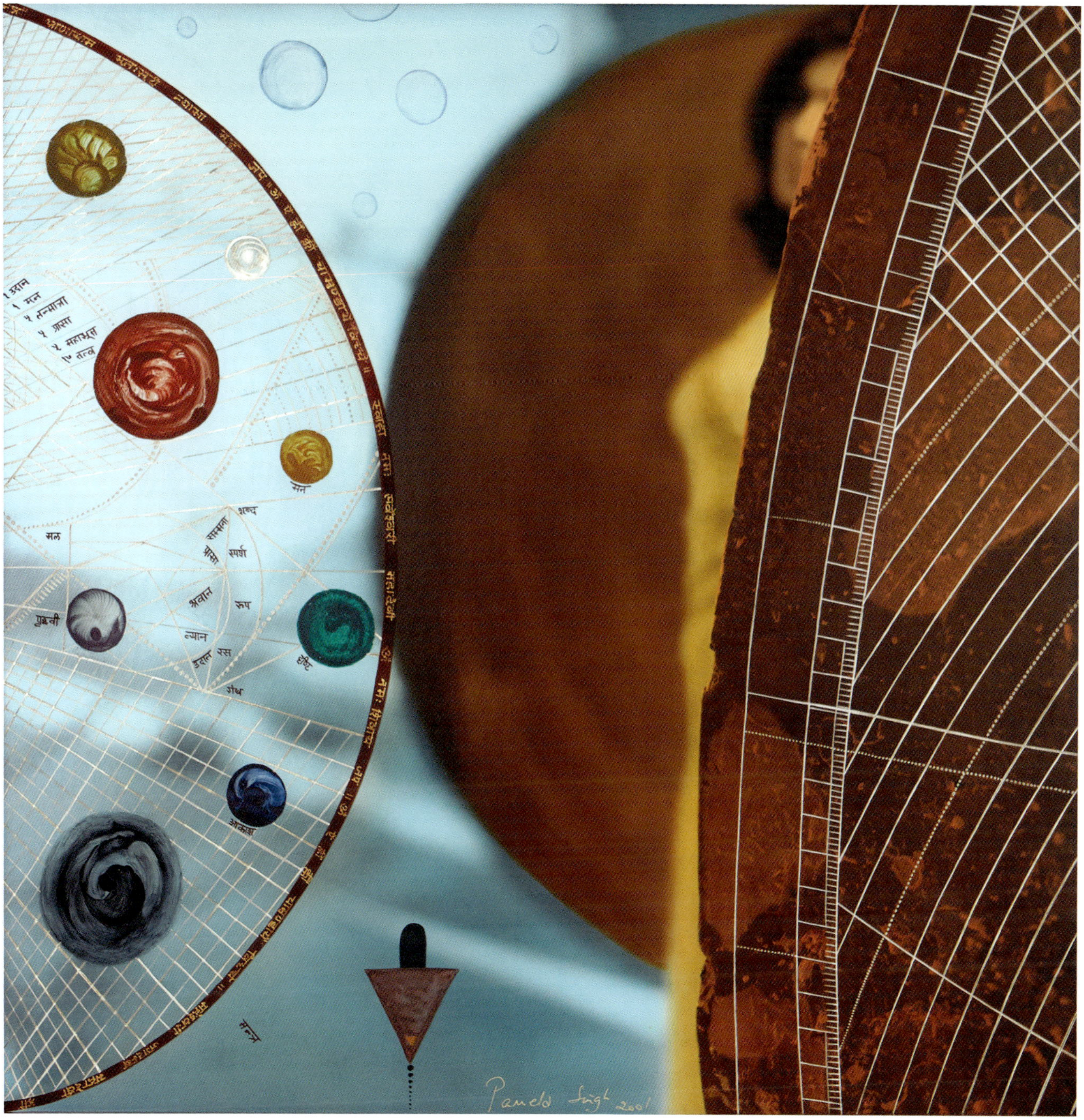

2

plain clothes during the day. The only trace of the artist in these so-called self-portraits is the shadow that falls in the frame. Where the sacred sculpture in this book gives concrete form to abstract concepts and superhuman qualities, Pamela Singh's photographs offer a way to atomize her own image and place our contemporary world in dialogue with a spiritual plane. | KGO

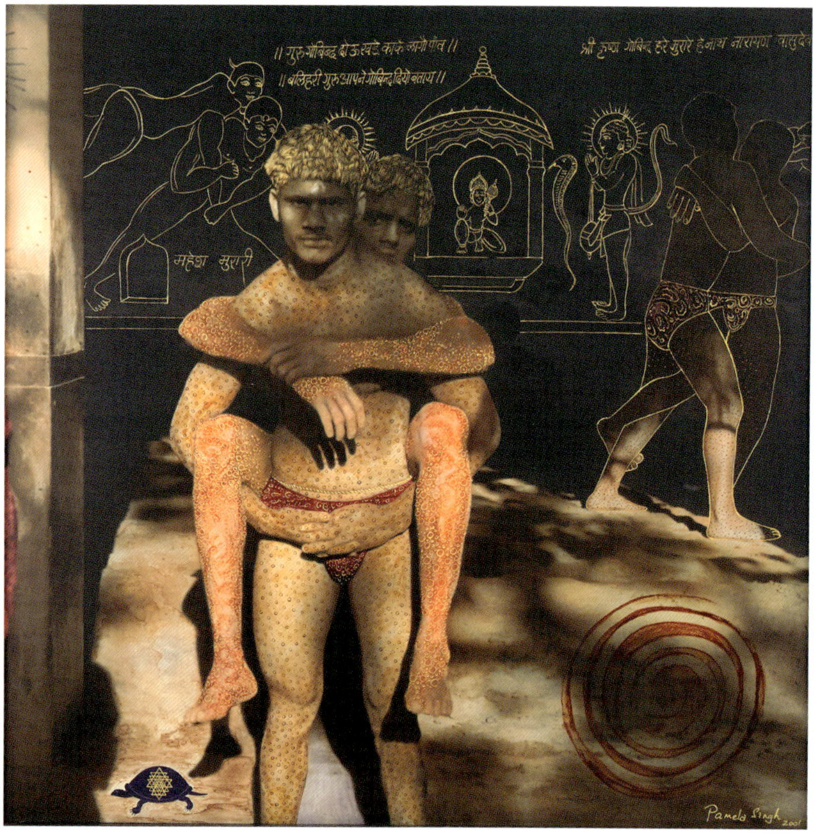

13

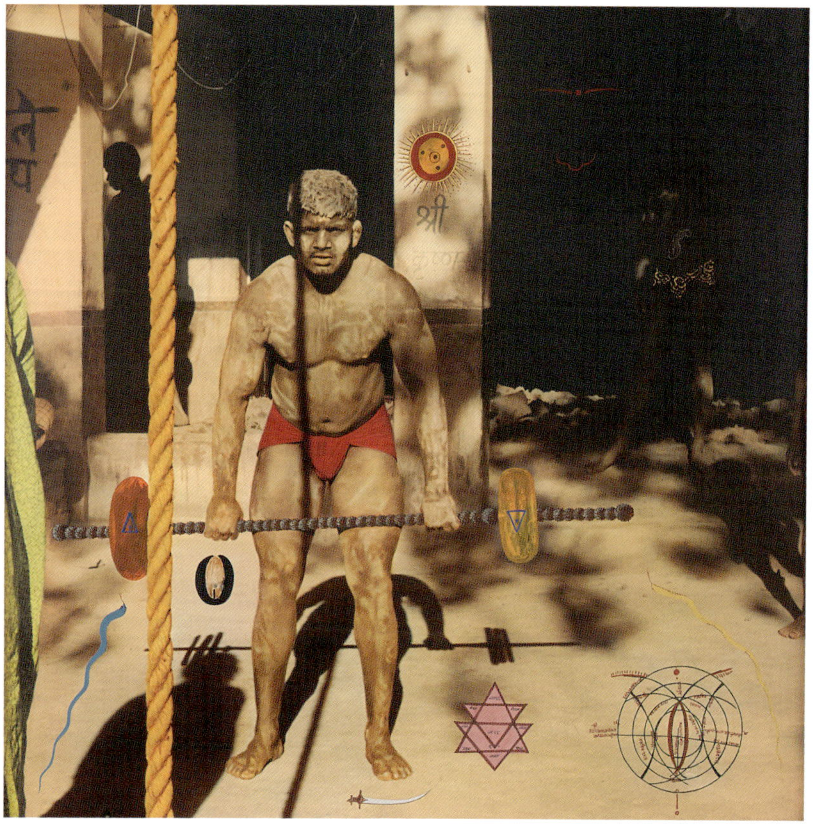

15

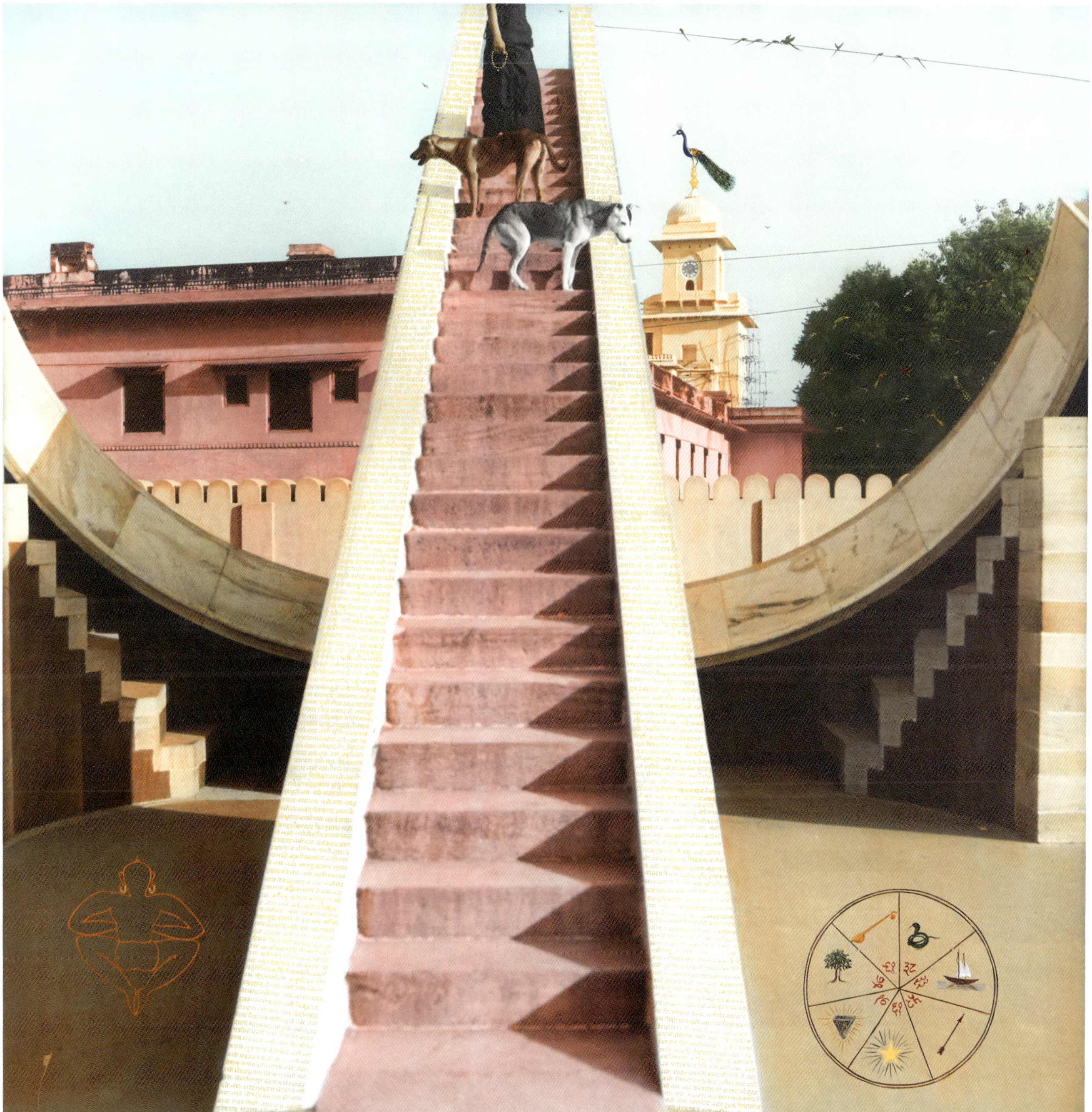

KHAJURAHO SERIES, 1965

BY VIVAN SUNDARAM (INDIAN, B. 1943)
Pen drawing on page removed from book
Various sizes, H. 14 cm x W. 8.9 cm to H. 20.3 cm x W. 5.7 cm
Lent by the artist and SepiaEYE Gallery, New York

CAT.
33

I found the reproductions in a modest government publication when I was traveling to Khajuraho. It was a small-size book, hardly 7-by-5 inches, of sculptures from Khajuraho. When I came back I continued to play around, fool around, with that imagery. —Vivan Sundaram[42]

Playfulness, humor, and irreverence intersect in Vivan Sundaram's *Khajuraho* series. In this youthful project, he took photographic reproductions depicting sculpture from historic Indian temple complexes and drew cartoon-like images on top of them. The result is somewhere between comics and the Surrealist drawing game/technique known as exquisite corpse. The new composite figures, adorned, coiffed, made up, and accessorized, emphasize or expose elements of the original sculptural compositions that might not otherwise be apparent. The pensive gaze of a female deity in *Khajuraho_8* is rendered more melancholy by the artist's humanizing additions of dramatic eye makeup and a simple modern bob, then it is transformed again into an image worthy of an LP cover or movie poster with the phrase "Hey! Let's Twist Again." In *Khajuraho_04* an image of a sculptural couple is transformed into a would-be ad bearing purposefully clunky phrases: "everything handled with care. comfort cosy caress. Speed. Air India." Sundaram appropriates the visual and verbal language of advertising—like the photographic reproductions of sculpture, so dependent on the female form—and mixes it with his own dry wit.

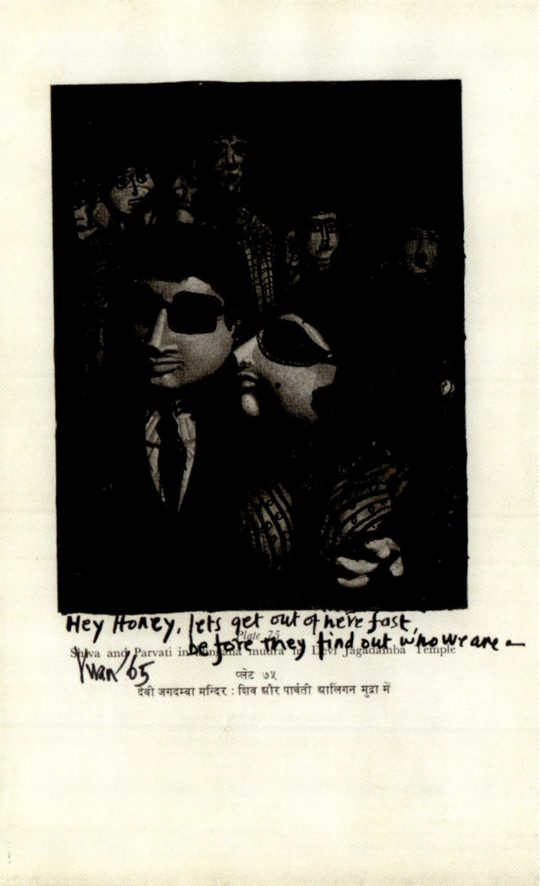

1a

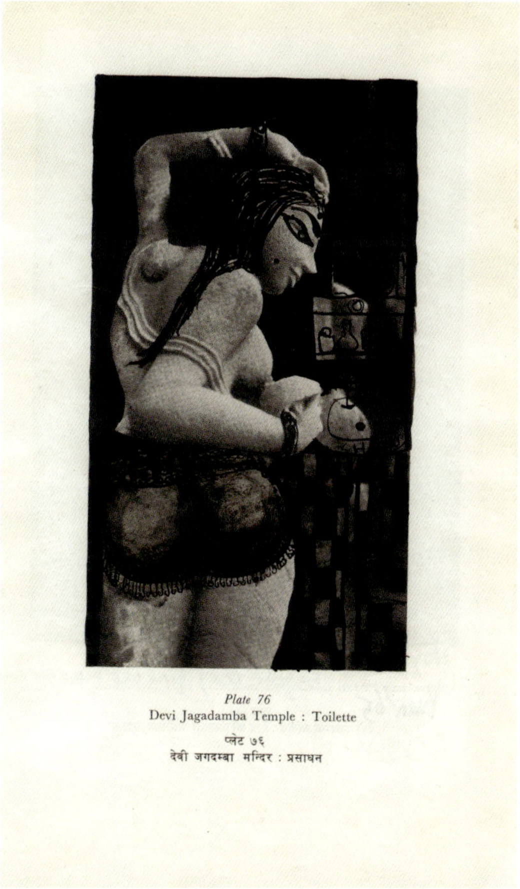

1b

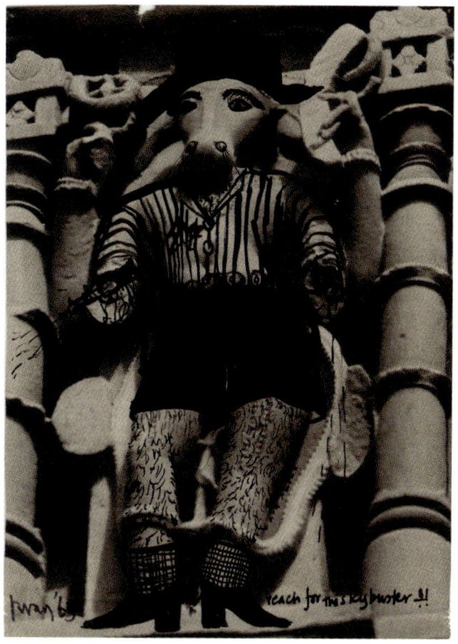

2

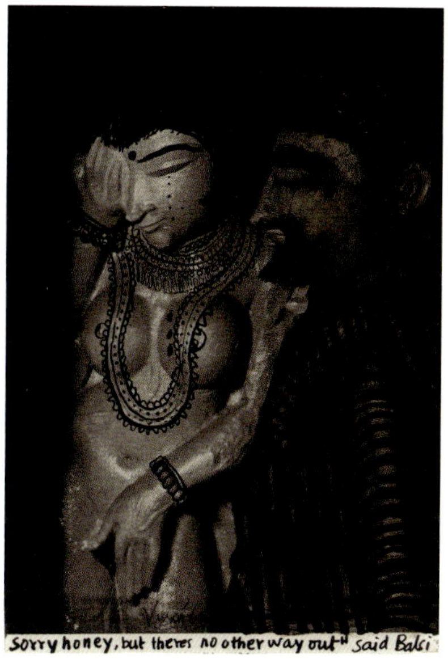

3

Asked about his use of photographic reproductions as "found objects" at this time, Sundaram replied, "In 1965–66, the word or the concept of found objects wasn't part of my vocabulary. I…was part of what we called pop art, which had aspects of graffiti, a kind of playful iconoclastic kind of working.… I found something and then scribbled over it, and, as I said, we didn't designate it as a found object, but of course now pop art and found objects can be linked."[43]

The postmodern mélange of global and local, ancient and contemporary, found and created, divine and human, somber and playful in Sundaram's art may at first seem like a simple game of remixing, but it is more than that. It is a reminder that seemingly small-scale exercises can embrace big themes, and that the monuments of the past can be the materials for questioning the present. | KGO

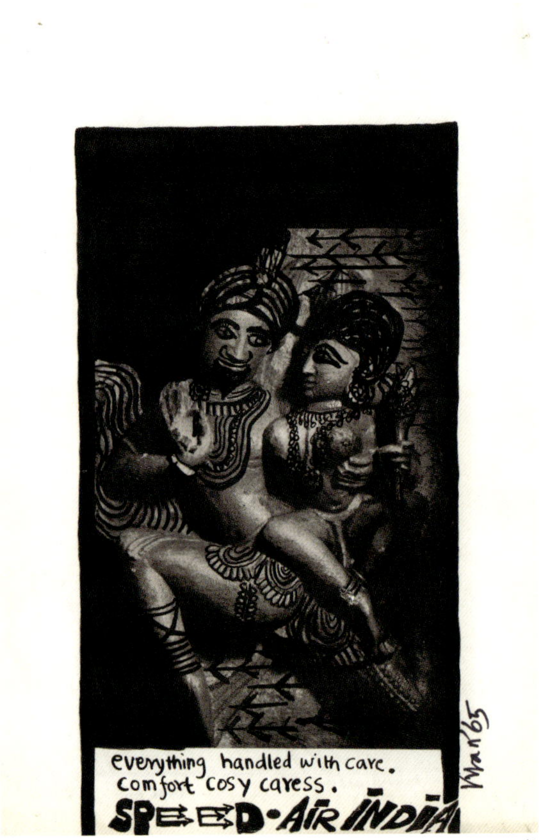
everything handled with care.
comfort cosy caress.
SPEED-AIR INDIA

4a

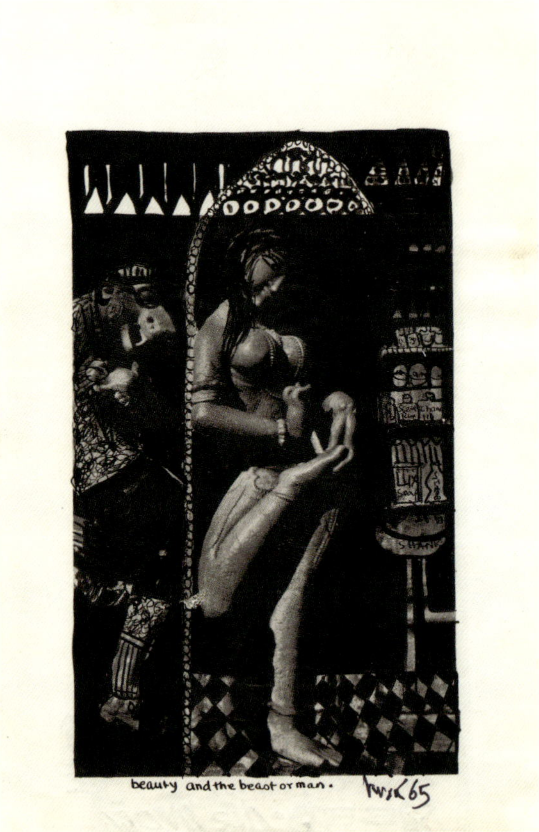
beauty and the beast or man.

4b

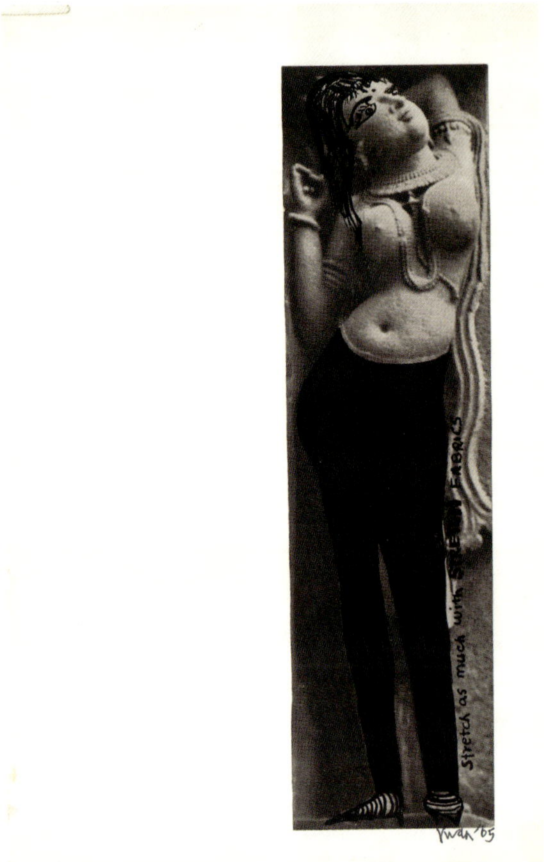
stretch as much with

7

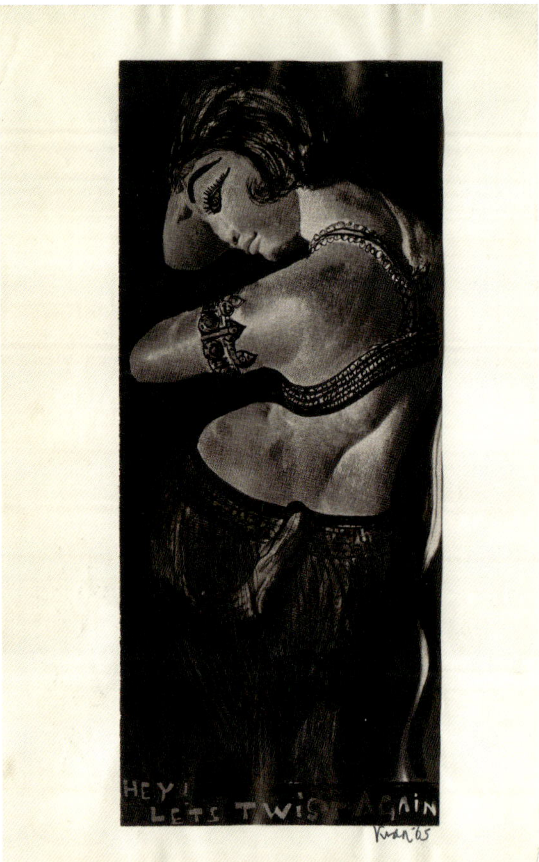
HEY!
LETS TWIS AGAIN

8

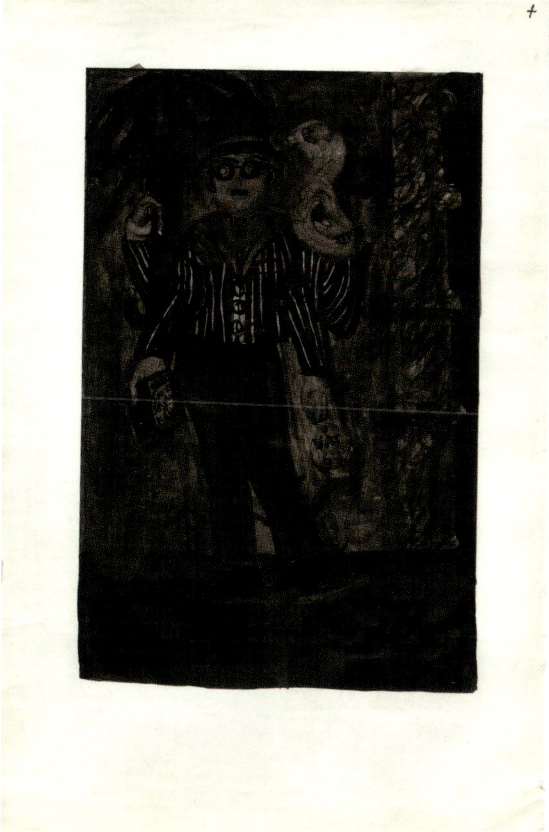

9a

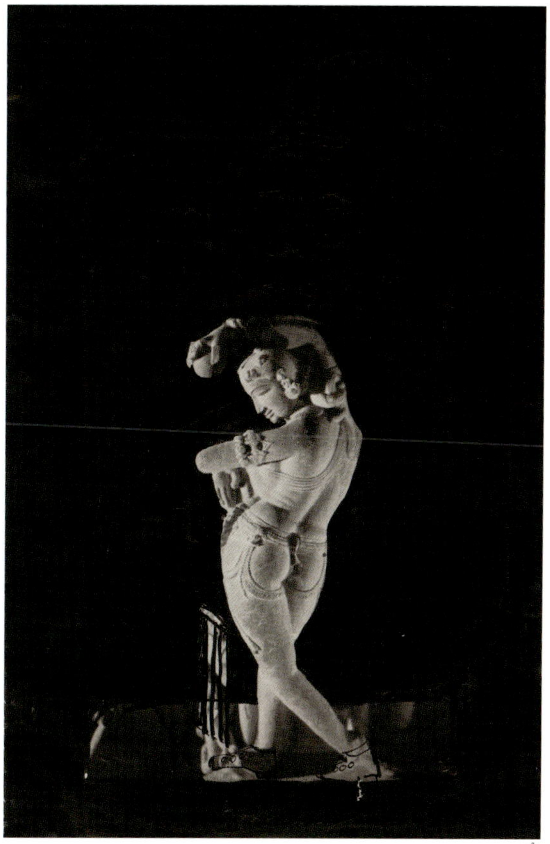

9b

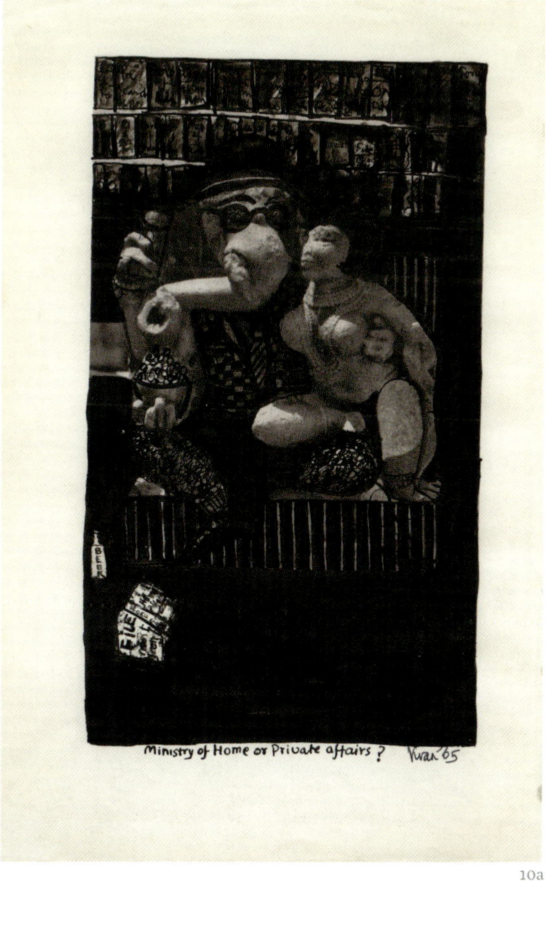

10a

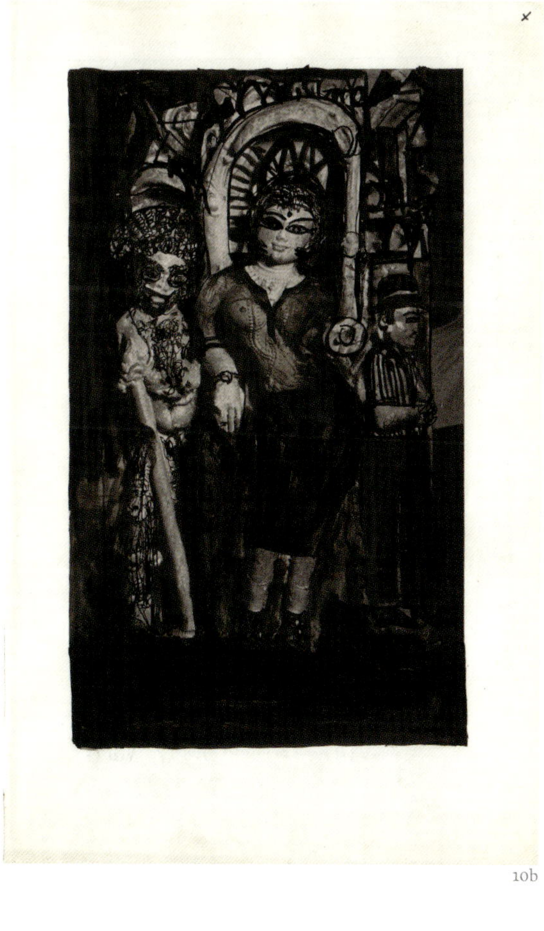

10b

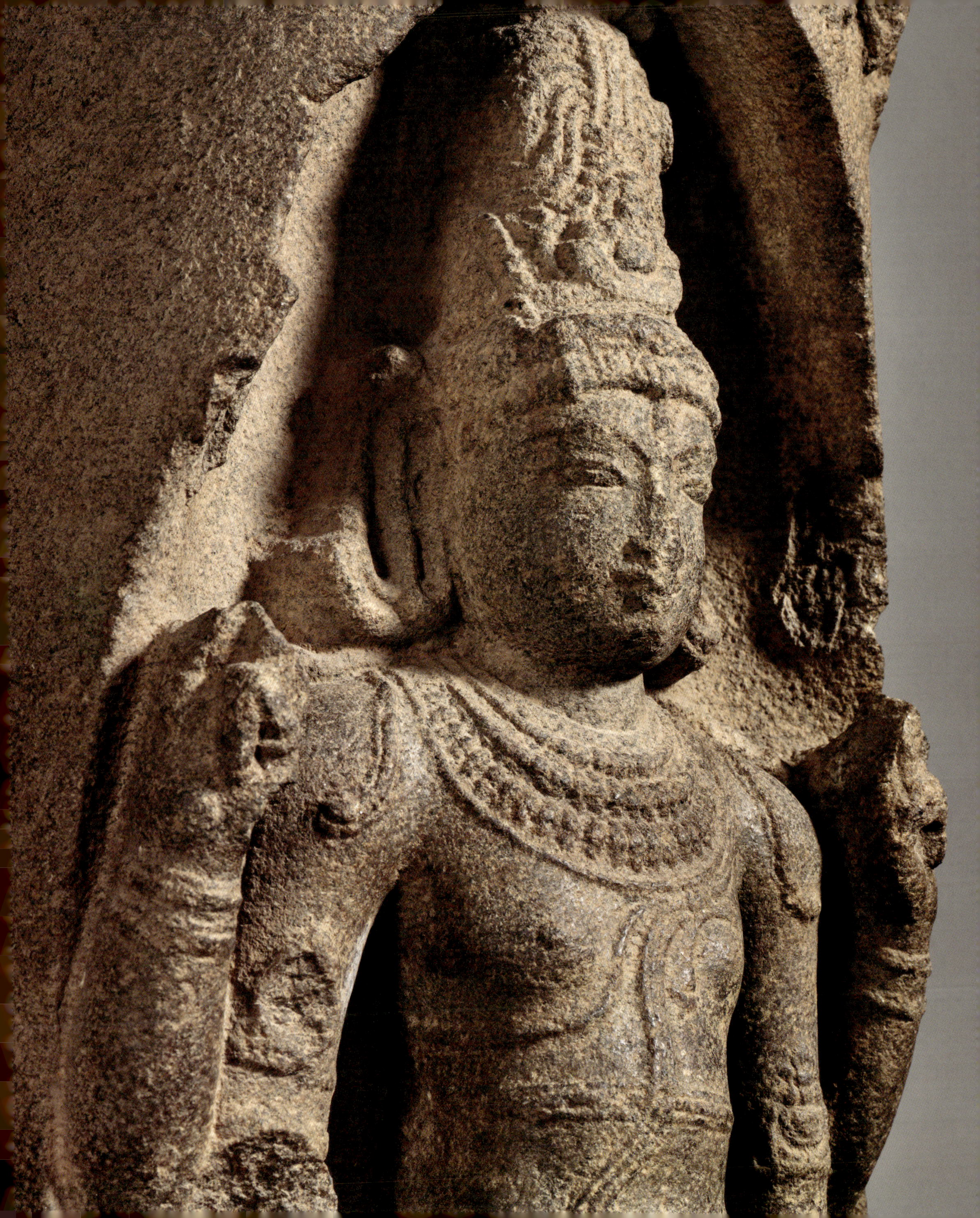

It is fatal to be a man or woman pure and simple; one must be woman-manly or man-womanly.... Some marriage of opposites has to be consummated.

—Virginia Woolf, English writer (1882–1941)

Divine Metamorphosis

There is nothing permanent except change.

—Heraclitus, Greek philosopher (fifth century BCE)

THE BODHISATTVA AVALOKITESHVARA (GUANYIN)

CAT.
34

APPROX. 1100–1200
China
Song dynasty (960–1279)
Wood (paulownia) with pigments
H. 132.1 cm x W. 106.7 cm x D. 63.5 cm
The Avery Brundage Collection, B60S24+

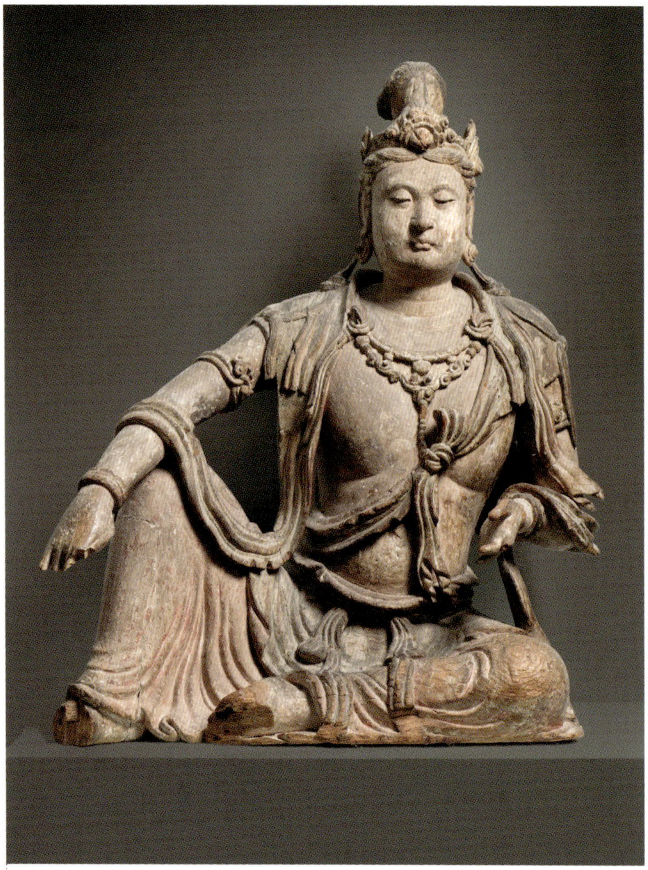

One of the most popular and multifaceted of figures from the pantheon of bodhisattvas described in the Buddhist Mahayana sutra literature is Avalokiteshvara, "the lord who gazes down" with compassion. This large-scale wooden sculpture would originally have been placed in a temple environment where worshipers could quite literally see him "looking down" on them. This sculpture depicts one particular manifestation of the deity: the Water-Moon Guanyin, which is a Chinese form of Avalokiteshvara. According to some scholars, the deity's full chest and flowing robes suggest the Water-Moon Guanyin has incorporated qualities that, in Chinese thought, were considered feminine, such as compassion.

There are, however, important aspects of Avalokiteshvara's gender ambiguity that have to do with philosophical rather than sociocultural issues. In the *Vimalakirti Sutra*—a text that provides a philosophical basis for full equality in the dharma for the laity and women—a divinity does indeed change gender. The deity in question does so, however, to demonstrate that all conceptions, including the dichotomy between male and female, rest on conventional rather than substantive distinctions. Similarly, by the very ambiguity of his form Avalokiteshvara embodies the realization that apparent opposites are not contradictory but rather complementary poles along a continuum—another key tenet of Mahayana Buddhism.

The emphasis on reflection in the imagery and mythology surrounding Water-Moon Guanyin likely has many sources. For example, the reflection of the moon on the water is one of the ten metaphors for the empty nature of the cosmos presented in Mahayana Buddhist literature. It is also likely that Water-Moon Guanyin evolved in tandem with artistic products based on imagery contained in the *Avatamsaka* ("Flower Garland") Sutra. In this ornate text, the Buddha describes a universe of reflections, where every cosmos contains itself and all others in microcosm, ad infinitum, and vice versa. Thus, the cosmos may seem to be multifarious but in fact subsists as a singularity—just like the moon reflected in water. | JD

THE BODHISATTVA AVALOKITESHVARA

1800–1900
Tibet
Colors on cotton
H. 77.2 cm × W. 59.7 cm (image);
H. 152.4 cm × W. 104.5 cm (overall)
Gift of the Friends of Richard Davis, 1988.34

CAT.
35

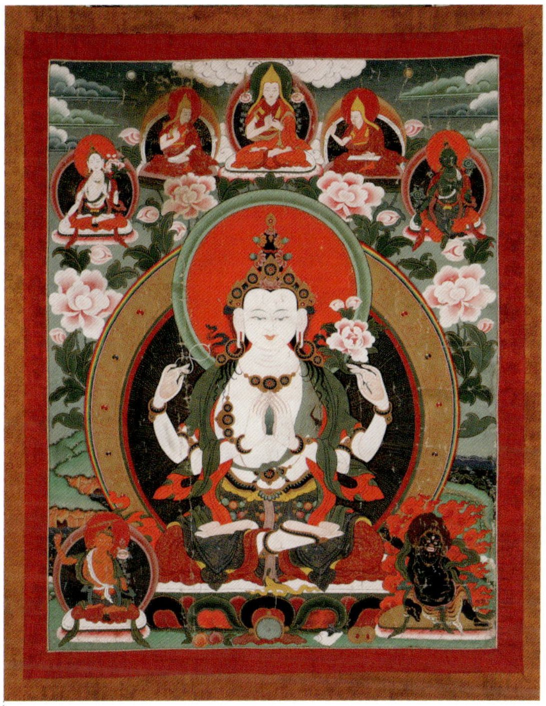

From his lotus seat at the center of this painting, the great bodhisattva Avalokiteshvara continually radiates universal compassion from his four-armed body. He is one of the best-loved and most important of Buddhist deities, especially in the Himalayan regions that practice the meditation techniques characteristic of Vajrayana, the Esoteric Buddhist tradition whose name translates as "Thunderbolt Vehicle." While earlier forms of Avalokiteshvara do not reveal any physiognomical peculiarities, the four-armed Avalokiteshvara inhabits a body quite unlike anything with which we might be familiar in ordinary reality.

The text that describes his form is called a "visualization" (*sadhana*) and might best be understood as a guided meditation. According to the *sadhana*, the four-armed Avalokiteshvara is white in color and seated in royal garments in the lotus posture. In his upraised left hand he bears a pink lotus (*padma*). At the center of his chest, between his palms, he holds a jewel (*mani*). And in his upper right hand, he holds a meditation rosary, according to which six syllables are recited: *Om, mani padme hum*.

This phrase is Avalokiteshvara's mantra, which translates as "Om, the jewel is in the lotus, hum." This may be cryptic to the uninitiated, but when combined with proper and attentive visualization, the recitation of Avalokiteshvara's mantra is understood to invoke both the presence and the power of the great being, first into the meditator's field of awareness and thence into the world at large.

For Himalayan Buddhists, Avalokiteshvara plays a uniquely engaged role in both the ordinary world and the world to come. He is the being who incarnates into the lineage of gurus known as the Dalai Lamas, and, as such, he can be understood as a bodhisattva directly involved in the affairs of the world. On a more cosmic level, the might of his compassion was so extraordinary that he entered every one of the six realms of existence—that of the gods, demigods, humans, animals, ghosts, and hell-beings—and appeared to the denizens of those realms as a saving buddha. Indeed, each syllable in his mantra corresponds to one of those six realms. | JD

THE BODHISATTVA AVALOKITESHVARA

APPROX. 750–850
Thailand; Plai Bat Hill, Buriram province
Copper alloy
H. 94 cm x W. 33 cm x D. 25.4 cm
The Avery Brundage Collection, B66B14

CAT.
36

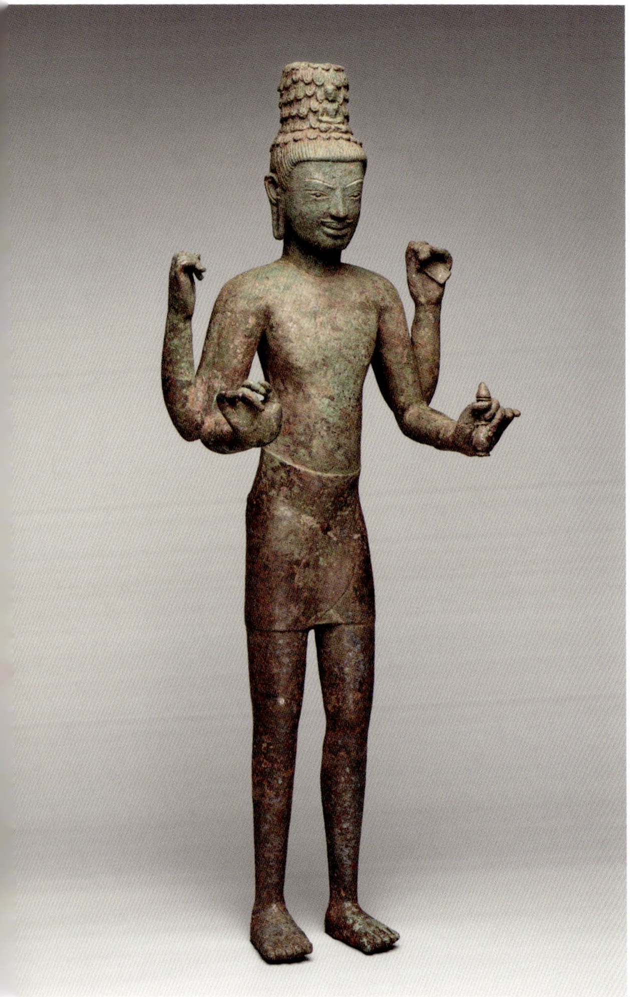

Avalokiteshvara first appears in the textual traditions of Mahayana Buddhism around 100 CE. There, he is described as a bodhisattva: a being who has vowed to save all sentient beings from the endless cycle of rebirth (*samsara*) before he himself enters the bliss of nirvana. In the *Heart Sutra*, arguably the key philosophical text of Mahayana Buddhism, he presents the essence of Buddhist teachings, the "perfection of wisdom" (*prajna-paramita*), as "form is emptiness, emptiness is form." Further, another manifestation of Avalokiteshvara saves sentient beings from the "eight great fears," including death by any number of causes. Thus is Avalokiteshvara intimately associated with both the central philosophy of the Mahayana, emptiness, and its central ethic, compassion. This connection appears in Southeast Asia in sculptural form. A number of triadic sculptures from the region feature a central Buddha—a still-mysterious figure often seated on a serpent—flanked by Avalokiteshvara on the one hand and by the goddess Prajnaparamita, embodying the perfection of wisdom, on the other.

Nowhere in the Perfection of Wisdom literature is Avalokiteshvara described as having the extraordinary four-limbed physiognomy we see in this Thai bronze. How then did he acquire it? One hypothesis holds that, as stories and imagery surrounding this important savior figure began to accumulate, Buddhist scholars and artists codified these forms, thus rendering them visually iconic and narratively canonic. What we are seeing here, then, is one such codified form. But which one? Usually, as with the four-armed Avalokiteshvara so important in Tibet (see cat. 43), it is possible to find a text that describes precisely how to visualize the deity and what its symbolism means. But as no source text for this form has yet come to light, how the symbolism of this form of Avalokiteshvara worked in southeast Asian thought remains a mystery. | JD

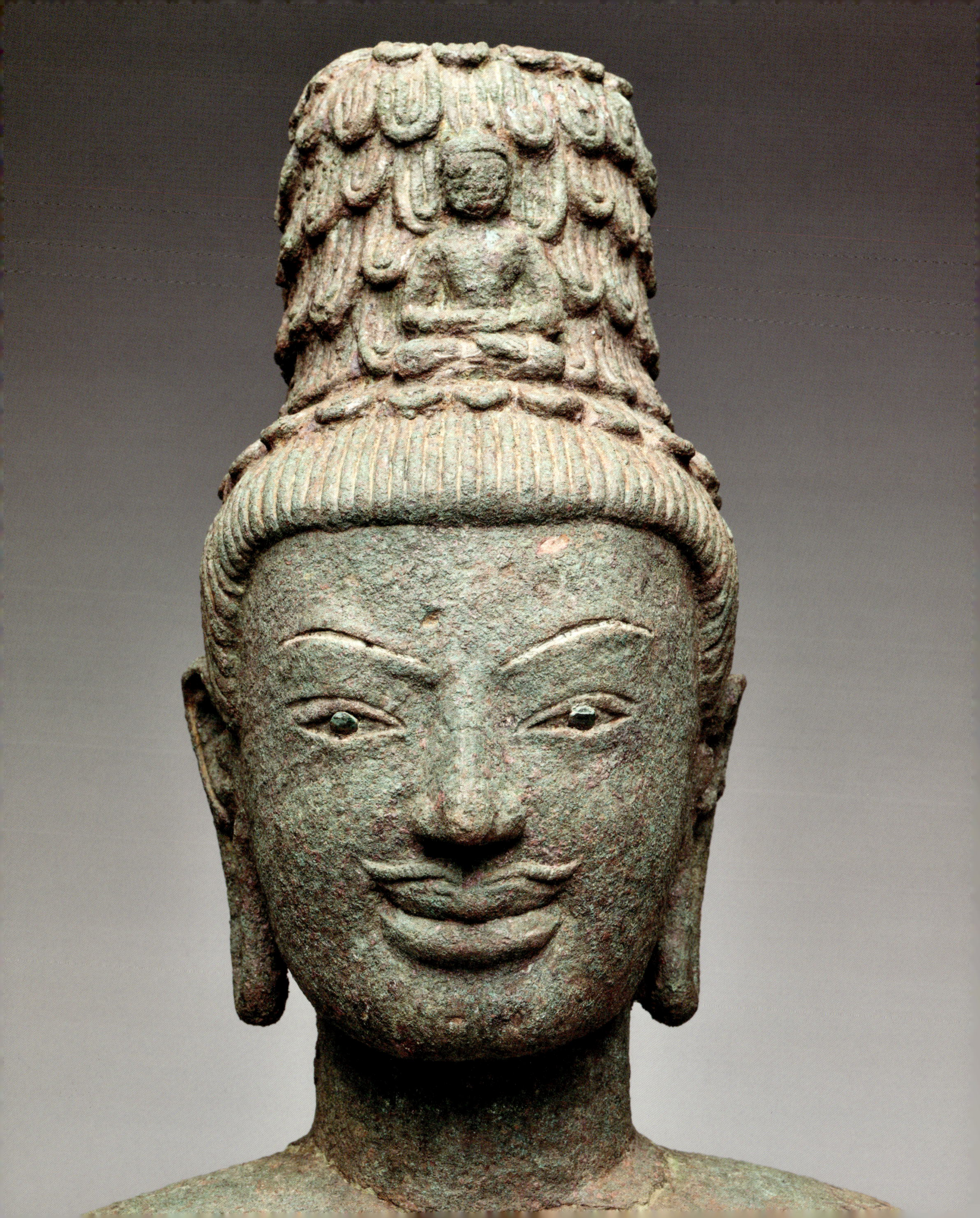

THE BODHISATTVA AVALOKITESHVARA

CAT.

37

APPROX. 1300
Western Tibet; Ladakh region
Bronze with gilding and inlaid copper, silver, turquoise, and semiprecious stones
H. 34.3 cm x W. 19.1 cm x D. 5.7 cm
The Avery Brundage Collection, B60S231

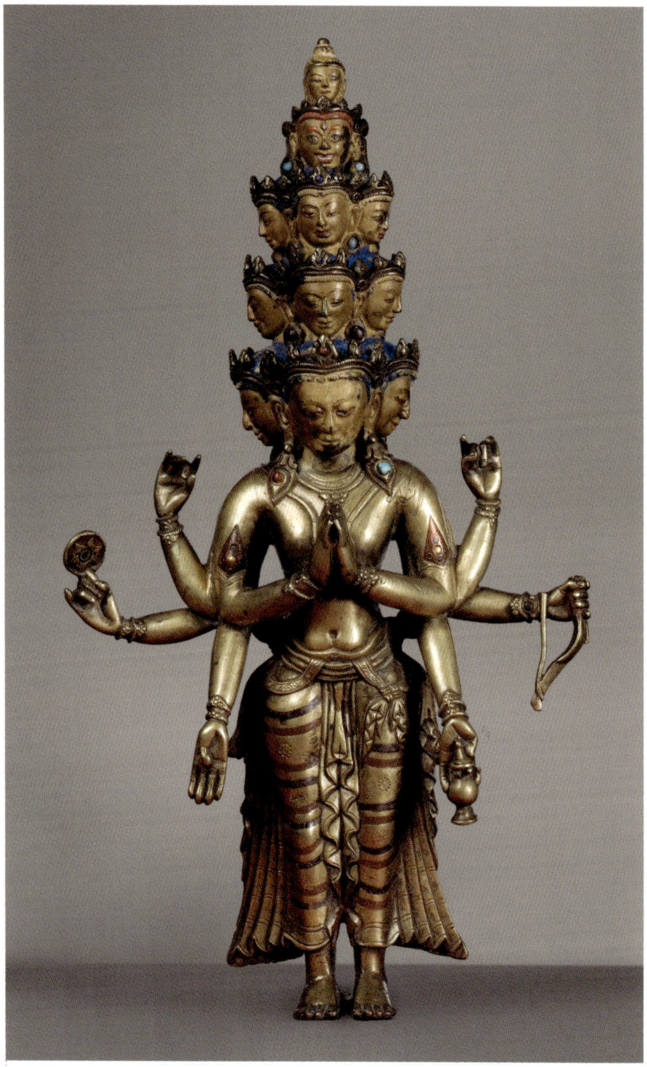

As with mythic figures in many traditions, one of Avalokiteshvara's special abilities is the apparent ease with which he alters the configuration of his body. And as with such figures, his key characteristic finds itself on display in a wide variety of mythic contexts, from East Asia to India and the Himalayas. Avalokiteshvara long ago took the vow of "mind of enlightenment" (*bodhichitta*): the altruistic resolution to save all suffering beings from the torments of *samsara* before himself entering nirvana. Perhaps the wide appeal of this vow across Asia explains why Avalokiteshvara has, art-historically speaking, taken on so many different forms across time, culture, and even gender.

This early bronze sculpture illustrates Avalokiteshvara's shape-shifting nature. Note the striking physiognomy, with his head split into eleven pieces. The myth behind this extraordinary manifestation describes a vision in which the compassionate bodhisattva perceived all at once the sum total of living beings' suffering. It was simply too much for him, and Avalokiteshvara's head forthwith split into pieces. His spiritual father, however, was the red buddha Amitabha of the west, who healed each of Avalokiteshvara's heads so that each might once again function.

Still, Avalokiteshvara could do nothing about the suffering he saw. In response, his arms then split into a thousand limbs, each bearing an eye with which to behold the sufferings of beings throughout the multiverse. Again, the buddha Amitabha came to the rescue, giving Avalokiteshvara the power not merely to see suffering beings but to actively aid them in their quest to escape from *samsara* to nirvana. Thus does the body of this divinity encode an entire mythic episode. | JD

THE HINDU DEITY VISHNU

1200–1300
India; Karnataka state
Stone (chlorite schist)
H. 105.4 cm x W. 57.1 cm x D. 29.8 cm
The Avery Brundage Collection, B70S5

CAT.
38

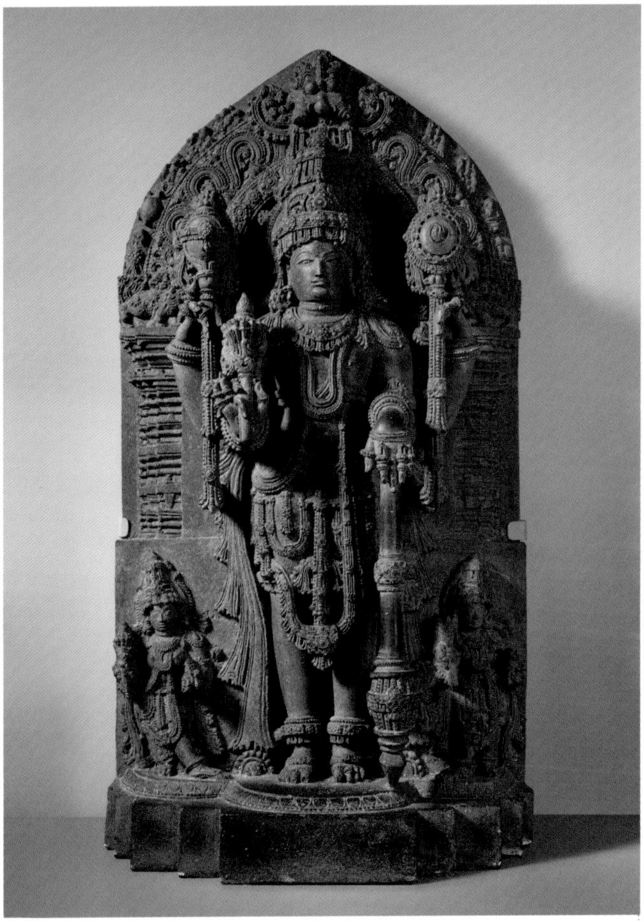

Vishnu is one of Hinduism's most prominent and widely worshiped deities, and according to many accounts he is the creator of the universe.[44] Vishnu is also the preserver of order in the cosmos, defeating all forces of chaos and entering the terrestrial world at mythic moments in one of ten human, animal, or hybrid forms—or avatars—to overcome obstacles that threaten order (see cats. 39 and 40). For his followers, Vishnu is limitless in power, the embodiment of all truth, the soul within each of us, beyond human comprehension. According to his devotees, all other gods, including Shiva, are subsidiary to Vishnu and perform his bidding.

In temples dedicated to the god, the central devotional image is that of Vishnu standing erect in a frontal pose, with firmly planted feet and four arms in which he holds his attributes: a discus (*chakra*), a mace (*gada*), a conch shell (*shankha*), and a lotus flower (*padma*). Sometimes, as in this example, a hand gesture (mudra) signifying reassurance or the granting of a wish replaces the lotus. These symbols reflect the various qualities that mark Vishnu as a supreme protector, a deity who can be compassionate or angry, as the situation requires. His tautly held body reminds viewers that Vishnu "the preserver" has also been described as the "cosmic pillar," the axis of the universe that holds the heavens and earth in place. He is usually dressed as a king, with a crown and jewelry that denote his place in the hierarchy of deities as the lord of all gods. Vishnu's ten avatars frame the central figure on this sculpture. These details arrayed on a single visual plane unite his different forms to emphasize his limitless power and remind devotees that what they see are only fragments of the all-encompassing god.

While most standing Vishnu figures include the iconography described above, individual sculptures often look very different. This Vishnu is typical of sculptures produced during the later centuries of southern India's Hoysala dynasty (approx. 950–1346). Vishnu's body type resembles other contemporary Hoysala images and likely reflects a local physiognomy. Likewise, the crown and jewelry, as well as the style of carving, with its profuse and minute decoration, also relate closely to regional examples. | QA

THE HINDU DEITY VISHNU IN THE FORM OF KRISHNA

CAT.
39

APPROX. 1400–1500
Southern India; former kingdom of Vijayanagara
Granite
H. 119.4 cm x W. 66 cm x D. 26.7 cm
The Avery Brundage Collection, B64S9

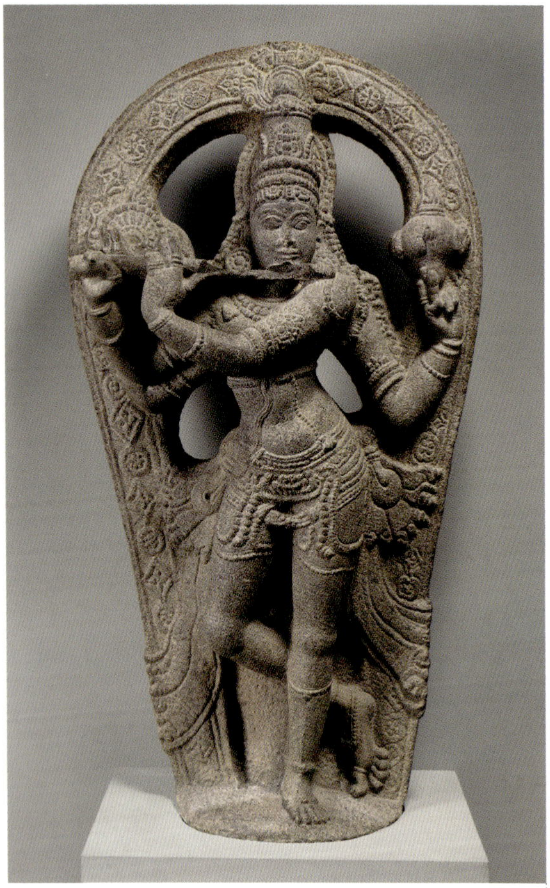

Krishna—Vishnu's eighth avatar, a human incarnation—is perhaps the most beloved of the Hindu gods. Over the centuries numerous traditions developed featuring the blue-skinned god as the central focus of personal devotional practices, or bhakti. Krishna, in many ways, is the most approachable of all deities: he is a mischievous child (cat. 29); a charismatic and flirtatious flute-playing youth; a cowherd; the ideal lover of Radha, his favorite among the village's cow-herding women; the devoted brother of Balarama. But in addition to all these seemingly lighthearted roles is Krishna, the powerful king of Dwarka, the demon slayer who can see through their deceptive guises, the brilliant statesman and warrior of the epic Mahabharata, whose advice to the hero Arjuna comprises Hinduism's core text, the *Bhagavad Gita*. Krishna is also Vishvarupa ("the universal form"), within whose body resides all of creation—the universe, its heavens, earth, and cosmic underworlds.

Krishna's most recognizable appearance is as a flute player. Here, he stands in a dance-like posture, the artist having inscribed a sense of dynamic motion into the stone. Krishna wears a crown and jewelry around his neck, arms, waist, and ankles; the edges of his transparent garment (dhoti) are denoted by beaded outlines on his legs. Krishna's divinity is made visible through his four arms, two of which hold Vishnu's attributes, the discus and the conch shell, whose supernatural powers are visualized as flames.

Texts describe how Krishna's charm, beauty, and music captivated the hearts of the women of his village. Their love, symbolic of the devotee's longing for spiritual union with the divine, became the subject of much Hindu poetry. Adoration for Krishna and Vishnu is often expressed in terms of erotic love, as seen, for example, in the following verses dedicated to Vishnu by the twelfth-century South Indian poet Vedanta Desikar. | QA

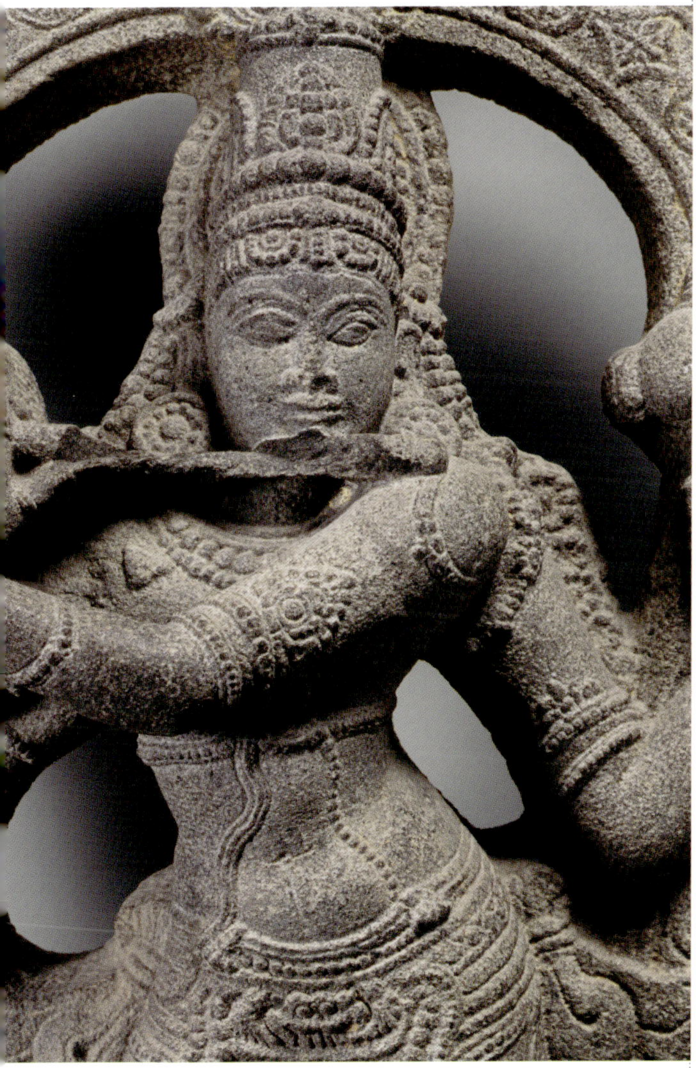

So my mind touches the lotus feet of Ranga's Lord [Vishnu],
Delights in his fine calves, clings
To his twin thighs and, slowly
Rising, reaches
The navel.

It stops for a while on his chest,
Then, after climbing
His broad shoulders,
Drinks the nectar of his lovely face
Before it rests at last
At the crown's flowery crest.[45]

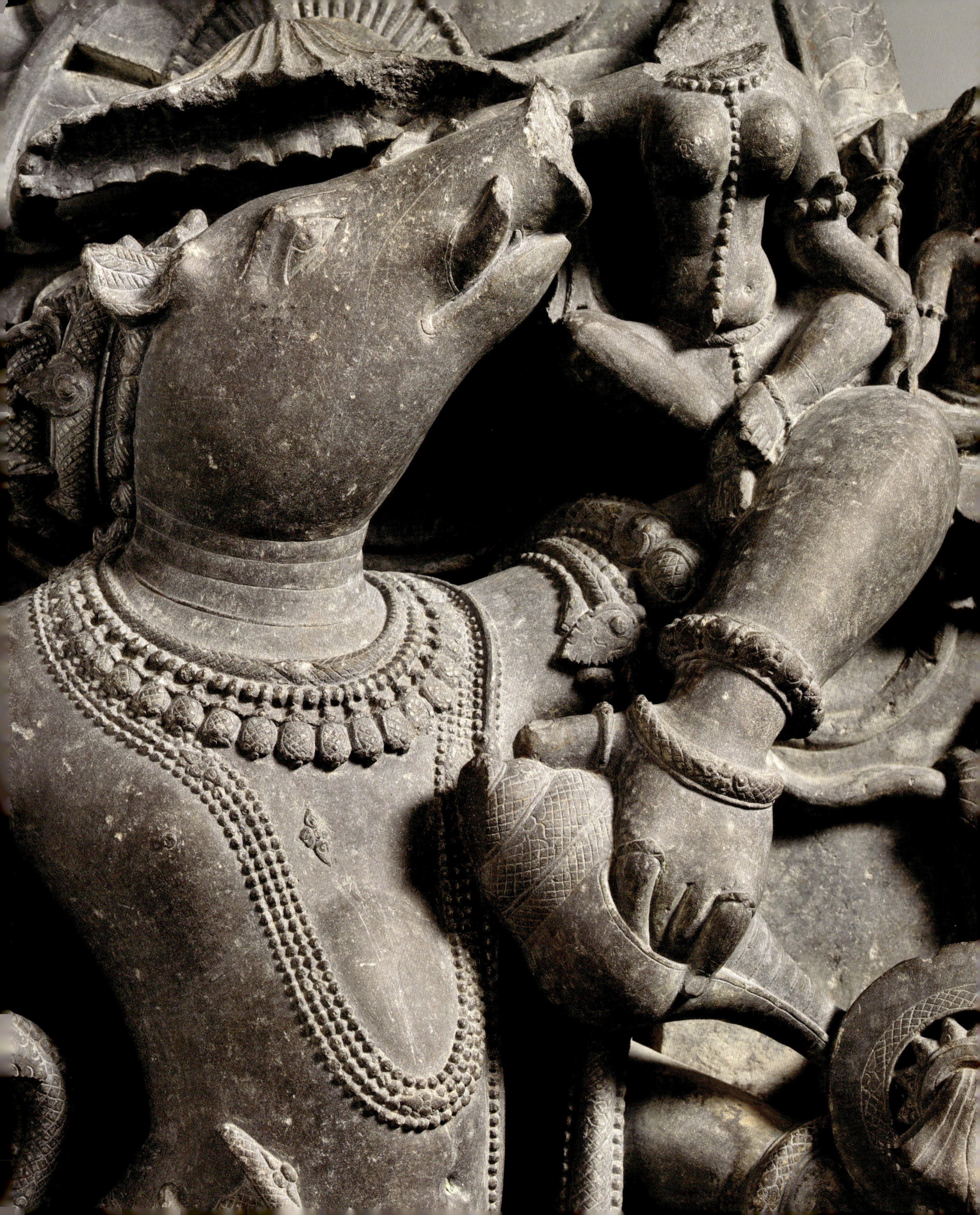

THE HINDU DEITY VISHNU IN THE FORM OF A BOAR (VARAHA AVATAR)

APPROX. 1000
India; probably northern Rajasthan state
Stone (schist)
H. 83 cm x W. 43.8 cm x D. 15.2 cm
The Avery Brundage Collection, B62S15+

CAT.
40

Here Vishnu appears with a boar's head and a four-armed human body. According to textural sources, when the earth, personified as a woman (Bhu Devi), was trapped at the bottom of the sea Vishnu took the form of a boar to dive beneath the waters, free her, and carry her to the surface. The earth goddess (her head now broken) is seated at Varaha's upper left elbow, affectionately patting his snout. He is identifiable as Vishnu by his four arms and standard symbolic implements: a club, a conch shell, and a discus. The waters through which Varaha has dived are symbolized by four half-human, half-serpent beings who twine near him and by the lotus leaves, flowers, and stems behind him.

In most religious imagery, a given depiction encapsulates a narrative (or combination of narratives) that would be familiar to its audience. Such representations include the key details that enable the story's identification and, therefore, serve as reminders of its underlying moral lessons. In the hands of a skilled artist, the impact of the story can be intuited even if one is unfamiliar with its details. Varaha's cosmic power and majesty are immediately discernable here through his diagonally aligned body ornamented with jewelry, taking a strident step upward, with the goddess poised on his elbow. | QA

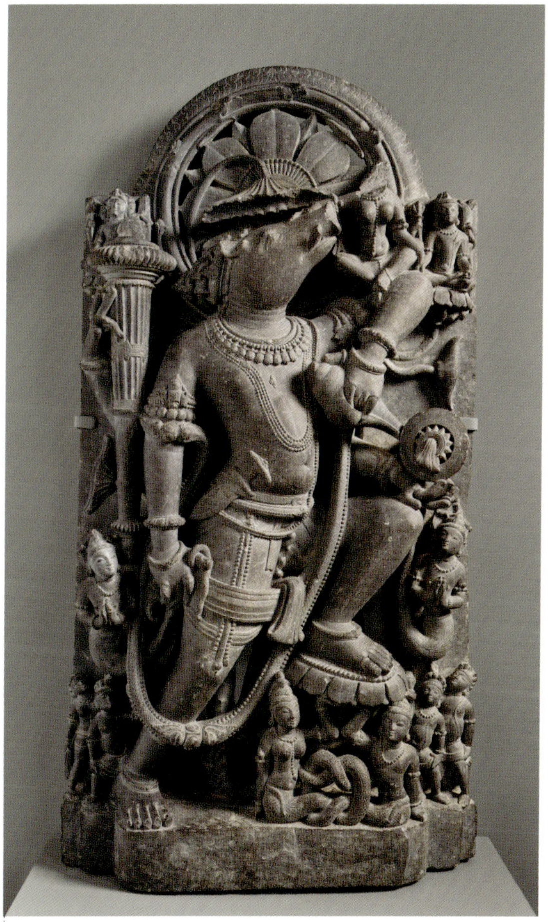

THE HINDU DEITY SHIVA

APPROX. 400-500
India; Madhya Pradesh state
Sandstone
H. 147.3 cm x W. 25.4 cm x D. 36.8 cm
Museum purchase, B69S15

CAT.
41

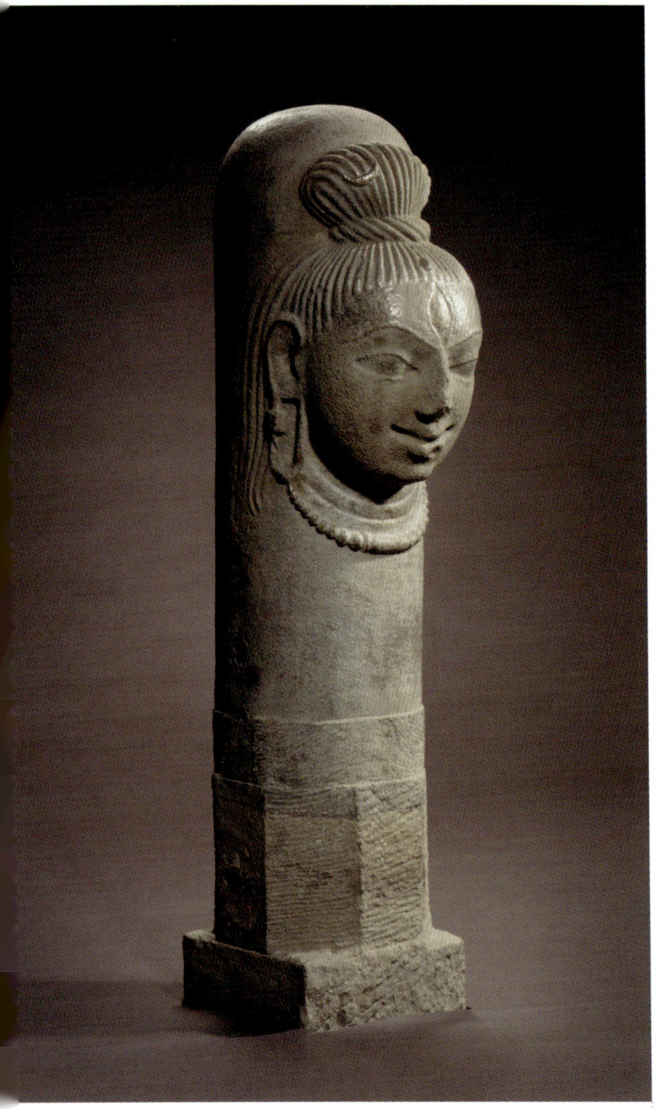

Shiva is perhaps the most complex god of Hinduism. He embodies a range of contradictions: he is creator and destroyer, great ascetic and supreme lover, teacher and wandering beggar. While Shiva does not have avatars in the same way Vishnu does, each of Shiva's different aspects has its own elaborate textual traditions, its own manifest form, and sometimes its own distinct name, which devotees of Shiva may worship as their personal god.

Temples devoted to Shiva often contain in their innermost sanctums a linga, or phallic emblem of this deity. A highly complex symbol, the linga represents the generative powers associated with Shiva. While most linga are plain in appearance, some—like this example—depict Shiva's face. It also includes other recognizable emblems of Shiva: matted hair (representing his asceticism and detachment from worldly concerns), the crescent moon in his hair (sometimes interpreted as a symbol of time), and the third eye in his forehead (indicating Shiva's penetrating vision and wisdom that pierce worldly illusions).

Shiva's association with the linga form derives from his asceticism. In Indian culture, ascetics were thought capable of attaining extraordinary powers—sometimes rivaling those of the gods—through meditation, austerities, and strict self-denial. Because their practices included celibacy and control of reproductive fluids, the upright phallus came to represent accumulated stores of energy and creative ability. Shiva, the foremost of ascetics, possesses powers vast enough to generate creation. The linga refers both to this ability and to asceticism's potential rewards, which include escaping rebirth. | QA

THE HINDU DEITY SHIVA WITH THE DEITY PARVATI

APPROX. 600–700
India; Bihar state
Stone
H. 53.3 cm x W. 35.6 cm x D. 17.1 cm
The Avery Brundage Collection, B62S9+

CAT.
42

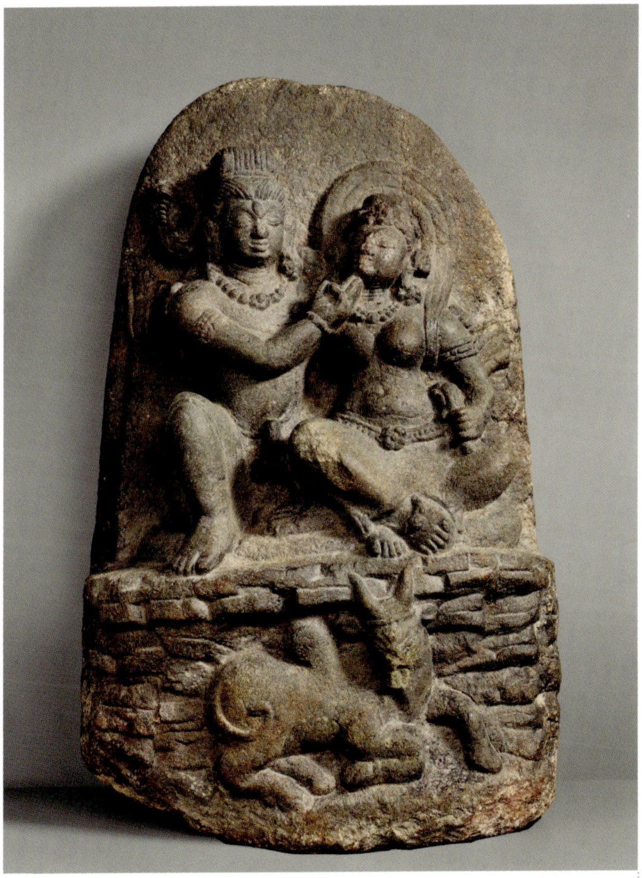

In many representations Shiva and his wife Parvati are shown as a loving couple. Adorned with jewelry as befits the gods, and with Shiva recognizable by identifiers such as his third eye, matted hair, trident, and cobra, the divine couple sits at leisure, absorbed in each other. With their bodies adjoining and arms around each other, the figures of Shiva and Parvati form a single visual unit. Their union is further emphasized by Shiva's erect phallus. The depiction of gods with sexual symbolism expresses the totality of the forces of creation, where Shiva represents the male principle and Parvati stands for the female principle. No creation of animate or inanimate life is possible without both in equal measure. The loving couple also stands as a metaphor for the unity between the individual and the Absolute.

The information and external references that artists encode onto the surface of their images are familiar to their intended viewers. Songs, poetry, well-known stories, and other forms of orally transmitted knowledge reinforce these nuances. Descriptions of the intimacy between Shiva and Parvati have been the subject of literature from at least the fifth century, as exemplified by the works of the famous Sanskrit poet and dramatist Kalidasa. Although criticized by some later commentators as inappropriate portrayals of the divine, Kalidasa described the couple's lovemaking in his *Kumara-sambhava*: "Though as they loved, the moon suffered when she seized / His hair and they tried to outdo each other scratching / Where nail marks should not be made and Parvati's belt-string / Easily opened to him, still he was never satisfied."[46] | QA

THE HINDU DEITIES SHIVA AND PARVATI COMBINED AS ARDHANARISHVARA

CAT.
43

900–1100
India; Madhya Pradesh state
Sandstone
H. 66 cm x W. 31.7 cm x D. 12.7 cm
The Avery Brundage Collection, B73S16

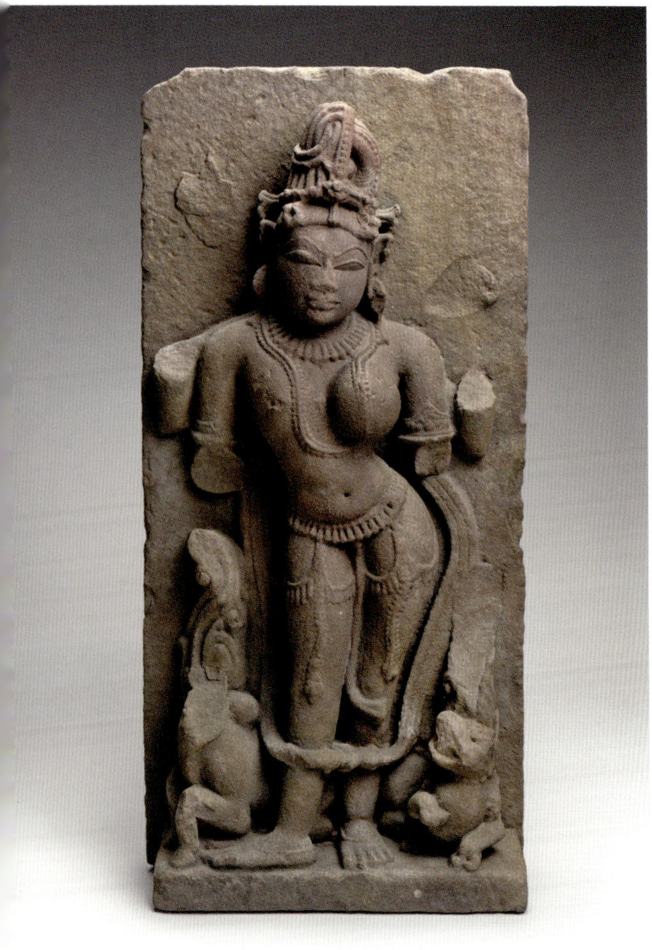

Matters of gender are well defined in Hinduism—and Indian culture more broadly—with clear boundaries articulating male and female roles in a variety of religious and social contexts. Yet in ancient Indian Samkhya philosophy, which forms the basis of the complex of theologies that we know today as Hinduism, cosmic creation is understood as a combination of male and female principles. The male consciousness (*purusha*) remains inert without the power of female energy (*prakriti*).

This concept takes a potent visual form in Ardhanarishvara, "the lord who is half female." Here, Shiva and his wife Parvati are shown combined into a single figure. Divided vertically, one half shows the feminine aspect and the other depicts the male: the headdress has contrasting halves, there is one male breast and one female breast, and at the god's feet lie two different animal mounts, Shiva's bull (its head now broken off) and Parvati's lion.

While Hindu texts and myths include episodes in which Shiva or Vishnu change into female guise, either by assuming a new form or by dressing in women's clothing, the meaning of the image of Ardhanarishvara is more elemental than temporary shape-shifting or cross-dressing: it represents nonduality and suggests that qualities that may appear to be contradictory are in reality two aspects of a single unity. | QA

THE HINDU DEITY SHIVA REVEALED IN THE LINGA

APPROX. 1050–1150
India; Tamil Nadu state
Granite
H. 125.7 cm x W. 40.6 cm x D. 30.5 cm
The Avery Brundage Collection, B65S3

CAT.
44

This sculpture is a powerful encapsulation of the views of Shiva's followers, who perceive their lord as the most superior of all gods. While they recognize deities such as Vishnu and Brahma, devotees of Shiva consider them secondary divinities. Here, the glorious Shiva reveals himself from within a linga, his nonrepresentational, phallic form. Near the top, Brahma is depicted as a goose, the bird he usually rides, while at the bottom is Vishnu in the form of his boar avatar, Varaha (see cat. 40). According to texts, Brahma and Vishnu saw an immense fiery pillar that appeared to have no beginning or end. In order to investigate its source and cause, Brahma rode skyward and Varaha dove into the ocean, but both failed to find the top or bottom of the column. It was only when they gave up in puzzlement and despair that Shiva revealed himself as the flaming axis of the universe, asserting his role as the cosmic creator and sustainer.

Here, Shiva's power and glory are made visible through different conceptions and representations of bodies inscribed on the stone's surface. The first is the linga, which represents the abstract nature of the essence of the Absolute. Carved into its side is the yoni, a stylized representation of the female genitalia, symbolizing *prakriti*, the feminine cosmic energy. Together, the linga and yoni symbolize creation, in both cosmic and human terms, and frame the resplendent figure of Shiva in human form. The matted hair piled crown-like on his head denotes him as the supreme ascetic (*mahayogi*); his body is adorned with jewelry as befits the god's inner beauty. Shiva's supernatural status is indicated by his four arms, each of which holds a symbolic implement; the skull cup in his lower right hand denotes his fierce form as Bhairava (see cat. 24). The balanced and firmly rooted four-armed Shiva further recalls images of the standing Vishnu (see cat. 38), which is no coincidence but rather a clear statement of Shiva's supremacy. This point is further emphasized by the depiction here of Brahma and Vishnu in animal form, their marginal placement on the sculpture, and their carving in low relief. | QA

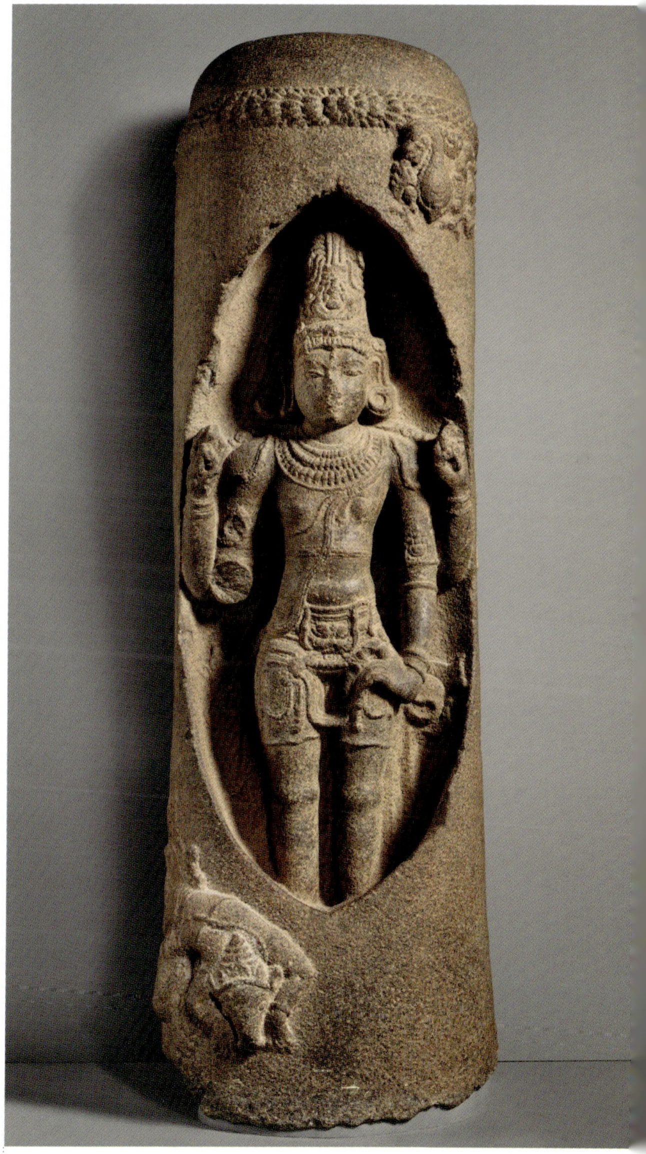

MONA AHMED SERIES, 1999–2017

BY DAYANITA SINGH
(INDIAN, B. 1961)

CAT.
45

I met Mona very early in my career, in 1989, on a routine assignment on eunuchs in India, commissioned by the *London Times*. For me, this was a way to establish my credentials as a photojournalist, to show that I was on par with the boys in my male-dominated profession. When you work for the media, which tend to see India only as either exotic or a disaster, a story on eunuchs is a must, along with a story on prostitution, child labor, dowry deaths, and child marriage. There are one million eunuchs in India; around 5 percent were born as eunuchs (with deformed genitals), the rest are all castrated boys. Obviously, this aspect of Indian culture lends itself to all kinds of myths and prejudices. Every few months, the "true story" of a eunuch is published somewhere, yet eunuchs are very media-savvy and will allow journalists and researchers only limited access, if any—always strictly controlled by the eunuchs themselves....

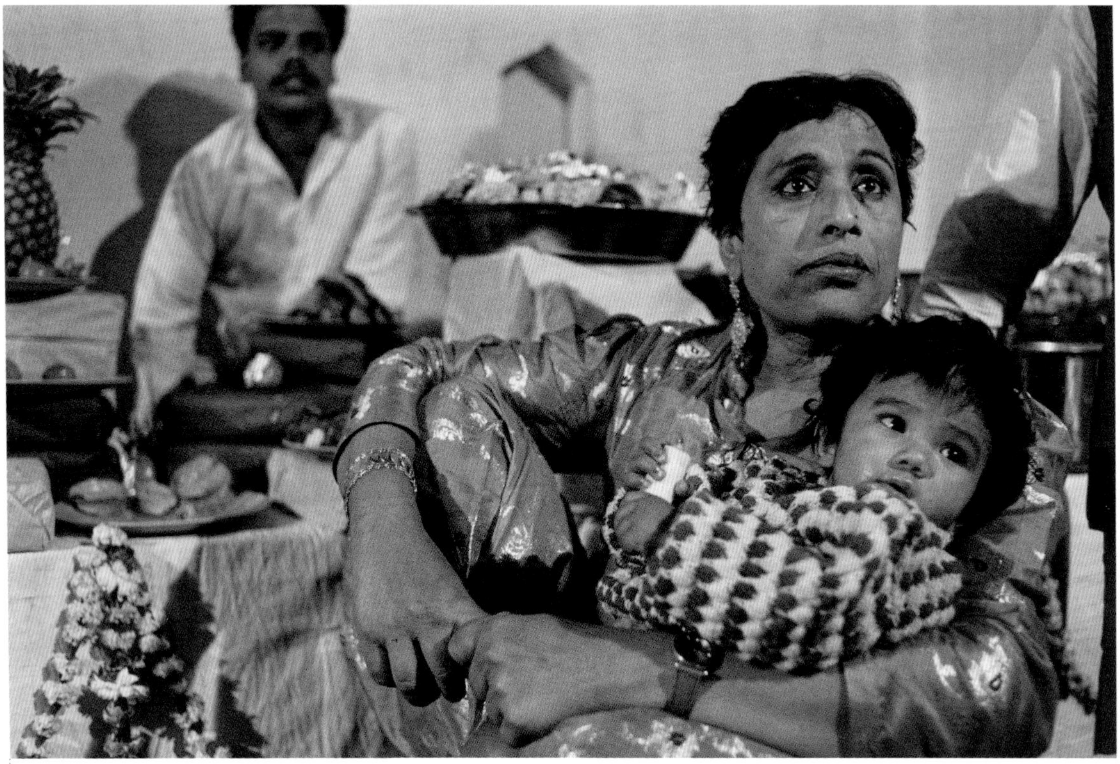

Myself Mona Ahmed, 2008
Gelatin silver prints
H. 30.5 cm x W. 45.7 cm (each image)
Museum purchase, 2017.46.a-.u

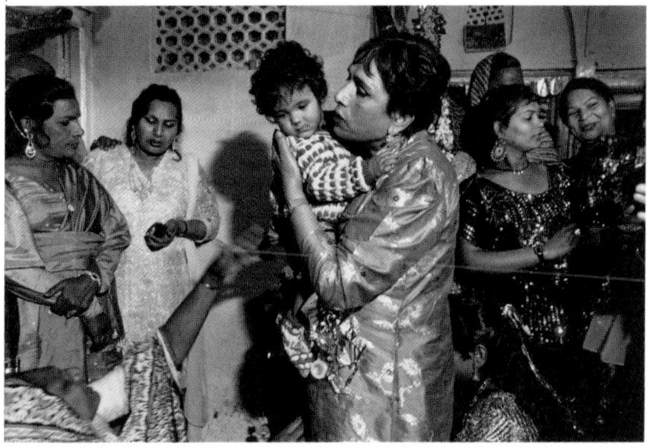

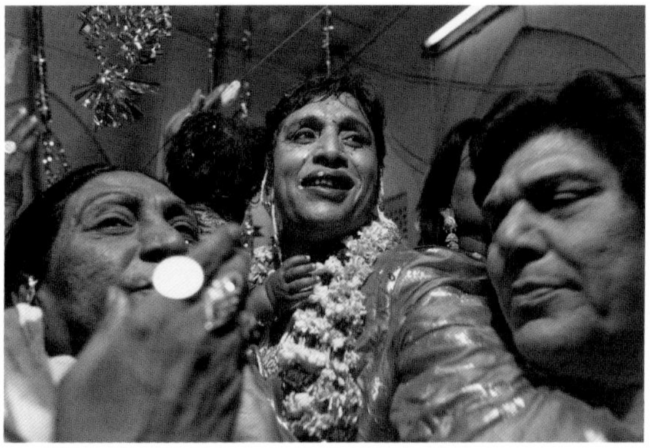

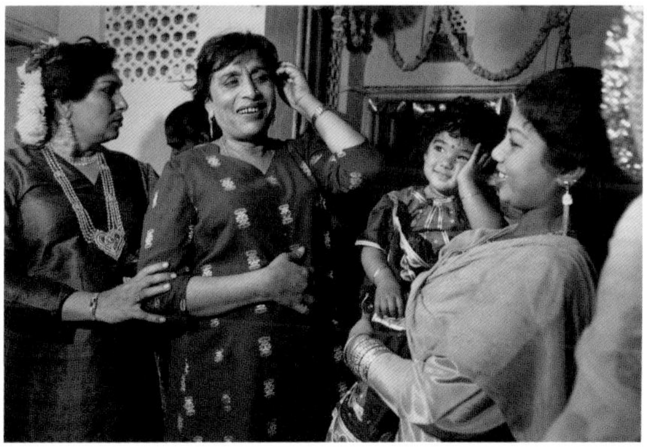

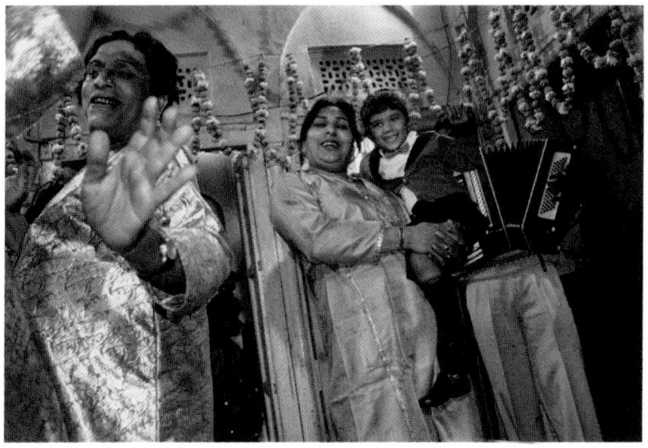

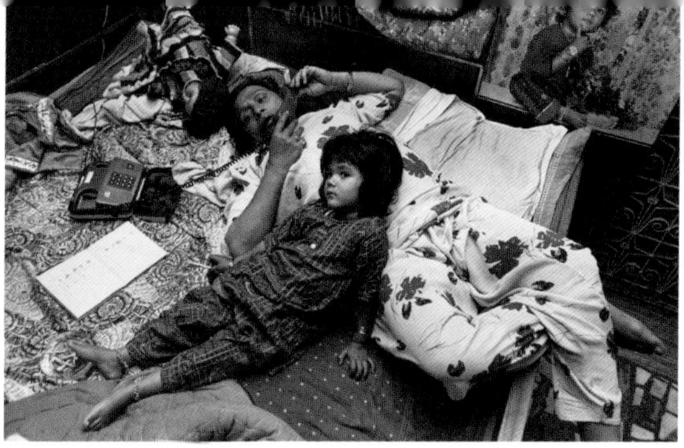

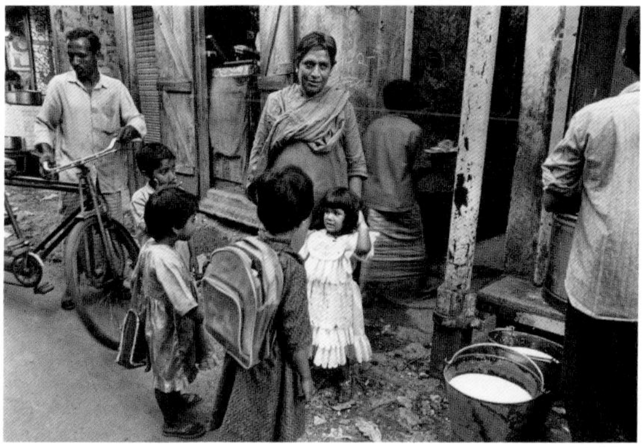

Over the years, I photographed her off and on, with no intention of ever publishing the photographs. It was only many years later, after Mona was thrown out of the eunuch's community and she became an outcast among the outcasts, that she told me she wanted to tell her own story....She wanted to tell the story of being neither here nor there, neither male nor female, and finally, neither a eunuch nor someone like me. She would always ask me, "Tell me: what am I?" I first assumed that a writer would have to tell her story, but after she dictated some emails, I realized that I probably underestimated her and that she could tell her own story, weaving together fact and fiction.[47] | DAYANITA SINGH

I was born on the 9th of November in Old Delhi. In my family we have a book where all birth dates and death dates are written down.

I was born at home, in a middle-class family. I came after two sisters. Everyone was very happy that after two girls a boy was finally born in the family, especially my father. He fed 200 people to celebrate his son's birth. I was naturally his favorite child, but once I started to grow, he started to feel I was not a boy and started to distance himself because I had very female mannerisms. Even I never felt as a boy and always sought the company of girls....

At the age of 12, my mannerisms were completely like a woman's. This angered my father a lot. People in the area started to realize I was a eunuch. This broke my heart, and the boys in school would taunt me. God gave me a man's body, but he also gave me a woman's spirit. That's why they would all call me hijra (eunuch).[48] | MONA AHMED

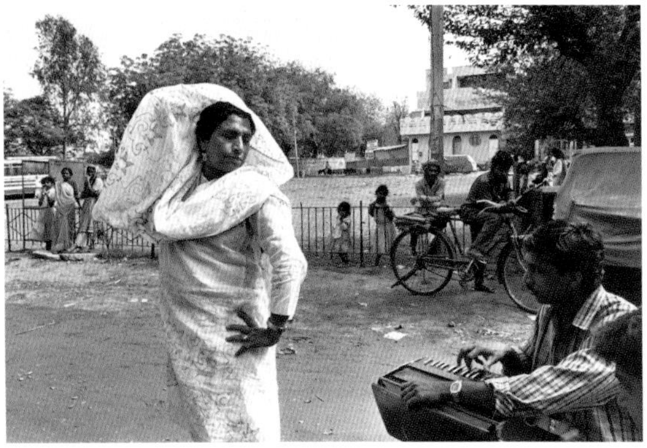

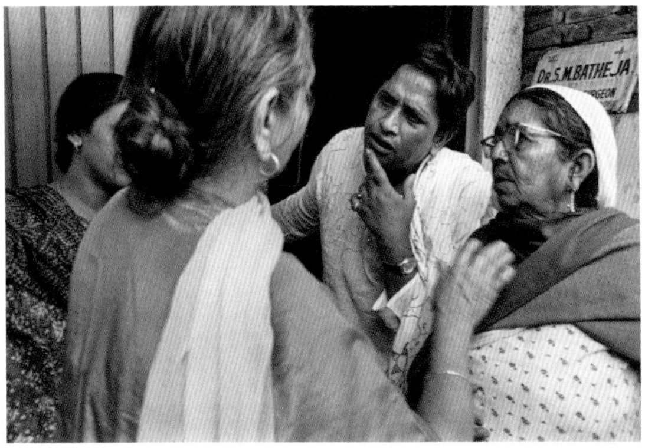
Dr.S.M.BATHEJA

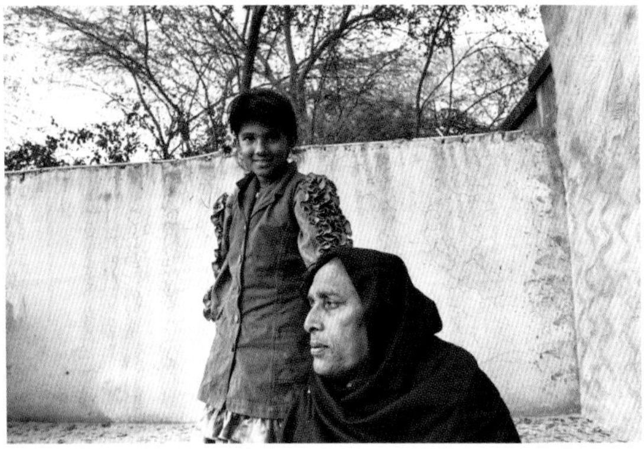

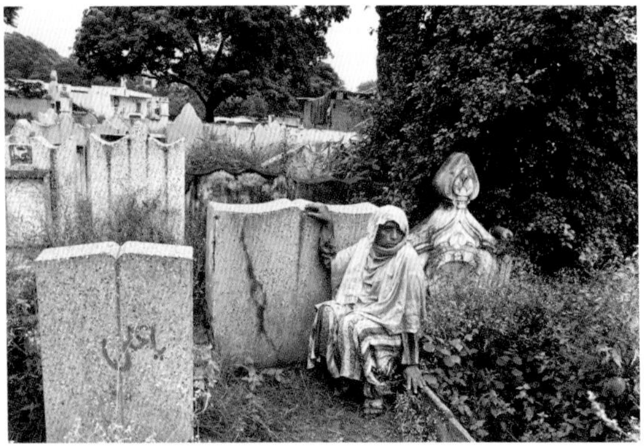

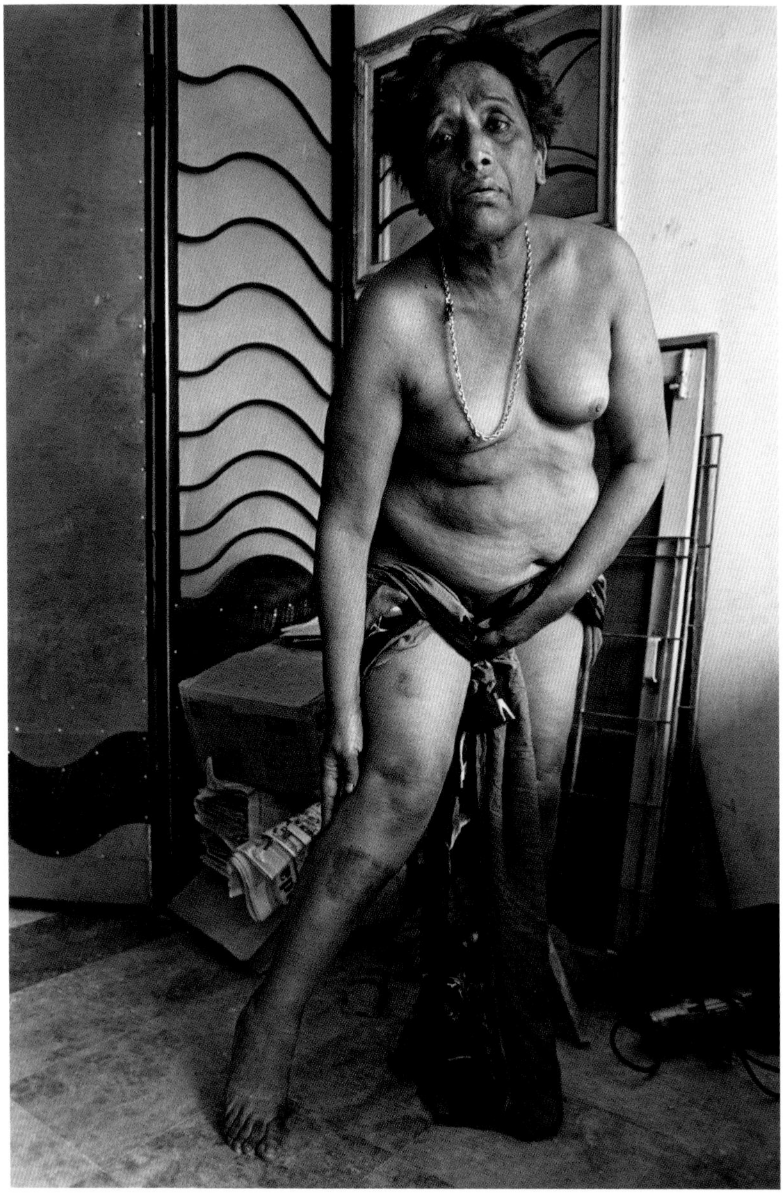

MYSELF MONA AHMED, 2008

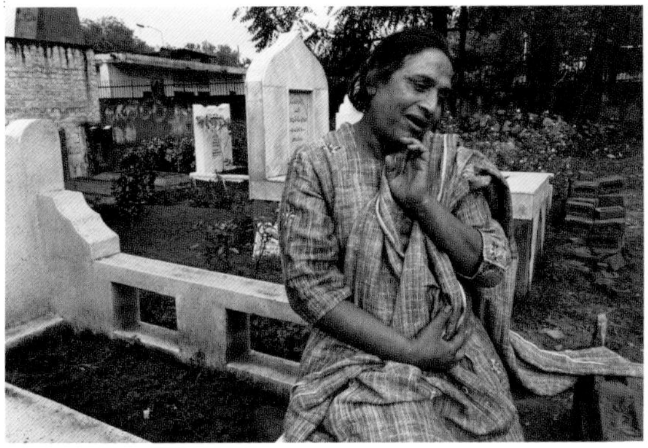

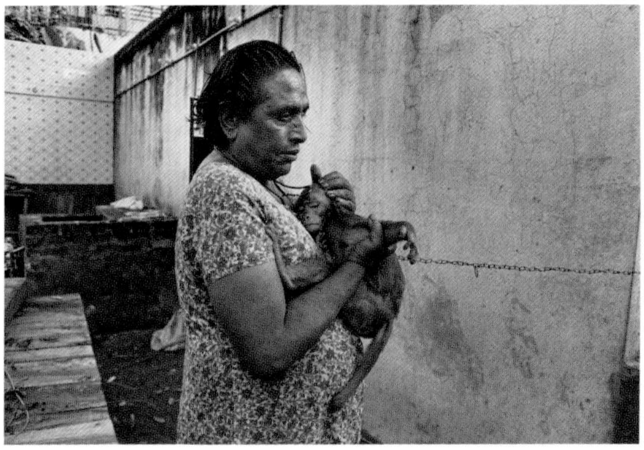

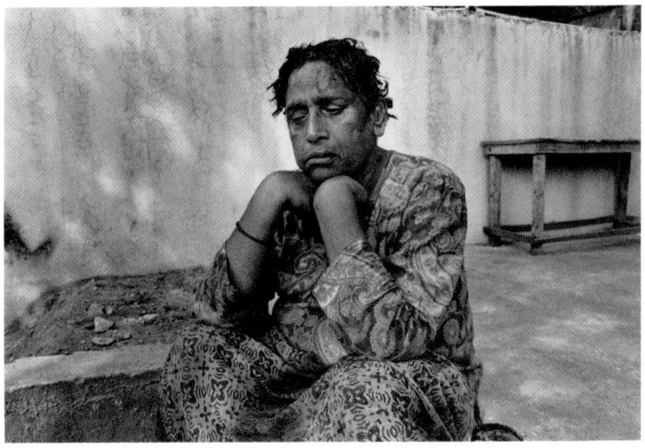

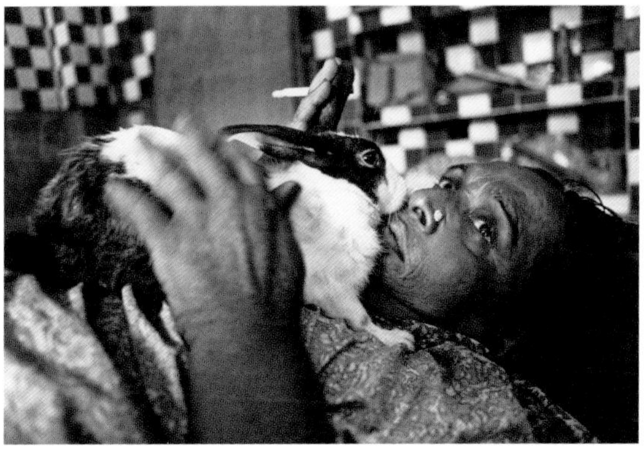

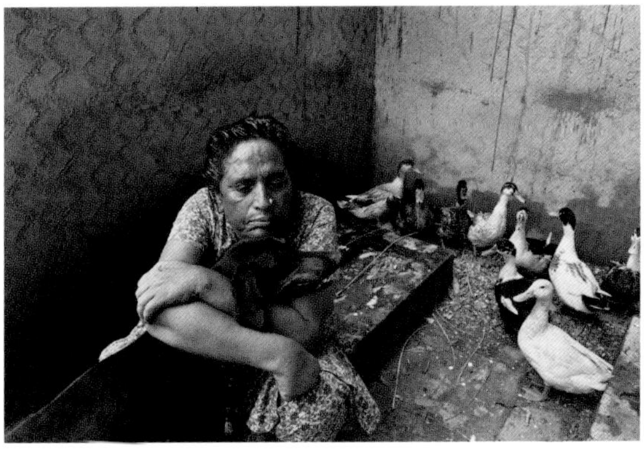

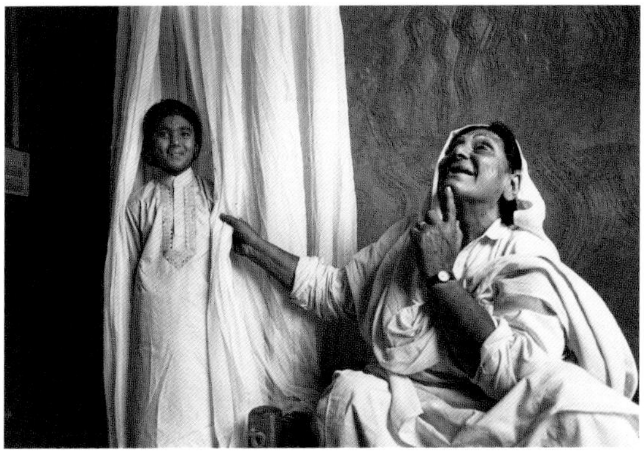

MYSELF MONA AHMED, 2008

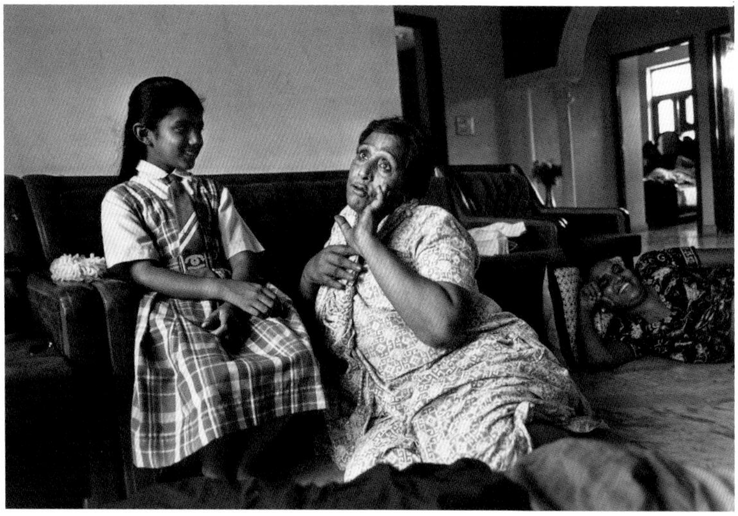

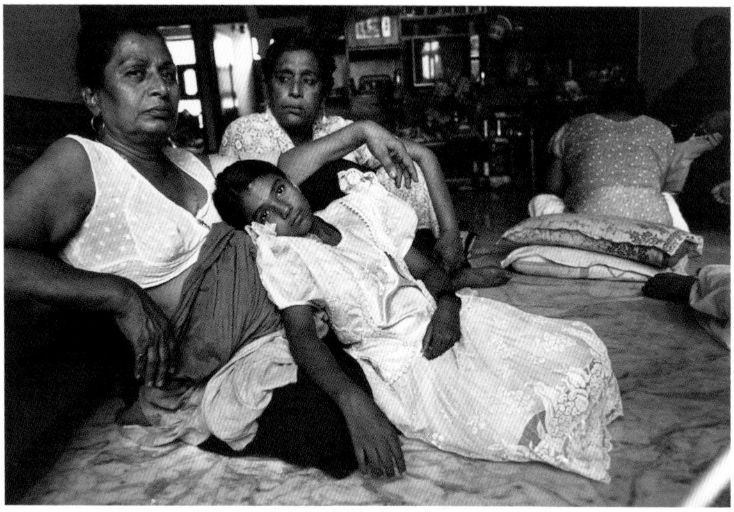

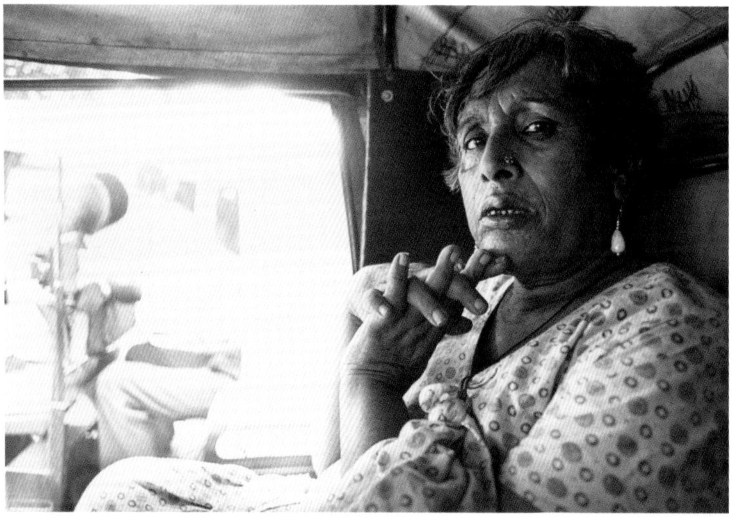

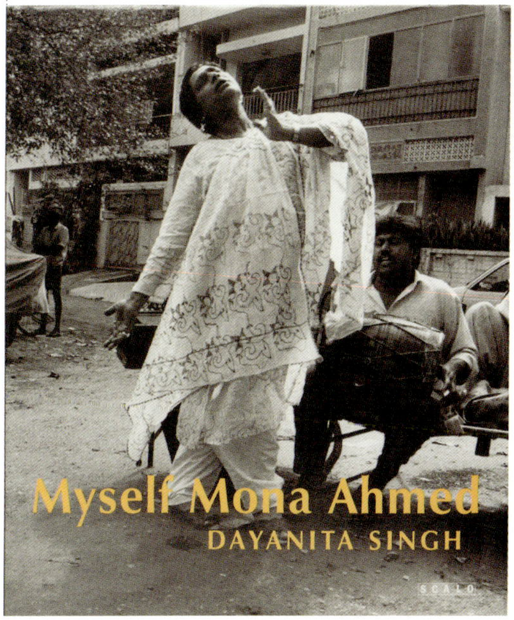

Myself Mona Ahmed, 2001
Printed book
H. 20.3 cm x W. 17.8 cm x D. 1.7 cm
Lent from a private collection

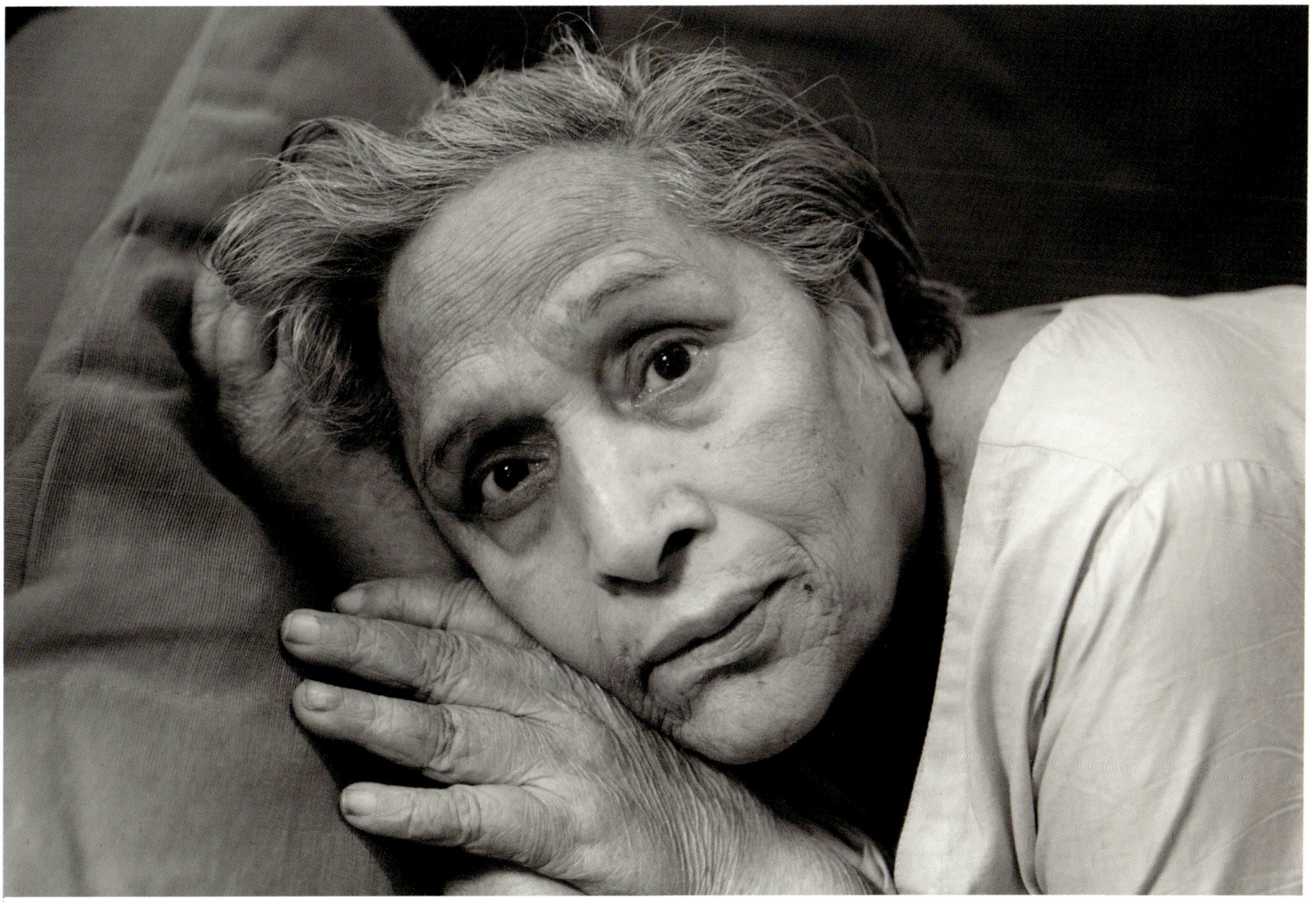

Mona and Myself, 2013
Single-channel video with sound, 3:45 min.
Lent by the artist and Frith Street Gallery, London

COSMIC BUDDHA

China
Tang dynasty (618–907)
Limestone
H. 101.14 cm x W. 45.7 cm x D. 40.64
The Avery Brundage Collection, B61S66

CAT.
46

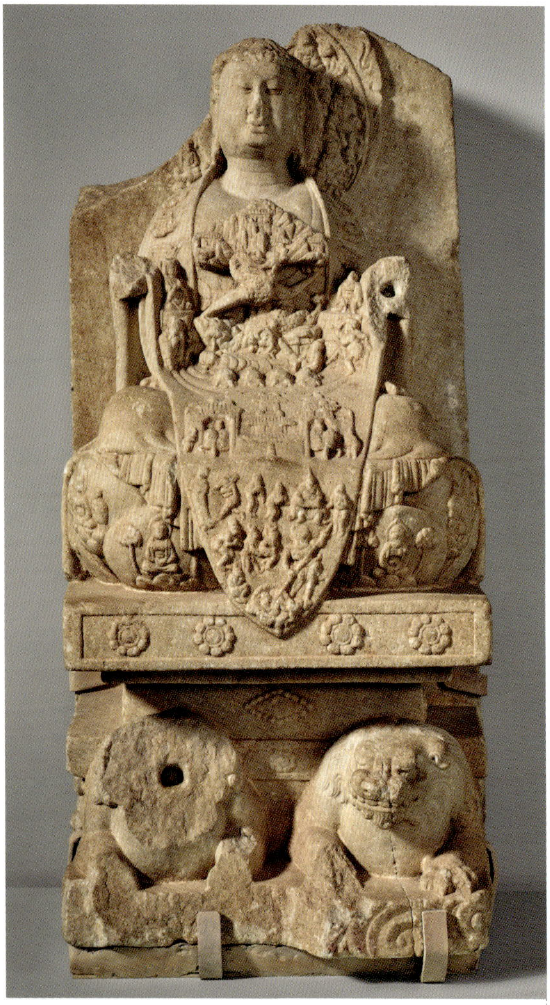

This sculpture includes not one but several divine bodies—or rather the divine body of a buddha appearing simultaneously in several different contexts. Most obviously, and despite his missing forearms, the main image here is clearly a buddha; from his topknot of hair (*ushnisha*) to his elongated earlobes, this figure bears all the signs of buddhahood. But this sculpture is clearly not the historical Buddha Shakyamuni. To begin with, the hourglass-shaped throne upon which he sits signifies the setting as Mount Meru, the center and summit of the Buddhist cosmos. Seated on top of this cosmic mountain, the buddha gains an all-embracing view of the entire universe. How the sculpture depicts this revelation, in terms of both artistic technique and philosophical sophistication, is a remarkable feat with a surprising twist.

In order to reveal his comprehensive vision, the main seated buddha has opened his robes. Within them, we see nothing less than the entire Buddhist cosmos. From his chest emerges, in elevation, Mount Meru itself—the very one upon which the large buddha is seated. Its peculiar triangular morphology is home to the mansions of the gods, beings who have achieved their status by generating good karma. It is supported by a mythic crocodile called a *makara*. Its two front legs support Mount Meru, while the scaled bulk of its body bulges outward as if crushed by the mountain's weight.

In contrast to the heavens, the panel of the buddha's robe hanging below his crossed legs depicts a Buddhist hell. At the top right, the king of hell—recognizable by his pointed hat—judges a group of sinners; eventually, they all make their way to the very bottom, where a bull-headed demon stirs a cauldron filled with sinners. Finally, between the buddha's legs and arms, the human world is represented. Accordingly, a number of episodes from the biography of the historical Buddha Shakyamuni appear here. Around the knees, the young Buddha-to-be is shown riding out from his father's palace twice for two of his fateful "four great encounters." In these he sees, for the first time, an old man, a sick man, a dead man, and a monk and resolves to begin a career of spiritual endeavor.

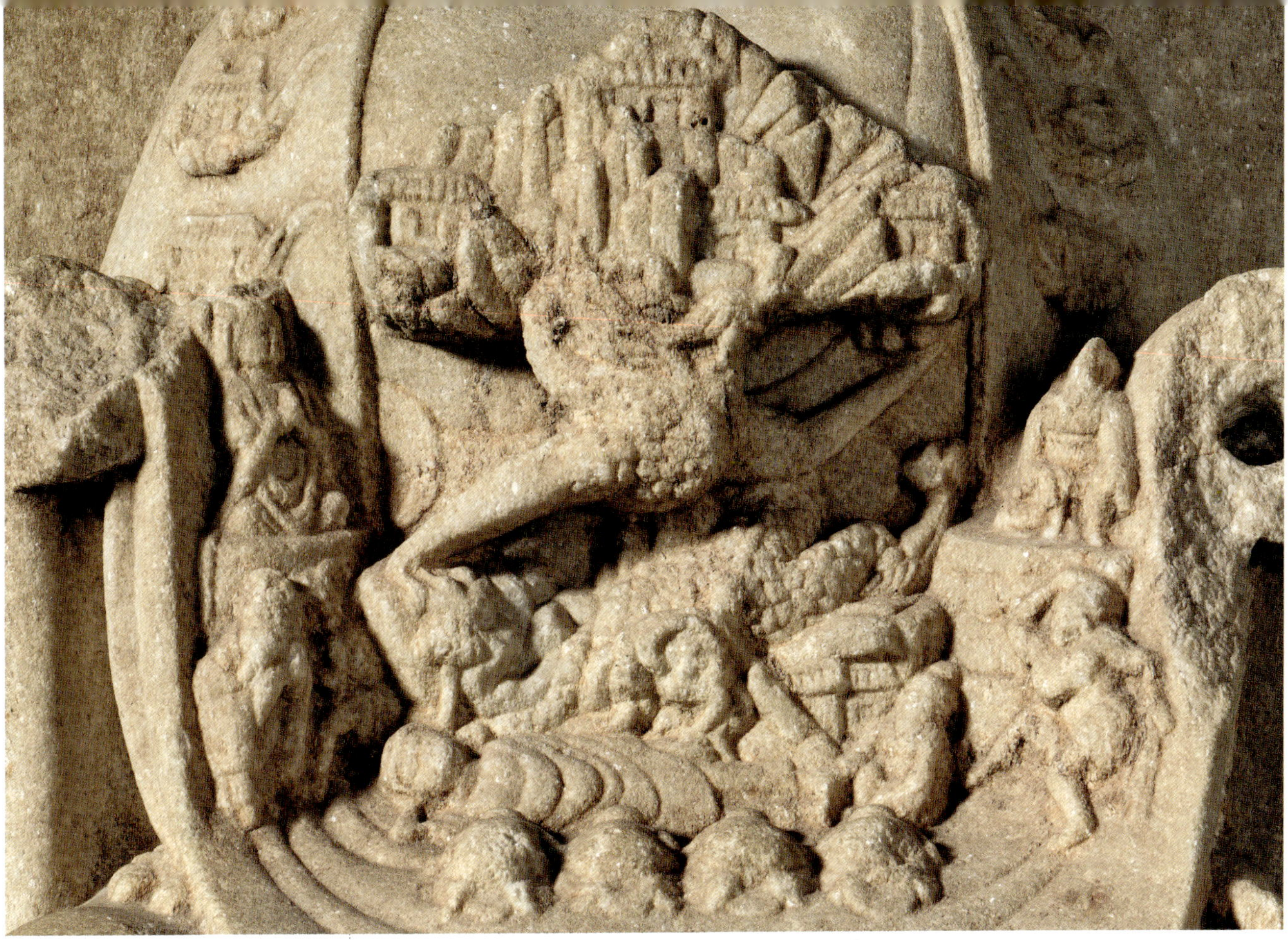

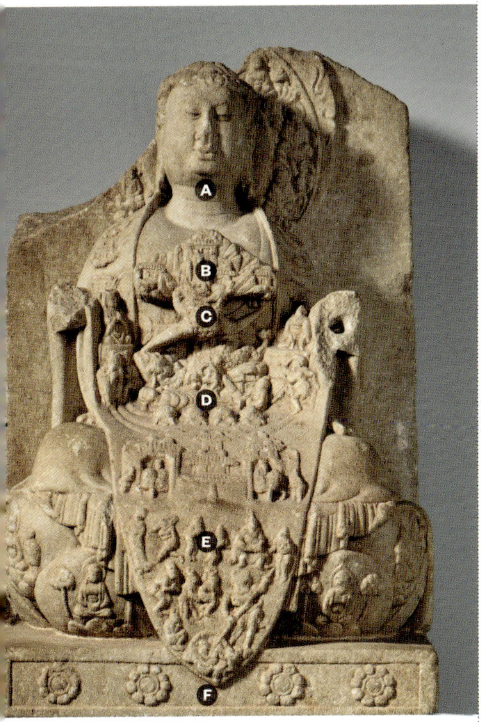

A. Cosmic Buddha

B. Mount Meru, central axis of the cosmos: divine realms

C. mythic crocodile (*makara*) supporting Mount Meru

D. dying Buddha with devotees: human realms

E. horned demon and the damned: hellish realms

F. pedestal representing Mount Meru

Above these scenes, at the lap, appears the terminus of the historical Buddha Shakyamuni's earthly career. Having long since achieved buddhahood and spent decades teaching the insights he has gained, he has now died, and his disciples surround his deathbed to mourn his passing. Four monks can be seen from the rear, bowing forward before him on their knees. Thus is it clear that the Buddha is in the buddha, just as Mount Meru is depicted within the robes of the buddha sitting at the summit of Mount Meru. In both cases, we have an instance of recursion, where a given object contains a simulacrum of itself. This is precisely the situation we encounter when we experience embodiment: within our minds, we encompass simultaneously a vision of the world and of ourselves—a miracle so familiar that we are hardly surprised to find ourselves in a world and in a body. | JD

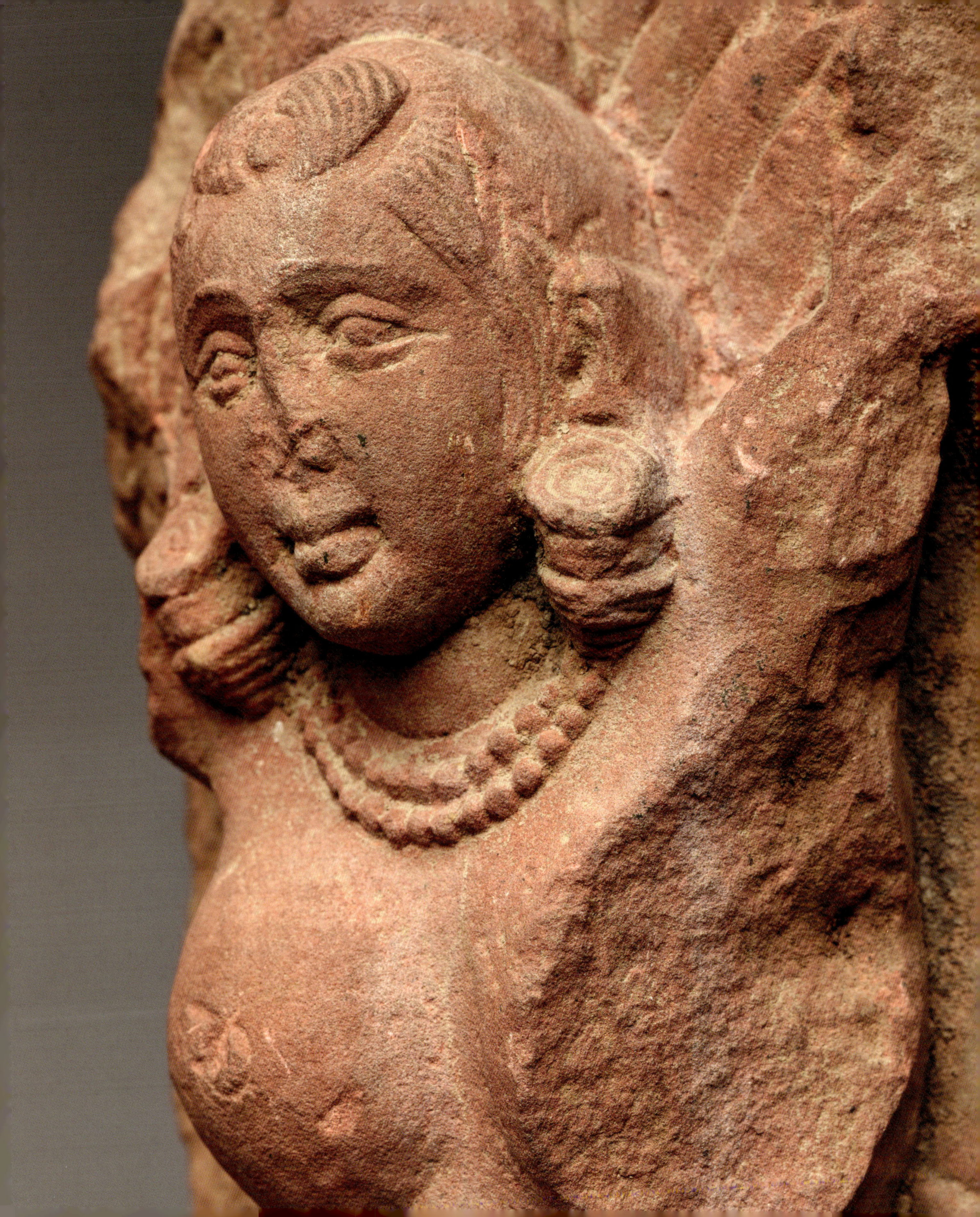

NOTES

Seeing in a Sacred Manner the Shapes of Things in the Spirit

1 For our current project, we are not including religious traditions of Asia—such as Islam, Judaism, and Sikhism—that do not rely on figural imagery in worship.

2 Robert DeCaroli, *Image Problems: The Origin and Development of the Buddha's Image in Early South Asia* (Seattle and London: University of Washington Press, 2015), 8.

3 Diana L. Eck, *Darśan: Seeing the Divine Image in India* (New York: Columbia University Press, 1998).

4 Jan Assmann, introduction to *Representation in Religion: Studies in Honor of Moshe Barasch*, ed. Jan Assmann and Albert I. Baumgarten (Leiden: Brill, 2001), xvii.

5 Veena Das, "Paradigms of Body Symbolism: An Analysis of Selected Themes in Hindu Culture," in *Indian Religion*, ed. Richard Burghart and Audrey Cantlie (London: Curzon Press, 1985), 181.

6 Representations of the Buddha appear fairly late in Buddhist artistic traditions, several centuries after his death. The earliest Buddhist art indicates the Buddha's presence only through symbols. See DeCaroli, *Image Problems*.

7 Robert E. Buswell Jr. and Donald S. Lopez Jr., eds., *The Princeton Dictionary of Buddhism* (Princeton, NJ: Princeton University Press, 2014), 506, 1094–95.

8 Debra Diamond makes this observation about North Indian paintings of ascetics, but the underlying principle can be equally applied to broader Buddhist artistic traditions that, through pilgrimage and monastic sites, enabled the exchanges of material culture, texts, ideas, and people across vast distances. Debra Diamond, "By the Grace of Jalandranath: Politics and Painting in Jodhpur," in *Holy Madness: Portraits of Tantric Siddhas*, ed. Robert N. Linrothe (New York: Rubin Museum of Art and Serindia Publications, 2006), 150.

9 Doris Meth Srinivasan, *Many Heads, Arms, and Eyes: Origin, Meaning, and Form of Multiplicity in Indian Art* (Leiden: Brill, 1997), 3.

10 See also the concept of *anatman* ("nonself" in Sanskrit), which is of key importance in Buddhist philosophy. Buswell Jr. and Lopez Jr., *The Princeton Dictionary of Buddhism*, 42.

11 Vidya Dehejia, *The Body Adorned: Dissolving Boundaries between Sacred and Profane in India's Art* (New York: Columbia University Press, 2009), 65–66.

12 Vishnu's ten avatars are Matsya (fish), Kurma (tortoise), Varaha (boar), Narasimha (man-lion), Vamana, Parashurama, Rama, Krishna, Buddha, and Kalki. See Joan Cummins, ed., *Vishnu: Hinduism's Blue-Skinned Savior* (Ocean Township, NJ: Grantha; Ahmedabad: Mapin; Nashville, TN: Frist Center for the Visual Arts, 2011), 20.

13 Robert Zwijnenberg, "Presence and Absence: On Leonardo da Vinci's Saint John the Baptist," in *Compelling Visuality: The Work of Art in and out of History*, eds. Claire Farago and Robert Zwijnenberg (Minneapolis: University of Minnesota Press, 2003), 117.

Body and Cosmos

14 Mircea Eliade, *A History of Religious Ideas*, vol. 1, *From the Stone Age to the Eleusinian Mysteries*, trans. Willard R. Trask (Chicago: University of Chicago Press, 1978), 6–10.

15 E. E. Evans-Pritchard, *Theories of Primitive Religion* (Oxford: Oxford University Press, 1965), 23–24.

16 J. Clottes and D. Lewis-Williams, *The Shamans of Prehistory: Trance and Magic in the Painted Caves* (New York: Abrams, 1998), 99.

17 Mircea Eliade, *Shamanism: Archaic Techniques of Ecstasy*, trans. Willard R. Trask (London: Arkana, 1989), 110–44.

18 Malcolm Hamilton, *The Sociology of Religion: Theoretical and Comparative Perspectives* (London: Routledge, 1995), 47.

19 Rudolf Otto, *The Idea of the Holy* (Oxford: Oxford University Press, 1923), 12–39.

20 Mircea Eliade, *Patterns in Comparative Religion*, trans. Rosemary Sheed (Cleveland: Meridian, 1958), 62–63.

21 Joseph Campbell, *The Masks of God*, vol. 1, Primitive Mythology (New York: Penguin, 1989), 147.

22 Eliade, *Patterns in Comparative Religion*, 77. Indeed, the name Zeus derives from the Sanskrit name for the Vedic sky-deity Dyaus, whose name is itself derived from the Sanskrit root *div* ("to shine").

23 X. Liu, *Ancient India and Ancient China: Trade and Religious Exchanges AD 1–600* (Delhi: Oxford University Press, 1997), 114–15.

24 G. Schopen, *Bones, Stones, and Buddhist Monks: Collected Papers on the Archaeology, Epigraphy, and Texts of Monastic Buddhism in India* (Honolulu: University of Hawaii Press, 1997), 135, 154–55.

25 *The Long Discourses of the Buddha: A Translation of the Digha Nikaya*, trans. Maurice Walshe (Boston: Wisdom, 1995), 441–60.

26 *Buddhist Mahayana Texts*, trans. E. Cowell (New York: Dover, 1969), 6–11.

27 *The Middle Length Discourses of the Buddha: A New Translation of the Majjhima Nikaya*, trans. Bhikkhu Nanamoli and Bhikkhu Bodhi (Boston: Wisdom, 1995), 979–88.

Bodies of Work

28 Walt Whitman, "I Sing the Body Electric," in *Leaves of Grass*, 1855, https://www.poetryfoundation.org/poems/45472/i-sing-the-body-electric.

29 Contemporary American artist Jeff Koons has spoken of the Venus of Willendorf as the visual and conceptual inspiration for his 2012 work *Balloon Venus (Magenta)*: "The Venus of Willendorf is truly a symbol of fertility because it can procreate on its own." Quoted in Nicolai Hartvig, "'It's Somebody Having Sex': Jeff Koons Bares the Subtext of His Art in Brussels," Blouin ArtInfo, October 15, 2012, http://www.blouinartinfo.com/news/story/832783/.

30 Giorgio Vasari so praised Michelangelo's *David* in 1550: "[N]or has there ever been seen a pose so easy, or any grace to equal that in this work, or feet, hands and head so well in accord, one member with another, in harmony, design, and excellence of artistry." Giorgio Vasari, *Lives of the Painters, Sculptors, and Architects*, trans. Gaston du C. De Vere (New York: Knopf, 1996), 2:655.

31 Sundaram created the *Khajuraho* series after graduating from the Maharaja Sayajirao University of Baroda and before moving to London to pursue his graduate studies at the Slade School.

Catalogue of Works

32 G. Schopen, *Bones, Stones, and Buddhist Monks: Collected Papers on the Archaeology, Epigraphy, and Texts of Monastic Buddhism in India* (Honolulu: University of Hawaii Press, 1997).

33 David Hodge and Hi-Jin Kang Hodge, *Impermanence: Embracing Change* (Ithaca, NY: Snow Lion Publications, 2008), 13.

34 The Buddha was born as Prince Shakyamuni (also called Siddhartha), who gave up his life as a royal to find ways to end human suffering. For more information on the Buddha's life, see John S. Strong, *The Buddha: A Short Biography* (Oxford: Oneworld, 2001).

35 See the entry on "*Mahapurushalakshana*" and the appendix, "List of Lists: Thirties," in *The Princeton Dictionary of Buddhism*, ed. Robert Buswell Jr. and Donald Lopez Jr. (Princeton, NJ: Princeton University Press, 2014), 506 and 1094–95, respectively.

36 For further discussion on this subject and a detailed bibliography, see John Guy, ed., *Lost Kingdoms: Hindu-Buddhist Sculpture of Early Southeast Asia* (New York: Metropolitan Museum of Art, 2014).

37 Debra Diamond, ed., *Yoga: The Art of Transformation* (Washington, DC: Arthur M. Sackler Gallery, Smithsonian Institution, 2013), 131–37.

38 Vidya Dehejia, *The Body Adorned: Dissolving Boundaries between Sacred and Profane in India's Art* (New York: Columbia University Press, 2009), 87–92; for discussion of *yakshi* figures on Buddhist architecture, see 75–86, 92–98.

39 Ibid., 119.

40 For an account of the story, see Stella Kramrisch, *Manifestations of Shiva* (Philadelphia: Philadelphia Museum of Art, 1981), xvii.

41 Cited in Thomas B. Coburn, "The Threefold Vision of the *Devi Mahatmya,"* in *Devi: The Great Goddess*, ed. Vidya Dehejia (Munich and London: Prestel, 1999), 49.

42 Vivan Sundaram, interview by Nandita Raman, March 2016, International Center for Photography, www.icp.org/interviews/vivan-sundaram.

43 Ibid.

44 For a succinct account, see Cummins, *Vishnu*, 101.

45 *Singing the Body of God: The Hymns of the Vedantadeshikan in Their South Asian Tradition*, trans. Steven Paul Hopkins (Oxford: Oxford University Press, 2002), 157–60.

46 Kalidasa, *Origin of the Young God: Kalidasa's Kumarasambhava*, trans. Hank Heifetz (Berkeley: University of California Press, 1985), 130; cited in Dehejia, *The Body Adorned*, 147.

47 Dayanita Singh and Mona Ahmed, *Myself Mona Ahmed* (Zurich: Scalo, 2001), 9, 16.

48 Mona Ahmed, email to Walter Keller, ibid., 46–47.

BIBLIOGRAPHY

Ahuja, Naman P. *The Body in Indian Art and Thought*. Antwerp: Ludion, 2013.

Assmann, Jan, and Albert I. Baumgarten, eds. *Representation in Religion: Studies in Honor of Moshe Barasch*. Leiden: Brill, 2001.

Barthes, Roland. "Death of the Author." In *Image–Music–Text*, translated by Stephen Heath, 142–48. New York: Hill and Wang, 1977.

Baxandall, Michael. *Patterns of Intention: On the Historical Explanation of Pictures*. New Haven, CT, and London: Yale University Press, 1985.

Belting, Hans. *Likeness and Presence: A History of the Image before the Era of Art*. Translated by Edmund Jepcott. Chicago and London: University of Chicago Press, 1994.

Berger, John. *Ways of Seeing*. London: Penguin, 2008.

Buck-Morss, Susan. "Aesthetics and Anaesthetics: Walter Benjamin's Artwork Essay Reconsidered." *October* 62 (Autumn 1992): 3–41.

Buddhist Mahayana Texts. Translated by E. Cowell. New York: Dover, 1969.

Buswell, Robert E., Jr., and Donald S. Lopez Jr., eds. *The Princeton Dictionary of Buddhism*. Princeton, NJ: Princeton University Press, 2014.

Campbell, Joseph. *The Masks of God*. Vol. 1, *Primitive Mythology*. New York: Penguin, 1989.

Clottes, J., and D. Lewis-Williams. *The Shamans of Prehistory: Trance and Magic in the Paleolithic Caves*. New York: Abrams, 1998.

Cummins, Joan, ed. *Vishnu: Hinduism's Blue-Skinned Savior*. Ocean Township, NJ: Grantha; Ahmedabad: Mapin; Nashville, TN: Frist Center for the Visual Arts, 2011.

Davis, Richard H. "Indian Image-Worship and Its Discontents." In Assmann and Baumgarten, *Representation in Religion*, 107–32.

———. *Lives of Indian Images*. Princeton, NJ: Princeton University Press, 1997.

Dehejia, Vidya. *The Body Adorned: Dissolving Boundaries between Sacred and Profane in India's Art*. New York: Columbia University Press, 2009.

———, ed. *Devi: The Great Goddess*. Munich and London: Prestel, 1999.

———. *The Sensuous and the Sacred: Chola Bronzes from South India*. New York: American Federation of the Arts, 2002.

Dehejia, Vidya, and Charles Allen. *India through the Lens: Photography 1840–1911*. Washington, DC: Freer Gallery of Art and Arthur M. Sackler Gallery, Smithsonian Institution; Ahmedabad: Mapin; Munich and New York: Prestel, 2000.

Diamond, Debra, ed. *Yoga: The Art of Transformation.* Washington, DC: Arthur M. Sackler Gallery, Smithsonian Institution, 2013.

Eliade, Mircea. *A History of Religious Ideas*. Vol. 1, *From the Stone Age to the Eleusinian Mysteries*. Translated by Willard R. Trask. Chicago: University of Chicago Press, 1978.

———. *Patterns in Comparative Religion*. Translated by Rosemary Sheed. Cleveland: Meridian, 1958.

———. *Shamanism: Archaic Techniques of Ecstasy*. Translated by Willard R. Trask. London: Arkana, 1989.

Evans-Pritchard, E. E. *Theories of Primitive Religion*. Oxford: Oxford University Press, 1965.

Farago, Claire, and Robert Zwijnenberg, eds. *Compelling Visuality: The Work of Art in and out of History*. Minneapolis: University of Minnesota Press, 2003.

Feher, Michael, Ramona Naddaff, and Nadia Tazi, eds. *Fragments for a History of the Human Body, Parts 1–3*. 3 vols. New York: Zone, 1989.

Goldin, Nan, and David Armstrong. *The Other Side*. Zurich: Scalo, 2000.

Goldin, Nan, and Guido Costa. *Nan Goldin*. London: Phaidon, 2003.

Goldin, Nan, David Armstrong, Walter Keller, and Hans Werner Holzwarth. *A Double Life*. New York: Scalo, 1994.

Goswamy, B. N. *Essence of Indian Art*. San Francisco: Asian Art Museum, 1989.

Granoff, Phyllis. "Portraits, Likenesses, and Looking Glasses: Some Literary and Philosophical Reflections on Representation and Art in Medieval India," In Assmann and Baumgarten, *Representation in Religion*, 63–105.

Hamilton, M. *The Sociology of Religion: Theoretical and Comparative Perspectives*. London: Routledge, 1995.

Huntington, Susan L., and John C. Huntington. *Leaves from a Bodhi Tree: The Art of Pala India (8th–12th centuries) and Its International Legacy*. Dayton, OH: Dayton Art Institute in association with the University of Washington Press, 1990.

Kramrisch, Stella. *Manifestations of Shiva*. Philadelphia: Philadelphia Museum of Art, 1981.

Linrothe, Rob. *Ruthless Compassion*. London: Serindia, 1999.

Liu, X. *Ancient India and Ancient China: Trade and Religious Exchanges AD 1–600*. Delhi: Oxford University Press, 1997.

The Long Discourses of the Buddha: A Translation of the Digha Nikaya. Translated by Maurice Walshe. Boston: Wisdom, 1995.

Maniura, Robert, and Rupert Shepherd, eds. *Presence: The Inherence of the Prototype within Images and Other Objects.* Burlington, VT: Ashgate, 2006.

Meyer, Birgit. "Religious Sensations: Why Media, Aesthetics, and Power Matter in the Study of Contemporary Religion." In *Religion: Beyond a Concept*, edited by Hent de Vries, 704–23. New York: Fordham University Press, 2008.

Michell, George, ed. *In the Image of Man: The Indian Perception of the Universe through 2000 Years of Painting and Sculpture.* London: Arts Council of Great Britain, 1982.

The Middle Length Discourses of the Buddha: A New Translation of the Majjhima Nikaya. Translated by Bhikkhu Nanamoli and Bhikkhu Bodhi. Boston: Wisdom, 1995.

Morgan, David. *The Sacred Gaze: Religious Visual Culture in Theory and Practice.* Berkeley: University of California Press, 2005.

Otto, Rudolf. *The Idea of the Holy*. Oxford: Oxford University Press, 1923.

Paine, Crispin. *Religious Objects in Museums: Public Duties and Private Lives*. London and New York: Bloomsbury, 2013.

Promey, Sally M., ed. *Sensational Religion: Sensory Cultures in Material Practice*. New Haven, CT, and London: Yale University Press, 2014.

Schopen, G. *Bones, Stones, and Buddhist Monks: Collected Papers on the Archaeology, Epigraphy, and Texts of Monastic Buddhism in India*. Honolulu: University of Hawaii Press, 1997.

Singh, Dayanita. *Dayanita Singh: I Am as I Am*. Birmingham, UK: Ikon Gallery, 2001.

———. *Dream Villa*. Göttingen: Steidl, 2010.

———. *House of Love*. Cambridge, MA: Peabody Museum Press; Santa Fe, NM: Radius, 2010.

———. *Museum Bhavan*. Göttingen: Steidl, 2017.

Singh, Dayanita, and Mona Ahmed. *Myself Mona Ahmed*. Zurich: Scalo, 2001.

Singh, Dayanita, and Exilio Gráfico. *Dayanita Singh*. New Delhi: Penguin Studio, 2010.

Singh, Dayanita, and Britta Schmitz. *Privacy*. Göttingen: Steidl, 2004.

Singh, Dayanita, and Raghubir Singh. *The Home and the World / La Maison et le Monde*. Göttingen: Steidl, 2008.

Srinivasan, Doris Meth. *Many Heads, Arms, and Eyes: Origin, Meaning, and Form of Multiplicity in Indian Art*. Leiden: Brill, 1997.

Throckmorton, Jodi, and Atreyee Gupta. *Postdate: Photography and Inherited History in India*. San Jose, CA: San Jose Museum of Art; Oakland: University of California Press, 2015.

Weegee, and Miles Barth. *Weegee's World*. Boston: Little, Brown; New York: International Center of Photography, 2000.

Weegee, and John Coplans. *Weegee: Naked New York*. New York: Te Neues, 1997.

Weegee, and André Laude. *Weegee*. London: Thames and Hudson, 1989.

Westerbeck, Colin, and Joel Meyerowitz. *Bystander: A History of Street Photography*. Boston: Bulfinch, 2001.

CONTRIBUTORS

QAMAR ADAMJEE is Malavalli Family Foundation associate curator of art of the Indian subcontinent, Asian Art Museum of San Francisco.

JEFFREY DURHAM is assistant curator of Himalayan art, Asian Art Museum of San Francisco.

KARIN G. OEN is assistant curator of contemporary art, Asian Art Museum of San Francisco.